PRAISE FOR *SORRY F(*  ?

"Incredible . . . this story ripped my heart in two, had me grabbing for the tissues, and then put me back together again."

—Mindy Kaling

PREVIOUS PRAISE FOR FARAH NAZ RISHI

"Rishi . . . skillfully addresses complex contemporary issues on both the global (environmental damage, war, greed) and personal (identity, mental health) scales."

—*The Horn Book Magazine*

"Heart-wrenching, absorbingly clever, and beautifully written."

—R. F. Kuang, author of *Yellowface*

"Imaginative, funny, and frank . . . a must-read debut about love, loss, hope, and the real-world choices we make in our final days."

—Sona Charaipotra, author of *Magic Has No Borders*

"Examines human nature and how people react in the most desperate of times."

—*Publishers Weekly*

"Rishi . . . brings nuance and freshness to the familiar *You've Got Mail* dynamic with desi Muslim teenagers in this deftly layered novel."

—*Publishers Weekly*

"This coming-of-age tale deftly incorporates elements of desi and Muslim culture, grief, and overcoming trauma into a story about love and change, what it means to be a family, and how relationships can shift over time."

—*School Library Journal*

SORRY FOR THE INCONVENIENCE

OTHER TITLES BY FARAH NAZ RISHI

I Hope You Get This Message

It All Comes Back to You

SORRY FOR THE INCONVENIENCE

A MEMOIR

Farah Naz Rishi

MINDY'S BOOK STUDIO

Published by Mindy's Book Studio, New York

www.apub.com

Amazon, the Amazon logo, and Mindy's Book Studio are trademarks of Amazon.com,
Inc., or its affiliates.

ISBN-13: 9781662520969 (hardcover)
ISBN-13: 9781662520976 (paperback)
ISBN-13: 9781662520983 (digital)

Cover design by Tree Abraham
Cover illustration by Simone Noronha

Printed in the United States of America

First edition

For Stephen:
It was always you;
it will always be us.

A NOTE FROM MINDY KALING

There's nothing less romantic than a marriage of convenience. That's what Farah Naz Rishi tells herself when her best friend and roommate offers to help her out of a bad situation via a city hall ceremony. No matter that her mother is all too excited about her only daughter's overdue union, or that her best friend, Stephen, is the type of caring, handsome, loyal, charismatic man that comes along once in a lifetime. With so many ups and downs in her life, Farah has no idea what to expect in her marriage.

I was blown away by Farah's modern romance about family, friendship, and love. This memoir (that started with a TikTok video that went viral!) was so unputdownable, it was a story I needed on the Mindy's Book Studio list. It scooped out my heart and left me believing in the power of soulmates.

AUTHOR'S NOTE

Do you ever think about how you've never actually seen yourself? That the closest you'll ever get is seeing your reflection in a mirror? Yet we know how often mirrors mislead and distort our understanding of ourselves. *Objects in mirror are closer than they appear.*

Nonfiction, especially memoir, is like that. Nonfiction is writing based on *fact*, to be taken as whole truth; and certainly everything in this memoir is as I know it to be. I have done my best to recall what I can, though some dialogue has been condensed or otherwise summarized, and some names have been changed for privacy.

But, as my high school creative writing teacher so aptly put it, so much of what we refer to as "nonfiction" relies on our *perception* of the world and the events unfolding around us. Nonfiction is based on real things that actually happened, yes, but nonfiction is never exactly the *full* truth: it is our brains seeing ourselves in the mirror and wondering why our head is so big.

Any mistake in this memoir is the result of faulty depth perception, a failure to notice the details, or my own shaky human memory.

I would also ask that the reader take this memoir as no way representative of the entirety of the Pakistani American Muslim experience, nor should any of my personal experiences be taken as a reflection of Islam itself. I am simply one of many.

PART I

Rock upon Rock

CHAPTER 1

Like Summer

It's embarrassing to admit—and it's definitely up there with one of my more desperate, delusional moments in life—but one of the only reasons I decided to take a class at Haverford College was the prospect of meeting a boy. Preferably a nice Muslim boy my parents would actually approve of.

But as my fellow students filed into the classroom—ignorant of my silent appraisals as they simply minded their business—I realized none would be good enough for my parents. Hell, on most days, *I* wasn't good enough for them.

A minute before class had started, and already my hopes were shattered.

To be fair, it was my fault for holding such ludicrous expectations. Would the love of my life just *conveniently* waltz into the same class I was taking at Haverford—in a Japanese Civilization class, of all options? No. If he existed, he'd be in some premed class, like biochem or How to Save Babies 101. Or he wouldn't be on campus at all because he'd be busy saving some nice old lady's cat from a tree.

Only, I wanted to meet someone in college, and I couldn't do that at Bryn Mawr, the all-women's college I attended as a first-year student. And in my mind, I had to meet someone, if only to stop Mom from making snide comments about never finding anyone who could, in her words, "put up" with me.

So there I sat, in my Japanese Civilization class, sitting on my fingers to keep them warm (it was January, and freezing cold) and to stop myself from anxiously bouncing in my seat.

Finally—finally!—the last student arrived: a boy named Stephen, with warm, russet skin and close-cropped black curls, slightly smooshed on one side, like he'd just rolled out of bed. He wore flip-flops and khaki shorts in the middle of January, like he'd made the conscious decision to never acknowledge the existence of winter. And of all the available seats left, he chose to sit front and center—as if he hadn't just ambled into class over five minutes late.

I watched Stephen from my seat at the back of the classroom, baffled. Not because I particularly cared about the tardiness of other students, but because I swear I'd sensed the world ripple around me the moment he'd walked in with that easy smile of his.

It wasn't love at first sight. I don't believe in love at first sight. What even is that? A person can't love someone they don't know. Love is many things, but it isn't, by my definition, *instant.* What I felt was more of an inevitable, inexplicable connection. I'd felt the same thing before, recently: with Kaya—another first-year in my hall, and the only other Asian. When our RAs forced the first-years to do icebreakers the day we'd moved in, Kaya had looked ready to bolt, like she wanted to be anywhere else but there. Watching her felt like looking in a mirror, and, naturally, we became fast friends.

With Kaya, that feeling was reassuring. With Stephen, though—I felt myself *scowling.* Maybe it was the palpable way Stephen had stumbled into my life out of nowhere, tripping over my loose threads. A promise of an inevitable unraveling. When I saw him, that ripple in the world felt like a warning that this person was about to change my life, forever, and I couldn't predict how yet.

I dismissed the warning. It had to have been all in my head. After all, Stephen was emblematic of a Haverford boy: ridiculous and sloppy and inconsiderate. I mean, flip-flops in the snow? Being *that* unapologetically late to your first class? If anything, he was a perfect example of why I would never find my future husband at college. No, no, no, clearly the situation was hopeless. And as our professor read from the syllabus, I decided that if I wanted to avoid becoming like Mom and replicating her mess of a marriage, I was better off tossing the idea of marriage in the garbage altogether.

At least I could tell Mom I tried, and now I was free! No more talk of being introduced to young men from my family's Pakistani community! No more being asked if I'd somehow scared away all the good Muslim boys with my uniquely strong case of RBF! I did my due diligence, but there were simply no options, and now I could focus solely on learning and forging a path to self-sufficiency. What a concept.

I settled in my seat, pleased—at least until Professor Tanaka announced that we would be required to get into assigned groups for a project presentation. And like a ridiculous setup for some young adult rom-com novel, I was put in a group with *him*.

Our group had four people: me, Stephen, Cecilia, and Meg. I was the only first-year student. Cecilia was a Haverford student who'd been born and raised in France. Everything about her screamed French: she was tall, effortlessly pretty, and could probably wear a potato sack and make it work. Meg was a Bryn Mawr student and wore black combat boots (very cool, in my opinion) and a small neon-pink-and-black backpack with a Hello Kitty character, Badtz-Maru, on it. And Stephen was . . . someone I'd rather avoid.

It took the four of us weeks to coordinate a time to meet, in part because no one wanted to be the first to reach out. Eventually it was Stephen who emailed everyone, and resorted to calling me when I never emailed him back. When I realized it was him on the other end of the line, I nearly dropped my phone in panic. I didn't want to talk to him. I just wanted to get through the project and be done with it.

Even though I'd come across as rudely frosty when I picked up the phone, Stephen remained relaxed, polite. Unbothered.

"So I'm thinking it'd just be easier to meet at Haverford," he said. "We probably only need one in-person meeting, and then we can coordinate the rest through email. What about you? What do you think?"

"Huh?" I'd been pacing around my dorm room, and his question stopped me.

"Have any thoughts on the plan?" he asked again.

"Oh. Um, no. It makes sense." It did mean Meg and I would have to take a ten-minute bus ride to Haverford, so that was annoying. But I kept my mouth shut. "Have you asked everyone else yet? Are Meg and Cecilia on board?"

"No, not yet," Stephen answered, hesitating. "I called you first, sorry. But I'll ask the others after this."

I couldn't help wondering why Stephen called me first, but I decided not to think any more of it. There was probably no significance to it.

"All right," I said. "Just text me if everyone's on board, and I'll see you there."

"Great!" Stephen's enthusiasm on the other line was palpable. "See you soon."

When I hung up, I felt confused. I'd thought of myself as someone who was fairly good at reading people. But I was starting to think that Stephen wasn't ridiculous or sloppy or inconsiderate at all. If anything, he was so disarmingly friendly I hadn't realized, until the phone call was over, that he'd effectively melted the frostiness I'd encased myself in.

I'd never met anyone like that before.

CHAPTER 2

Dislocation

The story goes that when I was around five years old, Mom and I were at the mall, and I wanted to get away from her. Who knows why; maybe I saw something I wanted at a store. Maybe I didn't want to shop with my mom anymore. Maybe it doesn't matter.

The point is, I wanted to escape.

My mother, seeing the impulse, shackled my wrist with her hand and pulled me close, but I pulled back. She pulled harder. I pulled even harder. Back and forth we went until eventually my arm let out a sickening pop. In the world's most pointless game of tug-of-war, my mom dislocated my elbow.

Mom said it happened because I was being stubborn.

"Isn't that funny?" she said. "You were always set in your ways, even as a kid. And you've never changed."

She told me this story for the first time when I was in my first year of college. I'd come home to visit family for the weekend, and I'd complained about not being able to do push-ups—a weird complaint, as far as complaints go, but at college I'd started enjoying exercise for the first time in my life. I found comfort in my campus's gym, which was far cleaner and quieter than the YMCA back home—one of the many perks of attending an all-women's college. There I discovered things like running on a treadmill were cathartic. I would arrive at the gym, change into some yoga pants and a frayed, ill-fitting T-shirt from H&M, lace up my sneakers, and then run, quite literally, from my problems. Essays and readings for class. My upcoming Japanese civ group project. Mom. Sometimes myself.

But no matter how hard I trained, I couldn't do push-ups. Every time I tried, I'd feel a pinch in my elbow, a searing pain all down my arm and up to my neck, and even I knew that wasn't normal.

"So that's probably why you can't do them," explained Mom, amused. "The doctors had to pop your elbow back in, but I guess the body never forgets."

Apparently, my skepticism with love was so deeply ingrained in me, it literally affected my bones. It was *almost* funny.

My mom often laughed at things most people would find inappropriate, but only behind closed doors. She'd laugh at things that I'd wished she comforted me for, like when I'd cried at the ending of a good book or video game. *None of it's real,* she'd say, amused. *Why are you getting so worked up?* When I lost my fourth-grade presidential election, even though I'd practiced my speech a hundred times in front of the mirror, Mom told me if I was going to cry about it, then I shouldn't have run in the first place.

I wanted the kind of mom I'd see on TV, or the kind of South Asian mom who oiled their daughter's hair and smothered their children in kisses—whenever they were proud, or whenever their child was sad. Or simply just because.

Mom was always different.

Though she was born in Pakistan and spent her childhood in England, she lived most of her life in the United States—culturally speaking, she considered herself more American than Pakistani. She had a college degree. Got her MBA, passed the CPA exam. She chose to work as a homemaker, but there was little she couldn't do if she'd wanted.

Mom was beautiful, too. She had a soft baby face and doll-like brown eyes that gave her a delicate, captivating look. She dressed well, always on top of the latest fashion trends by mimicking celebrities like Julia Roberts or Jennifer Aniston (my favorite of her outfits was a vintage gingham dress she'd wear over a black turtleneck). Time and the natural process of aging didn't dare touch her. When we walked through stores or attended dinner parties, people often commented that we could pass for sisters, their eyes never leaving hers. Several times I'd overheard boys my age openly, loudly, calling her hot, calling her a solid *ten*.

I, however, looked far more like my dad—something Mom reminded me of often. "You have your dad's big nostrils," she'd say mournfully. I had come to think that favoring my dad was another act of defiance: that somehow my genetics purposefully leaned in his direction.

Mom, unlike me, was extremely fit; she made push-ups look *easy*. "I can do anywhere from fifty to a hundred, depending on how I'm feeling that day," she'd once told me with a wink. Years of Pilates and yoga had sculpted her petite figure, and I'd often find her giving fitness advice to other women, who'd listen with rapt attention.

And to the outside world, Mom was charming. Her two younger sisters adored her; her entire extended family treasured her. She knew how to win people over: when to smile, when to ask questions. To nod at all the right places, in a gentle assurance that she was truly listening. She knew all the right things to say to puff someone up, to make them feel good. It made her an easy favorite in our Muslim community in Chester County, Pennsylvania. Hell, it made her a favorite to *anyone* she met.

I'd lost count of how many times other kids, at field trips or parties, had come up to me only to tell me how lucky I was to have her as my mom.

The irony, of course, was that Mom never really wanted to be a mom.

"Sometimes I wonder how my life would look like if Nani Jan hadn't married me off at eighteen," she once said to me, after she and Dad had had another fight.

Dad, who'd been born and raised in Pakistan, was a prime example of the American dream: a colonel in the US Air Force, a pathologist. Throughout my childhood, he traveled on weekends to teach at nearby air force base hospitals to give presentations on methodologies to detect breast cancer. I didn't see him much back then.

In many ways he was Mom's opposite. When I thought of my dad, I thought of Tetley tea and stale cake rusks from the Indian grocery, his favorite snack. I thought of newspapers: the smell, the crinkle of pages. I thought of big brassy glasses and cheap polos from Walmart. Though Dad had a doctor's salary, he was a man of simple pleasures. Of *practical* ones. But Mom wanted gold and glamour. She wanted what she could never have, growing up on her mother's—my Nani Jan's—7-Eleven salary. And where Mom was expressive and charming, Dad carried a permanently stern expression and rarely cared what other people thought of him (much to her dismay). Arguments in our household abounded.

Mom would usually talk to me after her fights with Dad, as a kind of auditing of his wrongs against her: about how she felt he was holding her back from things she wanted to do in life, like open her own business. Sometimes they'd argue over little things, like how Dad chewed food, like bananas, so loudly you could hear the click of his molars, or how my dad would offer unsolicited suggestions to make her cooking better. And sometimes they'd be far more serious: like how Dad wanted more kids, but Mom did not. This meant I'd often learn things as a child—admissions, secrets—that I wished she'd tell a friend instead.

"If I'd been allowed to have my own life . . . I don't know," said Mom after one of those fights. "I just don't think I was cut out for motherhood. I really don't."

I didn't say it then, but I agreed with her.

It made sense that Mom never wanted kids: her own childhood wasn't full of love or affection; she never really learned to love herself, let alone love another. The education she got was in discipline and meeting expectations. And she learned how to keep things bottled up, even when she shouldn't.

Mom told me about my grandfather—Nana Jan. He had schizophrenia.

"This was back in the old days. We didn't understand these kinds of illnesses the way we do now. We didn't have good medication; that's why your nana kept losing his engineering jobs and your nani had to work at 7-Eleven. We all had to find ways to deal with it."

"Poor Nana Jan," I said.

"Poor Nana Jan?" Mom looked at me dubiously. "*He* was fine. *He* eventually got help. What about us?"

Sometimes mental health seemed to be simply a matter of discipline to her, or lack thereof.

Nana Jan's worst episode, Mom said, led him to accuse my grandmother—Nani Jan—of being a spy sent by the government. She was going to kill him, he claimed. So he pulled out a kitchen knife, threatening to stop her before she could inform the government of his secrets.

Nani Jan screamed for my mom, a child of eight at the time, to take her little sister and hide. "And no matter what you hear, don't come out of hiding. Do you understand?" she'd instructed.

Mom obeyed. She and her younger sister, Amber, hid in a coat closet and waited quietly. Unable to let out even a whimper.

Meanwhile, Nani sprinted outside to get away from her husband and lure him from the house. She'd been a track star in Pakistan during her school days, and her skills came in handy.

Eventually the cops came and took my grandfather to the hospital for a spell—until he calmed down. And the next day my mom and her sister went to school like nothing ever happened.

It's why, I think, Mom was so good at pretending. Pretending her home life was normal, pretending to be a happy wife. A happy mother who had nothing to complain about.

But I think the times she laughed at her daughter's struggles were perhaps some of the few times she was being her true, honest self. After all, Mom had lived a difficult life, a *truly* difficult one. She'd spent her childhood learning to survive: survive an unstable childhood, survive a marriage at eighteen years old. I was given opportunities she never had: education, stability, the privilege of a relatively quiet household. To her, all my problems seemed trivial. I never once had to look over my shoulder and wonder if my own father was going to kill me.

So how could I complain?

"Oh, don't look at me like that," Mom had said after sharing the story about my dislocated arm. "Your arm is better, right? You're fine. You can just do girl push-ups."

Mom commonly decided her children were fine when they decidedly were anything but—the same way she'd tell me to just sleep off my fevers while my dad, if he were home, would rush to find some Gatorade.

"Yeah," I answered. "I guess that's true."

"Honestly, you should think of the pain as a reminder that you need to listen to me next time," she added, laughing. "Boys don't like buff girls, anyway."

I didn't want to fight with her. I'd just started my second semester of college and was already exhausted. *Maybe I* should *cut down on my workouts,* I thought.

"Fair enough," I said, before slinking into the basement to find my brother, Shaz—the only person in the house who'd understand why I felt so hurt.

❧

Cruelty can take many forms. When we think of cruelty, we tend to think of the obvious: the screams, the hits, the shredding of one's soul. The worst of it.

Except cruelty can also be stealthy and insidious. Like dismissing one's feelings, over and over again—until one day you start to forget how to feel anything. That's the kind of cruelty that is hardest to recognize. And even if you can point to it, name it, it's often too late.

The damage has been done.

I wish I'd asked my mom why she didn't let go of my arm that day. I wonder if the option to let go had simply never occurred to her.

Years after my mom died, my aunt Seema told me that she'd called my mom the day she'd given birth to me.

"So how does it feel? How does it feel being a mom?" Seema had asked excitedly.

"It feels good," Mom said. "Because now I have something that's all my own."

CHAPTER 3

In Rolls the Pencil

I went to Bryn Mawr College, a liberal arts college in Pennsylvania, about an hour from where I grew up. One of the biggest draws of Bryn Mawr was that it was part of the Bi-College Consortium, and students could also take classes at nearby Haverford College, starting in their second semester. So that was how, when my second semester rolled around, I'd come to sign up for a class at Haverford called Japanese Civilization that met every Tuesday and Thursday.

My mom was pleased I'd decided to take a class at Haverford. Hopeful, even. Surely at Haverford, I'd find a replacement for my ex, Kareem, whom she'd been certain I'd marry one day. But that relationship had fallen apart in ways I was still reeling from when I set foot in Japanese Civilization, much to Mom's disappointment.

The whole thing was very confusing. I'd chosen to attend a women's college to reassure my mom that I'd focus on my studies. But later, when I was knee-deep in classes, Mom'd told me I wasn't doing enough to meet prospective suitors, that I needed to think about marriage. After all, what would happen to me if my parents died and I was left all alone? Mom was adamant that if I wanted the happy marriage she never got—a point she made often—I should find a husband sooner rather than later and start building a solid foundation for our future. Whatever that meant.

If a foundation was needed for a happy marriage, my mother and father likely never had one. Mom had been only eighteen when they married, and the whole thing had been arranged by one of my dad's eight sisters, who'd already arranged a marriage between my mother's and father's families and decided to ride that high into arranging even more. A practical approach to matchmaking. When I'd asked why Mom had agreed to the marriage, she shrugged. "He was handsome and he was a doctor," she'd said. "And it was the only way I could get away from my mom. Back then, I was desperate. Marriage was the quickest way to escape."

Nani Jan—my mom's mother—ran not a tight household, but a strangling one. Once, when Mom was a child, and her younger sister, Amber, only newly born, Nani Jan had feuded with her relatives so much that she'd cut off all contact with them. Without telling anyone, she moved to England with her two daughters, leaving even her husband behind. In a different country, far from everyone they knew, my nani forced her daughters to rely on her and *only* her.

Eventually family pressure became too much, and they moved to the States to be closer to Nani's younger sister. But as Mom grew up, Nani Jan never let her daughters hang out with friends. She listened in on their phone calls to ensure they weren't talking badly about her or, worse, talking to boys. Mom attempted to keep a diary and wrote about a crush she had, but that didn't end well; Nani Jan read it and slapped Mom senseless.

So Mom rushed into marrying Dad. He was her only escape plan.

And with that, my mom, an eighteen-year-old bride, finally got her own home—but she didn't get the freedom she'd hoped for. Soon after they'd married in Pakistan, Mom and Dad moved to a small apartment in New Jersey. Dad, at twenty-five years old, was starting a pathology fellowship at Thomas Jefferson University Hospital, so he was rarely home. Meanwhile, his sister Fouzia needed a place to stay while she studied for her boards to work as a physician in the United States. Without asking my mom, Dad invited her to live with them, and the three of them—Mom and Dad, newly married, and my Fouzia phuppo—were crammed into a two-bedroom apartment, sharing a single bathroom.

"Your mom made us a lot of meat loaf," Fouzia phuppo told me years later. "She didn't know how to cook anything else. She was so young, after all."

That was the first year of my parents' marriage: Mom, forced to accommodate her new husband's wishes, and Dad, not yet even recognizing her own personhood.

I wouldn't be born for another five years.

❧

I remember sitting on the couch with Mom once after school, watching episodes of *Charmed*. It was the only way we bonded: watching TV for hours, occasionally commenting on the story and the ridiculous choices the Halliwell sisters made—until Mom asked if I'd finished my homework, and I'd scurry away.

"If I were a witch," she opined, "I'd fall in love with Belthazor, too." Her eyes remained glued to the screen, and I wasn't sure if she was talking to me or just thinking out loud.

I'd liked Belthazor—up until he kept breaking the trust of his love interest, Phoebe, played by Alyssa Milano. "But he's a demon! He's done awful things."

"Yes, but he's sexy, isn't he? He's *tragic*. He's endured so much. And despite everything, he loves Phoebe." Mom always fell for villains, the same way she always wanted what she couldn't have.

I think Mom wanted me to have a big sweeping *passionate* romance like in the TV shows she watched. She wanted to watch me experience

17

the world in a way she could not. In her eyes, I was the vessel for all the broken hopes and dreams so cruelly torn from her.

I still had to focus on school, of course. But I also had to find the love she couldn't someday. As if love was something that could simply be found, like a pretty pebble on the side of the road.

❧

In my mind, Haverford College is known for three things:

1. Its Quaker background, evident in its relaxed school policies and simple but charming architecture.
2. The amount of people who mishear it as Harvard and are promptly disappointed upon being corrected.
3. The way Bryn Mawr students make fun of boys from Haverford for being awkward at best, and positively repugnant at worst, as illustrated by the fact that Haverford long suffered a problem with a male student who reveled in smearing the walls of his dorm basement with his own shit.

The day of my first group meeting with Stephen—who I was grudgingly admitting might be more interesting than I'd expected of a Haverford boy—my mom and I got into a fight. We argued a lot while I was growing up, mostly about my inability to get straight As or complaints about visiting her side of the family for the seemingly hundredth time, but this—this one felt especially bad. "You don't call me anymore," she'd yelled into the phone. "You rarely pick up, you rarely text me. Can't you see why it makes me suspicious? Who knows what you're up to at college?"

"Why do you always do this? Why do you always think I'm lying?" I replied.

Boys. That was what she thought I was "up to." If I wanted to go somewhere with my friends, it must be because I was secretly meeting with a boy, or if I had a friend who was a boy, he must be my secret boyfriend. But being with a boy was not only a distraction from school, it was sinful. And I would be *used*.

I wondered if Mom had been talking to Nani Jan again. Nani Jan had begun listening to so-called Islamic scholars on YouTube with wild fringe ideologies that had no basis in the Quran. Every time she visited our home, she spent most of the weekend glued to her laptop in the living room, blasting these videos that claimed things like *It is permitted for Muslim women to be forced into marriage; it is sinful for them to disobey their husbands under any circumstances; any non-Muslims, regardless of how good of a person they are, would be damned to hell.* She was blasting them for *me*. She never told me to my face, but she'd told my mom a hundred times that when I was a child, I was too outspoken, too wild. My parents let me play outside for hours in our neighborhood, to play kickball with the neighbors' kids or climb trees in the Kennett Square woods—and Nani Jan felt they gave me far too much freedom.

Before I'd left for college, Nani Jan had told Mom to keep an eye on me. *It's not good,* she'd said, *to give a young girl too much freedom.* Mom had relayed this to me, shaking her head. After all, Nani Jan had said the same thing to her when she was growing up.

When Mom was a teen, she'd fallen in love with a boy—her second cousin. When she told me about him, and I'd made a face, Mom looked hurt. *But I wasn't allowed to talk to boys, and he was the first one who'd ever paid attention to me,* she'd said. *I really thought we'd get married.* When Nani Jan had found out about their burgeoning relationship, she'd slapped Mom and locked her in her room. Mom wasn't allowed to even *entertain* the idea of marrying someone Nani Jan hadn't hand-picked. After that, Nani obsessively read every letter my mom wrote, even letters she'd written to my dad after they'd gotten engaged.

Mom never wanted to be like Nani Jan. And yet Nani's words often changed Mom's behavior. Instead of asking me how college was or what new friends I had made, Mom's questions centered on where I was at all times and whom I was talking to and why wasn't I picking up the phone fast enough anymore?

But her yelling only reinforced my desire to put some space between me and a home that had grown increasingly mistrustful and suffocating. I wanted to pull away from her, even if my arm broke in the process. I wanted to tell her that leaving for college was the best thing that ever happened to me, because it meant I could *finally* get away from her. Mom may have married Dad to escape her mother, but I didn't need that. College was *my* escape.

Except I bit back my words. Arguing with her would be pointless. It would only make her grip tighten, the way it always did. Instead, I told her I'd been busy (which was true), that I was sorry (which was also true), that I'd do better (which I'd try).

I hung up the phone, chewing my lip so hard it began to bleed, and hopped on the bus to Haverford for the group project meeting. To keep myself from fuming, I had to remind myself that my mom had grown up in a different time. Her own mother was abusive and paranoid, her own cheeks more familiar with vindictive slaps than soft kisses.

So who, then, could possibly blame her for doing the same every now and then?

⁂

During the meeting, Stephen, Cecilia, Meg, and I all sat around an open copy of our Japanese Civilization textbook, searching for a topic for the presentation. We were in a building called Stokes Hall, crowded in a tiny room that barely fit our chairs, with an even tinier coffee table in the center.

I was ready to focus on our work, ready to push back the storm in my head left behind by my argument with Mom. But in the first three minutes, I caught Stephen staring. He was sitting across from me, wearing a light, full-sleeved T-shirt and shorts—again, in January—and the bags beneath his big round eyes gave him the appearance of being mildly sleep-deprived.

Normally I'd glare at any boy who openly stared, but the way he was looking didn't strike me as creepy. It felt more curious, the way people look at a problem they're trying to figure out. To *solve*. Uncomfortable but not necessarily invasive. Still, I felt self-conscious beneath his gaze.

"Hey, what are you?" Stephen finally asked me.

Cecilia and Meg looked at each other and went quiet.

The question was so out of left field, I didn't know how to respond. "What?" I finally managed.

"What *are* you?" he repeated, sitting back in his chair, amusement tugging at his mouth. "Where are you from? What ethnicity? I genuinely can't tell."

I glared at him, after all.

As a Pakistani American Muslim, when people ask about my background, I'm immediately wary. In many cases the question isn't just *What are you?* The unspoken question they're asking is, *What are you so I can figure out if I should be racist toward you or not?* My dad's Kashmiri background and Mom's Pathani background had given me a somewhat paler complexion than most non–South Asians would expect (see: stereotype) of Pakistanis, especially in a post-9/11 world. On top of that, my last name, Rishi, was Hindu. I'd once asked Dad why his family hadn't changed their last name after our ancestors converted to Islam. He'd replied with a quote from Shakespeare: *"A rose by any other name would smell as sweet."* I'd groaned, and I'm sure if I repeated the same answer to anyone else, they'd groan, too.

Stephen, on the other hand, was Black, with a head full of dense, black coils and a strong, rounded nose. But the more I really looked at him, the more I recognized some of his features as South Asian, too. Something about those eyes, maybe—so sharp and startlingly big. Or maybe it was an internal homing beacon that helps people find their people. My instinct was especially strong, built over years of growing up in a small, majority-white town in the suburbs of Pennsylvania. I was searching, always searching, for anyone who looked even vaguely like me and my family.

Stephen waited for my answer, bright eyed and completely oblivious.

He didn't mean anything offensive by the question, I realized. He simply had no filter.

I relaxed a little. "I'm Pakistani," I answered. "I was born in DC, though."

He smiled broadly. So bright. "Oh, no way. I've never met anyone Pakistani," he said. "I'm half-Indian. Grew up in Jamaica, then moved here for college."

I was surprised. I'd never met anyone from Jamaica; he had no trace of a Jamaican accent, either. I suddenly felt humbled by how little I knew about that part of the world.

"I'm from France," piped up Cecilia cheerfully, in her unmistakably French accent.

"Cool," I responded, the only thing I could think to say—followed by a noticeable pause.

Eventually the four of us divided up the work for our presentation on the Tokugawa shogunate, a ruling military empire in Japan. Cecilia and Meg partnered up to write about agriculture and education, while Stephen and I opted for military and religion. Stephen and I would put the final presentation together, since he was confident in his PowerPoint skills, and I was confident in my note-taking and organization.

Halfway through our meeting, Stephen turned to me.

"Would you be comfortable taking meeting notes?" he asked. "I'd do it myself, but my handwriting is trash."

I nodded, digging through my bag, coming up with nothing.

"Shit, I forgot a pencil," I said. So much for organizational skills.

"I think I have one on me." Stephen quickly found a pencil—a proper, old-school #2—in his gray messenger bag and handed it over. "I may or may not have, uh, borrowed it from the chem lab. Just don't tell anyone."

I felt the tug of a smile. "In that case, I'm giving it right back when I'm done. I won't be an accessory to your crimes."

"Hey, I said *borrowed*, not *stole*—"

"Do we know what day our presentation is?" asked Meg.

"January 29," I answered immediately. "Coincidentally, my birthday." Which is the only reason why I remembered it off the top of my head. Having to do a presentation for class on one's birthday felt a little like being bullied.

Stephen's brows furrowed. "Seriously? Damn, I'm sorry. That sucks. You'll rush back to Bryn Mawr after class, right? To relax and celebrate?"

I was a little taken aback by his sudden sympathy.

"That's the plan," I answered.

"So, no celebratory lunch after our presentation?" Cecilia whined, her delicate eyebrows knitted together.

"No, probably not. Sorry."

To be honest, I wasn't sure what the point of a celebratory lunch would be. Once the semester ended, I'd probably never see any of them again—except maybe Meg, who went to my school. But we were just classmates who happened to be working on a project together. My roommate, Ava, and I had plans that involved a buttery-rich chocolate cake from the Bakery House that she'd promised would be waiting for me when I got back from class. *Nothing* would get between me and that cake and the comfort of my dorm room.

I felt Stephen's eyes on me again. Narrowed slightly, like he was trying to decide something.

Finally, he shook his head.

"Well, that's that," he eventually concluded, with a small, dimpled smile. "We'll just have to make sure everything goes smoothly so you can get outa there and celebrate."

"Yeah," I replied. "Thanks."

Maybe it would have been nice to hang out with them. But I guess I wasn't really looking to make new friends, anyway.

CHAPTER 4

Cryptophasia

One of the earliest gifts my dad ever gave me was a giant book of fables and fairy tales that he'd gotten off the bargain rack, each with a particular lesson at the end of every story: *A Treasury of Virtues*, with stories, the cover promised, about *courage, love, and honesty.* But it was the stories about love that stuck with me the most, like "The Velveteen Rabbit." I liked that the velveteen rabbit—a little stuffed bunny—had learned to be vulnerable through love, and even when he was abandoned by the boy who'd loved him, he was rewarded with finding himself, his "real" self. It was a story about the transformative power of love and heartbreak.

Not that I'd understood any of that at the time. But I wanted love. I wanted to love and be loved in return. I had no idea what it looked like, the forms it could take, the particularities. I knew there was romantic love and familial love and platonic love, sure. Even as a kid, I also knew that openly admitting to *wanting* love was a sign of weakness or girliness (the two things often conflated), and was met only with derision. Kids will tell other kids who want love that it means to have *cooties*; the same way adults will tell other adults, especially women, that to openly admit to wanting love is desperate, shameful even—a desire for airheads, not those with *ambition.*

But there was a certain kind of magic about it. Love was a powerful transformative force that could change people—could change stuffed bunnies into real rabbits. In some cases, it could even save the world.

A love like that, it seemed, had skipped my house entirely. Mom and Dad didn't act like the married couples I'd seen on TV or even in my fables. Despite Dad's love of teaching and talking—he was also a teacher and the principal of my Islamic Sunday school, beloved for his Socratic-style classes—Mom and Dad rarely spoke to each other. If they did, it was over dinner: usually about taxes or home improvements or drama in the community. Conversation mostly to fill the silence.

Nor had I ever felt that heady, transformative love. The only three things I loved were books, music, and my little brother, Shaz.

My brother and I bonded through video games. He was beside me the day I beat my very first game: a little-known Japanese RPG called *Okage: Shadow King*. It was a weird little game in the style of a Tim Burton movie about a boy named Ari who'd been possessed by an evil demon king, all to save his cursed sister.

When the credits rolled, I sobbed. I'd done it. I'd finished my first-ever game, and it had taken me months, and now it was over. It was more than reaching the end of a favorite book. I'd felt like I'd *lived* in this world, quite literally turmoiled through it, on my own. All those boss battles and untimely deaths, all those hours getting lost in dungeons and not knowing where to go. I'd done it all alone.

And, at the same time, I wasn't alone. There had been the characters I'd loved. Characters I now had to say goodbye to. And there'd been Shaz, patiently watching the entire time. Never once asking me for the controller, like he'd understood this was something I had to do.

As I sobbed, he watched me still. Maybe he was confused about why I was crying. Or maybe he understood more than anyone. Unlike our mom, he never once made fun of me for my tears, for being his older, dramatic sister who always felt too much about too much.

He placed his hand on my back. It was the first time I remember feeling like he was my *brother*. That even if he didn't understand me, he'd be there to awkwardly pat my back, and only later, when I'd calm down, lovingly call me *stupid* in the way only siblings can.

Granted, we still fought the way siblings do, too. When Shaz was only five years old, he'd found that book of fables and fairy tales, and scribbled all over its pages with a ballpoint pen. I didn't talk to him for almost three days—until one day he came into my bedroom with his copy of *Ketchup on Your Cornflakes?* (his favorite) and told me he'd let me draw all over it if it made me feel better.

We sat on the floor of his room and scribbled over its pages together.

Later, when he was seven, he got into a fistfight with a boy his age at a community dinner party. The boy had made fun of him for some-thing ridiculous, like his shirt or his favorite video game, the way mean boys do, and Shaz threw the first punch. It became an all-out brawl that had gotten so bad another boy at the party, named Sammy—a friend of Shaz's—tracked me down and explained what was happening so I could stop it.

I had to pin Shaz to the ground.

"Let me go!" Shaz grunted, desperately trying to push me off. "I'm gonna beat him up. I'm going to make him regret talking to me like that!"

"How's that going for you?" I hadn't budged an inch; a five-year age difference between us meant I was a lot bigger than my brother back then. "Freaking shrimp. I get that you're mad, but you need to calm down. It's over. You already taught the kid a lesson."

In fact, the boy Shaz had punched was now crying and threatening to tell his parents, to which Sammy retorted, *"But you started it!"*

Shaz had stopped thrashing, and I noticed it then: he had tears in his eyes, too. He was just trying to hold them back.

I realized then that, like me, Shaz *did* feel things, and felt them strongly. But unlike me, who cried at everything as if to slowly drain those feelings over time, Shaz kept his feelings locked up until eventu-ally, inevitably, they exploded.

§

When I was thirteen, my parents signed me up for piano lessons. Another attempt at getting a head start on college admissions. Colleges liked talented musicians, Mom told me. She'd have preferred I'd chosen the violin, but after a yearlong attempt, I showed not only zero interest, but zero talent. So piano it was.

I liked piano. It felt more intuitive. I liked how the keys felt under my fingertips. I liked the resonance, the reverberation of the sound throughout our living room. Unlike my violin teacher, who'd literally scream if I made mistakes, my piano teacher, Mrs. Rothfeld, was kind.

Except as I practiced, I felt my brother's interest grow. He'd watch me play, then ask if he could try, too. My parents were flabbergasted; Shaz had never shown an interest in anything, never took the initiative when it came to activities and hobbies. Dad couldn't even get him to come outside to play catch; he'd beg my brother to try, but Shaz would disappear into his room, so I'd have to offer to play catch with my dejected dad instead.

Music became Shaz's release. He immediately showed a talent for music that floored even his teachers. It wasn't long before he was playing Beethoven and Liszt. His favorite was Chopin's *Fantaisie-Impromptu*, one of the most notoriously difficult piano pieces ever written.

He should be playing in competitions, Mrs. Rothfeld had informed my parents. They eventually found a teacher from Russia who whipped him into shape, and soon Shaz was performing for northeast regional competitions. Despite having started piano later than most competitors, he'd ranked second.

Dad was especially supportive of Shaz's talent. He recorded my brother's performances and uploaded them to his own YouTube channel. *Everyone should hear his music,* he'd say. For Shaz's birthday, Dad got him his own Yamaha baby grand piano—used, of course, but *stunning.* Dad even reached out to his contacts to find gigs for my brother, and before long Shaz was getting paid to perform at church services and weddings.

"You're having Shaz play at a *church*?" I asked him, surprised. Dad was the principal of our Islamic Sunday school; it almost felt sacrilegious to have his own son play at a church service.

"Music knows no boundaries," Dad replied.

Dad was always the pragmatist. His relationship with his faith wasn't based on fear, but on love and respect. He loved God, read the Quran countless times, prayed five times a day. But he took time for himself, too: to garden, play golf, read history books. That was his policy, and the one he instilled in us: be steadfast with religion, but appreciate and enjoy the gift of life. And good music, he felt, brought us closer to God.

Meanwhile, I'd long given up on piano; I'd lost interest after seeing my brother's passion. It almost felt disrespectful to the instrument to play it when I hardly cared. It was much nicer listening to him play instead. I'd sit by him and listen to him practice, the way he once had when I played, unintentionally training my own ears to pick up on mistakes, on rhythm.

Piano belonged to Shaz, and I was happy he had something all his own.

"Are you sure it's not because you feel like Shaz took it from you?" Mom snidely asked me once.

I never understood why Mom did that sometimes, as if she were trying to pit my brother and me against each other. When Shaz was born, for example, she was convinced I was jealous of the attention he was getting because, as she put it, I kept *talking like a baby*.

"This voice you do—you can't do that just because you want attention, okay?" she said, sitting me down in my room for a talk. I cried, confused. I had no idea what she was talking about; it was just my *voice*. I was only five years old, after all.

A few years later, when Nani Jan stayed with us for a week, she spent most of her free time with Shaz. The two of them would play

UNO for hours. It was one of the only times I remember seeing my nani laugh.

"She spends a lot of time with Shaz, huh?" asked Mom. But I'd only shrugged. I didn't like spending time with Nani, anyway. I didn't like the way she talked only to my brother and boy cousins. The way she stared at me like she was sizing me up, and found me lacking.

❧

The problem was that neither of my parents viewed music, or the arts in general, as viable careers. To them, music was a hobby, one that should be taken seriously, of course. But one should never let a hobby get in the way of stability.

When Shaz was fourteen and I was home from college for the weekend, he got into a big argument with Mom and Dad.

"I don't understand why you always push me to practice and do these competitions and work my ass off when I'm not allowed to *do* anything with it!"

Shaz had always hated school. I'd gone to a public school, but my parents decided to enroll my brother in a private school in Delaware. He was smart, got straight As without trying, but school, and the culture of private school, seemed to drain a part of his soul. He was bullied for being brown. Bullied for being Muslim. I think the stress of it all made that inner rage Shaz secretly carried even thornier. Piano was the only thing that calmed it.

Still, Mom and Dad wanted him to go to med school. They wanted him to be a doctor, not the pianist he wanted to be. And yet they pushed him to practice for hours. If we had guests over, they'd yell for him to come down from his room and perform, as if Shaz's love of piano was a mere parlor trick, worthy only of being used to show off.

"It's because you have the talent!" Dad retorted, when Shaz told him he was sick of playing for their guests. "It's a *waste* not to use it!"

"For who?!" Shaz screamed back, his eyes red-rimmed, before storming off to his room.

As Shaz and I got older, I tried to step into their arguments, to defend my little brother. But this was an argument I'd already had with our parents time and time again—not just for Shaz, but for myself.

In high school, I'd told my parents I wanted to be a writer. I was an editor at my high school newspaper, and coeditor of our creative literary journal called *Portals*, which I ran with two close friends, Kristy and Caitlin. I wanted to try. But Mom and Dad told me the same thing. Writing was a hobby. Not a job.

It was a fight I'd lost, too.

After Shaz's big argument with Mom and Dad about his career, I put on the glow-in-the-dark sunglasses I'd gotten from Six Flags, burst into my brother's room, and danced poorly to Daft Punk's "Harder, Better, Faster, Stronger" blasting on my phone. I didn't know what I could say to make him feel better, but we both loved Daft Punk, and maybe that was good enough.

He'd done similar things for me before. One time I'd been depressed after a fight with Mom, and Shaz had walked into my room. *Got a gift for you,* he said, then proceeded to play a guided meditation narrated by Jeff Bridges on his laptop. When I'd asked why he thought I needed to meditate, he gave me a pointed look that said it all.

That's the beauty of siblings, I think. You don't need words. After growing up in the same dysfunctional household for years, you develop your own special telepathy, your own secret language: of facial expressions only the two of you can read, of inside jokes only the two of you understand, of memories only the two of you share.

You get each other, perhaps in a way no one else ever will.

From his bed, Shaz, with an exasperated look, watched me dance badly to Daft Punk. But at least there was a quirk to his mouth now.

"You're such a dipshit," he muttered.

It felt like a win.

CHAPTER 5

Great Expectations

Despite the assumptions I'd made about him the first time I saw him, during the project, Stephen and I worked well together. Really well.

We shot emails back and forth, then talked on Facebook chat, before Facebook was a hub for grandparents and conspiracy theorists and ten-year-old memes. Our chats were at first exclusively about the project, but over time we branched out to less related things. What shows and anime we loved. Our favorite characters to use in *Mario Kart*. Pakistan and Jamaica. How both of us had grown up eating similar foods, how people perceived him as more Indian in Jamaica, but more Black here. How I was Muslim, how he'd been raised Christian but never felt connected.

Stephen mostly drove our conversations—weird, meandering chats that sometimes went late into the night—but I didn't mind. I found him open and easy to talk to. Uncomplicated.

When the day of our class presentation finally came—my nineteenth birthday—Stephen kept his promise. Everything did, in fact, go smoothly. Perfectly, even. Not only had we worked well together, but I wasn't even a little nervous during the presentation. Stephen and I effortlessly bounced off each other, filling in each other's gaps. *So to add on to what my partner was saying . . . ,* he'd say, with that same goofy, unnecessary enthusiasm I'd begun getting used to. His energy was infectious.

With him, I didn't need to take our presentation seriously, to be anxious about stumbling over my words. It was as if it was just another one of our weird little Facebook chats, natural and effortless, and no one else existed.

When the applause came, and Professor Tanaka started giving feedback, I felt as if I were just waking up from a fugue state. The presentation was over. It was almost anticlimactic. Based on what Professor Tanaka—whom I was only half listening to—was saying, we were sure to get an A.

So why did things feel so unfinished?

Stephen was staring at me again. We were still standing in front of the classroom as our professor reminded the rest of the class that it was in their best interest to be taking notes during these presentations. Cecilia and Meg stood on the other side of the projector screen: Cecilia beaming and Meg's shoulders relaxed with relief.

"What?" I whispered.

"I, uh—" Stephen mumbled. "Your birthday. Isn't it today?"

"Oh. Yeah."

"Almost forgot." His smile was small. Shy. For a moment he seemed to struggle to find the right words.

"Well, happy birthday," he said finally. "I hope you have fun today."

"Oh. Thanks."

I stared ahead, deflated. Disappointed. Stephen had forgotten my birthday until now. Of course he had—how ridiculous and contradictory it was to think anything else. There'd been no deeper meaning in our silly little conversations. It wasn't like we'd somehow become *friends* after just a few late-night chats. We were project partners, and now the project was over. I was annoyed at myself for hoping for anything.

"How you do in school dictates your entire future," Mom had warned me while helping me study for a fourth-grade social studies test. I'd complained I was tired and wanted a break. "Your education is the only thing you can one hundred percent rely on. You don't need to think about anything else."

It stuck. I'd focused on school most of my life. I became increasingly withdrawn from my friends. I rarely socialized, unless it was related to school and clubs. I became afraid of socializing because I didn't want Mom to think I'd gotten distracted. I did it for her. Or I was doing it for me. I couldn't tell after a while.

But recently I'd started wondering what the point was. Mom and I never talked about what would come after I finished my education, what the end goal would be. What did success look like at the end of all this hard work? *You'd be a lawyer,* she'd probably answer. *You'd be a lawyer and make us proud.* But would I be happy? Fulfilled? Mom went to college and grad school and got her MBA; she got married. For the most part, she'd followed the same life plan she now laid out for me.

Was *she* happy?

That was a question I didn't dare ask her.

After class, I took the bus back to Bryn Mawr and trudged into my dorm room. Ava had kept her promise and got me a cake; we cut it into crooked pieces in the paper box she'd picked it up in, called over our hallmates, and ate it on the floor while I played music from my laptop. I laughed as Ava told us a story about her family back in Long Island. But I felt a little empty. As nice as it was to have my friends in my room, as delicious as the cake was, I kept mulling over the past few weeks and all those conversations I'd had with Stephen, which now felt pointless.

If this was where all those late-night Facebook chats got me, maybe what Mom had said back in fourth grade was true. Maybe all that mattered—all that ever mattered—was focusing on school.

But every few days Stephen would send me another Facebook message: about the shows he was watching, the plans he'd made with friends for the weekend. Mostly he'd ask about me and my life, asking questions like, *If you could be anything, what would you be?* (a writer, maybe); *If you could only eat one food for the rest of your life, what would it be?* (cereal, I think?). I wasn't sure what to make of it, especially since the project was over. Did he actually care? Was he that bored?

Was it too much to hope maybe he felt the same weird tug I did?

Almost two months after our presentation, Stephen invited me to his dorm room. Even though I didn't know what this—us—was, I accepted the invite, mostly out of curiosity to find out.

"Home sweet home," he said proudly. "Take a seat anywhere."

I looked around the room. It was surprisingly neat, though a little threadbare, devoid of any decor or even a single poster on the wall. Like he was ready to pack up and leave at a moment's notice. There was nowhere to sit, either, but a single chair in the corner and his bed.

Stephen had called me over to blow off some steam playing *Mario Kart*, and I'd agreed without thinking. But now that I was here and alone with him, panic began to settle in. What if *Mario Kart* was actually a euphemism for something dirty, and I'd just failed to realize it? I knew hookups happened at college all the time, but I didn't want that. For me and my first-year hallmates, our idea of a good time was doing karaoke on the weekends in the common room and eating ice-cream cupcakes from Cold Stone Creamery, or listening to a tipsy Ava tell us another gloriously wild story about her friends in Long Island, which is the only reason why I know what Purple Drank is.

So what was the *protocol* here?

The last time I'd been alone with a boy, it had ended in a nightmare I was still recovering from.

Mom's accusing voice rang through my head. *How many times have I told you? Never be alone with a boy. It's for your own protection.*

I suddenly felt sick.

I sat on the floor.

"You okay?" asked Stephen.

"Uh, yeah." I fidgeted. "Can we leave the door open?"

"Of course." Stephen pushed the door open a little wider. He didn't seem annoyed by my anxiety. Didn't question it. Instead, he simply began hooking up an extra Nintendo 64 controller, excitement wafting off his shoulders as he whistled.

He handed me the controller and sat beside me.

"So remember when you told me you'd beat me in *Mario Kart?*" he asked, grinning.

I scanned my memories, trying to recall some of the last couple of late-night Facebook chats. I had, in fact, told him I could *kick his ass* in *Mario Kart.* Mostly false bravado, not that Stephen needed to know.

"Yes . . . ?" I answered.

"Time to eat your words."

We played for hours. The upbeat music of *Mario Kart* filled Stephen's room, punctuated with our trash talk. And as the hours slipped by, I realized that Stephen lacked any ulterior motives: we were there to play video games. No secret agenda, no strings attached.

Just *playing.*

Something in my chest unfurled. Transitioning to college had been hard: sharing a bathroom with thirty other people, removing hair balls that weren't mine from the shower drain, rushing to class and constantly wondering if I'd forgotten to do homework or study for an exam. Even though it was an escape from home, I was on edge all the time. Making new friends was a painful process, too; I'd grown up with the friends I'd made in elementary school, and they had all gone their separate ways. Now I had to remember how to do that awkward song and dance of small talk with strangers.

But sitting there, with Stephen, ignoring midterms and wasting time on a game I hadn't played since I was a kid, felt bizarrely normal. I was actually *enjoying* myself, in an unselfconscious way I hadn't for a long, long time.

It was different from when I'd hang out with Ava, Kaya, and the rest of my hallmates. I liked them, and I wanted them to like me, too— desperately. But that *want* added a painful, completely unreasonable pressure filtering everything I'd say. I'd analyze every second I spent with them, looking for how I might have inadvertently given them cause to dislike me. Sometimes I'd convince myself I had, for no good reason.

With Stephen, though, I didn't put that same pointless pressure on myself. There were no expectations for us, not even a word for what we had—a kinship? Was that it? But whatever it was, it felt fleeting. Transient. We'd just happened to fall into this weird companionship of ours, and now it simply existed: some floating, nameless, jellyfish-like thing that carried no burdens, no desperation. It could just *be*.

"You know something funny?" Stephen said suddenly. "I almost didn't take this class."

"What, Japanese Civilization?" I asked. "Why?"

"I woke up one day with what I thought was a god-awful case of acne. Turns out it was chicken pox," he said. "I had to put on a giant hoodie and sneak over to the health center so no one would see me. They quarantined me in an apartment and everything. In all the chaos, I ended up missing the window to sign up for classes."

Up on the screen, my character, Luigi, got hit with a red shell. "This was right before the semester started?"

"Yeah. So by the time I finally signed up for classes, all the good ones were taken. The only one left was JCiv."

I shook my head in disbelief. "How did you even get chicken pox? Did you not get vaccinated?"

"Apparently no. My mom swore I did, though." He laughed. "How wild is that, though? All because of a freak case of chicken pox, I ended up in JCiv."

"And getting stuck with me for a project?" I asked, smirking.

"Hey, your words, not mine."

This time I laughed.

What *were* the chances he'd get chicken pox? What were the chances that JCiv would be the only class left? What were the chances we'd be put together on a group project?

I considered myself a Muslim, albeit a shamefully clumsy one: I'd pray as often as I'd remember to; I'd fast every Ramadan, for as long as my body permitted. I'd give zakat, or charity, when the chance presented itself. But the one belief I absorbed at Sunday school, from which I *never* wavered, was that although we had control over our own actions, the events of life came preordained: *"They were planning, and Allah was planning,"* my dad would quote the Quran, *"and Allah is the best of planners."* He'd mutter it sometimes—especially if we were running late for something, like a community dinner party or an interfaith panel he'd organized with local churches and synagogues.

Coincidences did not exist, I decided. Coincidences felt more like messages from the universe I hadn't learned to read just yet. And, as cheesy as it sounds, meeting Stephen was starting to feel like one of them.

Stephen tossed me a couple of blankets and asked me to build a fort while he set up a movie called *The Girl Who Leapt through Time* for us to watch (in his view, the best movies were meant to be watched beneath a blanket fort). I quickly cobbled together a lumpy, precarious fort of sorts; I had no future in architecture, but it stayed up.

While Stephen busied himself with digging up the movie file on his laptop, I crawled into the tent to wait. In seconds my eyes began to droop. I drifted, lulled by the faint sounds coming from other students out in the hall, returning from classes; the sound of Stephen clicking away at his laptop; the faint hums and whirs of a dorm in the middle of a semester, filled with life.

When I finally woke, it was dark.

I panicked all over again. I'd fallen asleep. I'd let down my guard and taken a *very* big risk. What if Stephen was a freak who took photos of my feet while I slept to sell on the dark web, or somehow slipped me a roofie while I was unconscious or something? I hadn't had *anything* to drink since I'd gotten to his room, which explained why my throat felt like sandpaper, but *still.* Something could have happened. And then Mom would kill me.

Stupid, stupid, *stupid.*

Except—there was a blanket over me that wasn't there before. Had Stephen done that?

I crawled out from beneath the fort and looked around the room. As my eyes slowly adjusted, I found a lump curled up by the adjacent wall, just a few feet away.

Stephen.

His eyes were closed, revealing surprisingly long lashes, and he was snoring softly. He must have found *The Girl Who Leapt through Time* after I'd fallen asleep and put it on, anyway—only, the movie had finished and now the credits were rolling, casting the room in a dim blue light.

I couldn't help it; I let out a laugh. It was ridiculous. Two college students, alone in a dorm room together, and we'd somehow fallen asleep like a couple of babies.

I was safe with Stephen. It wasn't so much because he hadn't done anything to me while I slept—God, the bar is so, so low—but more that I finally understood the idea would have never even occurred to him. That the only thought he'd had was to put a blanket over me to make sure I was warm.

The realization hit me with an onslaught of complicated emotions. I felt affection for this weird boy, my former project partner.

But we weren't just former project partners. It felt so obvious now. Stephen and I were friends. Simple, indisputable friends.

I could trust him.

CHAPTER 6

Something about Us

Stephen Griffiths: How's being home?

Stephen's texts, whenever I visited home, were a welcome distraction. A reminder that even though things might be bad there, there were people at school who cared about me. Who were waiting for me.

We'd also gotten closer since we played *Mario Kart*, and we were talking every day. Sometimes for hours.

Farah Naz Rishi: haha . . .

Farah Naz Rishi: food's solid

Farah Naz Rishi: my dad made seafood biryani

Stephen Griffiths: that sounds amazing

Stephen Griffiths: but the company . . . not so much?

I was typing up a response when Mom's voice came over my shoulder.

"Who are you texting?"

I quickly put away my phone, my spine leaping out of my body.

"A friend," I replied. I did not sound convincing.

"A friend . . . ?" she repeated.

"Yes. A friend."

"Then why are you hiding your phone?"

Mom had a point. We both knew there was only one reason why I wouldn't want her looking at my screen. We both knew the concept of privacy didn't exist in this house.

The only reason you'd want privacy is because you have something to hide.

It was a vicious cycle now, my interactions with Mom, and our relationship was getting worse the longer I was away.

College was changing me. And the truth was, I *did* want to hide my new friendship with Stephen. I wanted to protect it: this new, special, fluttering thing in my hand that I had yet to fully understand. I wanted it for myself.

And Mom—I thought Mom would try to ruin it.

I didn't know what a normal mother–daughter relationship was supposed to look like. What I do know is that the older I got and the more I learned about the world outside the house, the more Mom would pinch and prod at my every insecurity, as if daring me to react. If I tried to sleep in, she'd tell me I was being lazy. If I cleaned my plate at dinner, she'd comment that I ate like a man.

Once we'd been in her walk-in closet as she'd been getting ready for a dinner party. My family had recently moved to a new house in Chadds Ford, a bigger dream house that for years my mom had begged Dad for. It was almost twice the size of the old one, with tall ceilings and a giant staircase fit for one of those rom-com movie scenes where a girl would slowly walk down, revealing a gorgeous prom dress as the music swells and her family, and love interest, watch with mouths agape.

I didn't like the new house. It felt cold. Lifeless.

But I did like Mom's walk-in closet, which felt cozy and inviting. More than that, I loved looking through her dresses, her shalwar kameez, feeling all the material through my fingers.

"If you weren't so flat chested, I'd have loved to let you borrow some of them," Mom said, laughing as she slipped on her dazzling Chanel earrings. "I don't get it. No one else in our family has your chest, so I really don't understand what happened to you. It's such a shame."

I tried not to let it get to me. Maybe Mom realized she'd said something cruel, because a few weeks later, she bought me a dress: a gorgeous dark-brown dinner dress from Anthropologie. It fit perfectly.

"Not that you'll have any occasion to wear it," Mom said, laughing. "Miss Antisocial."

"Thank you. I really love it."

Mom looked pleased. "What would you do without me?"

But I was beginning to recognize that some of the things she'd say to me weren't right. That there was a dangerous, unhealthy pattern to her behavior: she'd act interested in me and my life—she'd act almost *motherly*—going so far as to ask what video games my brother and I were playing in the basement, and complain that she felt left out. Like she wanted to be involved but didn't know how. Mom was contrary like that.

But I almost liked that version of Mom.

I wanted to let her in. I would tell her things about my life, secret hopes and dreams I'd been too afraid to voice. I told her I loved writing. I told her other things, too.

Then she would say something bitter and scathing, seemingly out of nowhere.

You have no idea how good you have it, do you?

Your skin is looking awful. What are you doing to it?

And a few days later, she would do something to make up for it, like buy me a dress I hadn't asked for, and act like nothing had ever happened.

I was tired. In another world, I could talk to her about Stephen openly, without her thinking the worst, without her being hypervigilant and distrustful.

But that wasn't this world.

"It's like I said, he's just a friend," I told Mom again. "It's not a big deal."

That was the wrong response. I could feel the coming storm.

"He?" She let out a scornful laugh. "Let's be real, Farah. We both know what you mean when you say *friend*."

I could feel myself shutting down. I was an idiot to text Stephen out in the open, in the kitchen, where Mom could so easily find me.

"You shouldn't be talking to boys," she continued. "You should be focusing on school."

"I *am* focusing on school."

Mom was a minefield. One minute she'd be breathlessly asking questions like, *Have you met any boys?* Then they would become criminal accusations in the span of a week. *Find a husband* but *Don't think about anything except school. Hurry* but *Don't rush like I did.*

Stephen was not a marriage candidate. He was a friend.

Mom folded her arms across her chest. She always folded her arms when she was mad. "Clearly not. Who is he? How long has this been going on?"

Why did she *always* assume the worst?

"Mom, I can have platonic male friends. Just because I'm talking to one doesn't mean I'm *sleeping* with them."

"You said that about Kareem, and look what happened."

Her words had me in a choke hold.

Kareem was still my first and only real boyfriend. But using the word *boyfriend* would be reductive.

I had known Kareem since I was ten years old. We'd met in Sunday school, but for years we'd stayed clear of each other, even though we were in the same class. He was annoying, the way so many young, unchecked boys are. A *menace.* He and the other two boys in our class, Ahmad and Salim, would spend recess throwing hard green hedge apples (or, as they called them, monkey balls) at each other. And sometimes they threw them at me and the only other girl in my Sunday school class, Amina—until I screamed that I would tell on them to the principal, a.k.a. my dad.

Then everyone turned fifteen and began using AIM. Amina had discovered what Kareem's username was and planned an elaborate revenge plot for all the times he'd tormented us. I went to her house after school, and she suggested that we pose as secret agents who knew everything about him. We were certain he'd pee his pants in fear.

He figured out it was us in approximately three minutes.

Kareem and I kept talking after that. He even apologized for being so horrible when we were young. We fell for each other, hard and fast. People at Sunday school probably noticed the furtive, embarrassed glances we exchanged, the blushing. Our parents knew there was something between us and seemed excited by the prospect; his mother always went out of her way to talk to me at every dinner party and say how she wished I were her daughter. Still, Mom wouldn't allow me to openly meet up for dates or anything—propriety meant we had to wait until marriage—so Kareem and I settled instead for secret chats on AIM and MSN Messenger.

I could wait. Kareem and I would get married, I was sure of it—we'd told each other we would. And it made sense. We were an excellent match, at least on paper: we had similar interests, shared so many childhood memories, and could spend hours talking about nothing. We even shared similar traumas; my mom slapped me if my grades fell, while his dad would hit him with a belt. We both wanted to escape our parents.

Falling for him was easy. Kareem was whip-smart and funny and had the ability to say exactly what you wanted to hear. He knew how to get you to take down your own walls. Part of him, I think, was also incredibly lonely, and lonely people know what to say to other lonely people. After all, his family life was a nightmare, violent and unpredictable. He told me, once, how he dreamed of leaving Pennsylvania for good.

But every conversation we had felt intimate and profound and soul baring and meaningful. It felt like he saw me, all of me, when no one else did. He made me feel like I meant everything in the world to him. And I wanted to be that—to him. I hung on his every word. I relied on that feeling of importance. Of being valued.

And then he tore me apart. First by isolating me from my friends, telling me I didn't need them, that they couldn't be trusted. Then by suddenly acting cold and distant; if I pressed for answers, he'd bring up all the insecurities I'd shared with him—my own loneliness, my fear of not being good enough, for anything—as reasons why his change in behavior was merely all in my head. Sometimes he'd tell me about various girls at school who had flirted with him, who had expressed interest in him, who had asked him out. But if I expressed any jealousy, he'd tell me I needed to trust him, that I shouldn't make a "big deal out of nothing."

When one of my close friends in high school, Lexy, encouraged me to stand up for myself, Kareem texted her to tell her to leave us alone.

Surprising no one except me, he eventually cheated. Several times. I actually found out through an online video game, of all things; he'd asked me to play his favorite game, *Final Fantasy XIV*, with him, and as long as I had an internet connection, we could play together. Talk freely. But I was new to games and was far behind him. He abandoned me in the game to play with his friends while I tried to figure out how to play on my own. Eventually those very same friends of his found me in the game and told me he was cheating on me with someone in the game—someone he'd already met with offline, in secret.

When I finally confronted him about it and told him we needed to end things, he begged me to reconsider: "Why can't I have both? Why are you forcing me to choose? I don't want to lose either of you. I *can't*."

Us talking online, apparently, hadn't been enough for him. I almost felt guilty. He sounded so tormented, as if all of this was my fault. And now I was making him choose.

We were seventeen. We were at a dinner party my neighbors were throwing when he asked if we could talk, in private. I sneaked away with him, to my house across the street. To my bedroom.

There he said that he wanted me to "prove" that I loved him. That was why he'd cheated, after all: he didn't believe that I loved him, he told me. I was so cold, so closed off at times. But if he knew I loved him for certain, he wouldn't cheat anymore.

There was an easy way, he assured me, to give him proof.

Minutes into it—minutes that felt like hours—I started to cry. I couldn't find my voice at first, but when I finally did, I begged him to stop. This was wrong. I had wanted him, yes, but not this. Not like *this*. When he pulled away, he looked at me like I was the most disgusting, disappointing thing in the world. Then he left me on my bed, naked and crying and wondering, deep in the back of my mind, what had just happened and whether it was all my fault.

In situations of alleged assault, the world often blames the woman for putting themselves in that situation in the first place. Once, when Kareem and I went out for a walk during an iftari party at the Sunday school, a rumor that we'd been spotted alone—even though we'd just been talking, ten feet from the school—spread like wildfire. *You need to break Farah's legs,* one "uncle" suggested to my mom, loud enough for everyone to hear. *That's the only way you can control them.* Even Mom was so disgusted we left the iftari party early.

This is why you don't even put yourself in these positions. Do you see what people say? Mom told me on the way back.

But the shame of what happened with Kareem in my room became too much. I told my mom about everything. That the Kareem I'd known was long gone. Or maybe he'd always been an awful person, and I'd been too naive to see it.

And yet Mom continued to bring up Kareem like it was some mistake I'd made, some punishment for not following the rules.

"Holy *shit*," I said, my voice shaking. "I told you what Kareem did to me because I thought you would understand. Or at least try to. Not use it against me."

Her own voice rose. "I told you that when a boy and a girl are alone together, the devil is in the room with them. I told you a *thousand* times."

In this case, maybe it was true. It *would* have been smarter not to have been alone with Kareem. But I hated being in a world that demanded women protect themselves instead of punishing the men who would harm them in the first place.

"Are you *blaming* me? For what *he* did?"

"I'm saying you didn't listen to me then!" she yelled, gesturing to the phone I was trying so desperately to hide. "And you're still not listening!"

"You're my *mom*. You're supposed to be on my *side*."

"Who really knows what happened that day? What you're describing, what you're accusing him of—you could be misremembering. I'm not the kind of mother to blindly believe everything her child says." Mom said it like it was a point of pride for her.

"How could—" I felt my eyes swelling. My mom didn't believe me, even after everything I'd told her. My mom would rather believe Kareem over me. Or maybe it had nothing to do with Kareem—maybe it didn't matter who it was. She'd believe *anyone* over me.

What had I done to make her hate me so much?

I don't remember what happened after that. I shut down. But the next thing I knew, Mom was screaming about how I was making her out to be the *bad guy*, and my dad was in the room with us, trying to calm Mom, to little avail. *Samia, please, she's your daughter,* he said. A reminder. A plea. Dad, who never interfered in fights between Mom and me—who sometimes felt like a stranger to me—had finally stepped in.

As he tugged her away from me by the arm, our eyes met. I saw the shock on his face. I wonder if it mirrored mine.

Later Mom disappeared into her bedroom, and Dad came into the kitchen. He told me she'd agreed to go to therapy. That she knew our relationship depended on it.

"I didn't know how bad it was," said Dad, taking off his glasses and revealing tired eyes. "I knew the two of you argued, but not like this."

What a relief it was to finally have someone notice. My arguments with Mom happened so often those days, it was easy to forget that none of it was normal, let alone healthy.

"It's getting worse the older I get."

"You know why she's like this, though, don't you?" Dad had asked me. He was in teaching mode. He was trying to walk me through the logic of my own emotions, to see the situation clinically. The two of us were sitting at the breakfast table. The house was quiet.

"No," I answered.

"This behavior—the things she says to you—I've seen it before. Your nani Jan did the same to her. Worse. Not that I'm excusing it." Dad sat back in his chair. "But that is why she acts like this. Your nani Jan was jealous of your mom and would say all sorts of horrible things. After we'd gotten engaged, she would insult your mom, her cooking, her clothes, even when I was around."

"*What?*" I was no big fan of Nani. Perhaps it shouldn't have been so surprising; sometimes Nani'd ask me how school was going, and if I told her about my accomplishments, she'd get this weird, faraway look in her stern eyes. Like she didn't want to hear it. Like hearing about other people's successes bothered her.

Being jealous of her own daughter, though—it was unfathomable.

"Your nani once got involved in a big argument your mom and I had—this was a little after you were born—and encouraged your mom to take you in the middle of the night and leave instead of talking things out," Dad went on. "Your nani thinks the worst of people, and I think sometimes your mom does that, too. But it's learned behavior. It's not personal."

I've always hated that phrase. Half the time, whenever someone says *It's not personal*, it feels like a get-out-of-jail-free card. It's a way to refuse responsibility for hurting someone.

And in this case, it did feel personal. I was my mother's *daughter*. Of course it felt personal. I understood there was history, there was context I couldn't quite grasp, but if Mom didn't want to change for *me*, didn't want to break this cycle for the sake of her own kids, then maybe it meant only one thing.

Maybe she didn't care.

CHAPTER 7

Close Encounters

Mom did start going to therapy, just like Dad had said.

But she quit after a few weeks.

"I don't need it anymore," she'd told me over the phone. "I know what I need to do now. We just need to spend more time together. Rebuild."

Which was why, about a month or so after our huge fight, she planned to pick me up after my JCiv class. She wanted to grab lunch together at an afternoon tea spot she'd found just a couple of miles from campus. The food was supposed to be delicious—she'd even polled several of her friends for great recommendations for places—and it'd be good to get away from campus for a while. It was almost the end of my very first year of college, after all.

I was skeptical. Of course she'd polled her friends. It cemented the idea in other people's minds that she was a "cool mom" who went out of her way to take her daughter to nice restaurants. I could imagine that she would take a picture of us at the tea place just to post it on Facebook, or at the very least tell her friends what an exaggeratedly fabulous time we had. Mom did that a lot. I'd overhear her talking on the phone with her friends or even her sisters: "Farah and I are so close, you know. We tell each other practically everything!" Another time I overheard her telling a friend, "I swear, every time Farah and I go out together, someone tells us we look like sisters. Of course, Farah said she *hates* it."

Except I'd never said that. As someone who'd struggled with acne her whole life, I hoped to at least inherit Mom's youthful glow; it was something I looked forward to. I looked at Mom on the phone and gave her an annoyed look. She waved her hand away.

I never understood why lies would slip off her tongue so easily, why she wanted to paint a very different picture of the reality of our relationship. But if Mom was taking me out for afternoon tea, even just for show, at the very least I'd get some damn good scones—so what was there to lose?

Unfortunately, I'd completely failed to consider the prospect of my mom coming on campus, of her meeting my friends.

As class let out for the day, I found her in the hallway, just outside the JCiv classroom. She almost looked like any other college student, in a cute floral tunic perfect for spring, reading the flyers on a nearby bulletin board.

"Mom." I tried not to look surprised. "What are you doing here? I was just going to walk to your car—"

"Nothing wrong with me picking you up directly from class, right?" she said cheerfully. "Plus, I wanted to take a look around."

My stomach fell.

She was going to meet Stephen. I'd wanted to delay that from happening, preferably forever. All my life, Mom never went out of her way to get to know my friends. She'd be sweet to their faces when they came over, but would later tell me, completely unprompted, how my friends were *weird* or how she simply didn't like them, only to shrug her shoulders if I defended them.

I'd let Mom ruin my friendships before. When I was in high school, she told me she thought one of my closest friends since fifth grade, Anna, was too "obsessive" about us. *Don't you think you spend too much time together?* she'd asked. *I swear, she acts like she's in love with you or something.*

Like an absolute fool, I began to pull away from Anna. And when Anna realized it, she wrote me a heartfelt letter to assure me that whatever I was feeling, we could work through it together. But when I'd asked Mom for advice, she'd only scowled at the letter. As if it was *creepy*. What I hadn't realized until after we'd graduated from high school was that Anna had done nothing but be a good friend who simply enjoyed my company as much as I did hers. We had genuinely and openly cared for each other. And *that*—unselfconscious affection—was what Mom had found creepy.

It was bad enough that Mom meeting Stephen would confirm I'd been talking to a boy, something she'd told me time and time again to avoid doing. But if she could put a face to the name, she would bring Stephen up relentlessly, use him against me. If my grades ever fell, if I ever talked back to her, it would be because I'd let him into my life.

To her, Stephen wouldn't be his own person. He would be my moral failing.

"Farah?" said Stephen, coming from behind me.

Shit.

Stephen's eyes met my mom's. "Wait, is this—"

"Yeah," I answered uneasily. "This is my mom."

"Hey! Hi. I'm Stephen." He reached out a hand in friendly greeting.

Oh, Stephen. Sweet, oblivious Stephen. He had no idea he'd just walked into a spiderweb, and I'd failed to protect him.

I lost my appetite.

Mom plastered on a smile as she shook Stephen's hand. She'd barely touched it. "Hi, Stephen. It's nice to meet you."

"Stephen and I worked together on a project earlier this year. He's a friend of mine," I explained skittishly, emphasizing the word *friend*.

Mom gave me a sideways glance. I could tell she would have more questions for me later.

"God, Farah, if I'd known your mom was coming today, I would have worn a nicer shirt. I'm pretty sure I got this one from the kids' section." Stephen laughed, but it was different from usual. I wondered if he was nervous.

I laughed with him—it was either that or cry.

"It's a really nice shirt, actually," said Mom. Her voice had taken on a placatingly sweet and sugary coating, the kind of voice she used when speaking with friends. The one she used to ensnare other people into believing she was the nicest woman in the world.

My brother Shaz had called it her *Other* voice.

Stephen beamed. "Thank you! Cheaper, too."

I took a step back, maintaining desperate eye contact with Stephen. "Anyway, we should probably . . ."

"Right," said Stephen, picking up on my not-so-subtle hint. "I'm sure you have plans, and I don't want to keep you."

I nodded. "Yeah, we're going to grab lunch."

"Cool. Cool. Have a great lunch."

"Bye, Stephen!" said Mom before the two of us began walking to the parking lot.

Mom was silent until we got into the car. For a moment she said nothing.

I braced myself.

"What a fucking weirdo," she said finally, turning on the ignition. She was looking ahead, but I could tell her whole demeanor had changed. "He was clearly a nervous wreck, rambling on about that awful shirt of his. Are these the kinds of friends you're making here?"

I bristled. I didn't like that she could just casually insult my new friend like it was nothing. He didn't deserve that.

"He's really sweet," I whispered.

"Sure," she scoffed. She didn't say another word until we arrived at the tearoom, after which she talked about the new friends she'd made in the community, and how even though they were a little *backward* and a little too *fresh off the boat*, they seemed nice enough—friends, after all, were hard to come by.

"You never know who's secretly jealous of you in this community," she lamented, biting into another cucumber sandwich.

People *were* jealous of her; time and time again in the community, other aunties would copy the way Mom dressed, the way Mom decorated the house, even the way she did her hair. She was the aunty everyone liked, after all.

Sometimes it made me happy that Mom trusted me enough with her unfiltered thoughts about the people we knew. But I didn't like the way Mom talked about them in such a mean-spirited way, and then smile at those same people at dinner parties like they were the best of friends. It made me wonder if, even though she'd tried therapy to repair our relationship, deep down she was holding on to a secret disgust toward me.

The rest of lunch went without mention of Stephen. For now, at least, he'd been buried under the rug, safe and sound. It was better that way.

❧

"Your mom seems really nice," Stephen told me the next time I saw him in class.

Not you, too.

I swallowed hard. He'd meant it as a compliment, of course. But I had hoped—I'm not sure what I hoped. Maybe I wanted him to be an ally. Maybe I wanted him to see what I saw. That unlike everyone else, he wouldn't fall for that same fake smile. But he had.

It wasn't worth it, I decided, to tell him the truth. Of course I'd already told him that my mom and I didn't get along. But I never told him the full extent. I didn't tell him how whenever I was home, I imagined all the hypothetical arguments I'd get into with Mom, just to mentally prepare myself. That just by me talking to him, Mom would assume there was something sexual between us.

How does one even go about explaining that they're scared of their own mother?

It was easier to not get into it. He didn't need to be burdened with all *this*.

"Yeah," I lied, and looked away. "She can be."

❧

But even though I wasn't ready to talk about my mom, Stephen and I grew closer. After I was done with classes, and he finished tennis practice, we'd meet up—almost every other day—to do homework or watch a movie or play video games. Sometimes at his dorm. Sometimes at mine.

Stephen's arrival in my life had signaled a change I couldn't quite put my finger on. Except at the epicenter of so many of my happiest memories of college, there he stood.

It helped that he got along so well with my hallmates. My resident adviser, Rach, already knew him—they'd taken a bio class together. A few things about Rach: she was an artist who often came back from classes covered in paint. She was also a premed student, which meant she perpetually had circles so dark beneath her eyes you could see them through her glasses.

When I first told Rach about Stephen, she'd cackled.

"Of course I know Stephen!" she exclaimed. "He's the guy that always sits in the first row of the lecture hall and falls asleep, right in front of the professor!"

I smiled because I could imagine it so clearly.

"But he's a good kid," she assured me. "You should have him hang out with us."

And so I did. Which usually resulted in chaos.

Once, Rach had loudly announced to the hall that she had some clothes she wanted to get rid of, including a beautiful pink floral corset. Stephen happened to be with us that day. Kaya and Ava demanded that Stephen wear it—to get a better idea of how it looked on a person— which he did without complaint, much to Kaya and Ava's delight.

"Not gonna lie, it *is* kinda pretty," said Stephen, relenting.

Another time, Kaya got her hands on a water gun and decided the best way to test it would be on Stephen. It wasn't long before Stephen was so soaked he had to borrow one of my oversize T-shirts. But the next day Stephen showed up with a water gun of his own. The water gun fight that ensued in the hallway would live in infamy, and as far as I know, only a temporary truce was called. I couldn't remember the last time I'd laughed so hard.

I wondered if this was my hallmates' way of testing him, of making sure he was safe, the kind of guy who could roll with the punches. I'd told Kaya and Ava about my past, about what had happened with Kareem. Maybe it was their way of protecting me.

But if they were wondering about the nature of our relationship, they didn't push for answers. The truth was, I wasn't sure, either.

What I did know was that I felt secure around him. I knew I could talk to him about *anything*, and he wouldn't judge. When I'd gotten my period and run out of pads, for example, Kaya had lent me a tampon. Except I'd never used a tampon before; my mom had told me once that tampons were bad, that they could take a girl's virginity. I realized then it was probably something that Nani Jan had taught her, which was why it was so absurd.

"Can you teach me how to use one?" I asked Kaya, suddenly feeling determined to try one for the first time.

Stephen was hanging out in the hall with us.

"Is it weird to say I'm curious, too?" he chimed. "Like, how do they work? I just don't know anything about pads or tampons. Obviously." Stephen didn't have a sister, only an older brother, never even had a long-term girlfriend. He didn't know much about periods.

"You're basically an honorary Bryn Mawr girl at this point," Kaya replied. "Farah, go in the bathroom. I'll talk you through it." And she did, explaining to the both of us the magic of using a tampon.

Stephen wasn't grossed out by the natural processes of people with uteruses, the way some men (so *bizarrely*) are. This wasn't revolutionary; a guy not being weird about periods isn't exactly something to *celebrate*, per se. But I'd been raised in a home where I'd been taught to keep my period a secret, to wrap my pads up and hide them discreetly in the trash can. It was these tiny ways that Stephen showed respect—to me, to my friends. We could talk freely around him, and he'd take it as an opportunity to learn. That meant something to me.

I liked Stephen. A lot.

Even our first argument was novel. When spring rolled around, I invited him to a cherry blossom festival at Fairmount Park. At least that was the intent. Instead, I played it off as a casual, *I'll be there, and if you happen to show up, that'd be cool, I guess* open invite. The kind of open invite that was easy to misunderstand.

The day of the festival, I checked my phone for an update from Stephen; I'd texted him that morning but never got a response. It was a perfect spring day: sunny and cool, pink cherry blossoms fluttering in the wind. The distant sounds of taiko drums, of laughter, permeating the air. I recognized several other college students, eagerly waiting in line for fresh takoyaki.

The truth was, I wanted him to experience it. I wanted to experience it together.

I waited an hour. Then two.

Kaya, who'd come with me, along with her friend Ally, gave me a concerned look. "I thought Stephen was coming."

"Me too," I said.

Eventually the three of us went home.

Another hour later, I got a frantic text from Stephen, who apologized profusely. He didn't realize I'd wanted him there, didn't realize I'd been waiting for him. He'd been sleeping.

You should have known! I texted back. How was it not obvious?
How was that obvious?! came his reply.
I've been talking about it for days! I shot back.
I'm sorry. But I can't know what you don't tell me, he replied.

I don't know why I was so upset. I knew it wasn't fair to expect him to read my mind. I'd been the one who'd let my pride stand in the way of telling him how I really felt and giving him a proper invite. But perhaps that was the problem with finding someone whose company you enjoy; the world without them feels dulled. You become greedy for their presence, even when you're too afraid to ask for it.

After I'd cooled down, we talked about it face-to-face. It was the first time I'd ever had a difficult conversation with someone who really listened to me, who didn't gaslight me, who qualified their thoughts with *I feel* instead of *I know*. He spoke gently, every word laced with care. With him, I realized, arguments didn't have to be conflict, didn't have to be battles to be won. They could be about connecting and reconnecting.

After I apologized, I realized my biggest problem was that I was holding back when it came to him: the moment I'd open up, I'd be vulnerable, and being vulnerable meant being hurt, and that was *terrifying*. More importantly, if I got any closer to Stephen, Mom would use the friendship against me.

As for how he felt about me, I wasn't sure, either. Sometimes I'd catch him staring, not like the first time, during our group project meeting, but with a warm tenderness that would make me look away, embarrassed. Confused. But he was always so cool, easy, relaxed. Maybe this *was* just a friendship to him, nothing more. I had no way of knowing.

I soon found out.

We'd both taken several Japanese classes and decided to practice and pore over our Genki textbooks together. We'd been laughing about something, an inside joke, maybe. Or maybe it was nothing. Then he said it, a sudden burst from his chest, in Japanese: *I'm in love with you.*

He'd stopped laughing, but I didn't—until, after a frenzied minute, I realized he wasn't reading it from the textbook.

I finally recognized it for what it really was:

A clumsy confession.

For a moment I felt my heart flail excitedly. I could hardly believe it. Someone liked me. *Stephen* liked me. I hadn't even considered the possibility.

But the truth was, I think I liked him, too. Even if I hadn't considered the possibility of us being together, I did really love being around him. I loved talking to him and hearing his thoughts, his perspective.

Except . . . except it wasn't enough. I wanted to hear an *I love you* outright, with no fear of vulnerability, without cloaking it behind a language neither of us spoke. I wanted to hear it from someone who wasn't ashamed to say it in all its raw, proud truth. I needed to be certain of that love, especially if it meant we'd eventually have to face the terrifying prospect of my mom's judgment together.

But in the same way I was afraid to fully open up with Stephen, maybe he was afraid, too.

I looked at him then, really *looked* at him, fearful and hopeful and uncertain.

"Say it, then," I uttered. "Say 'I love you.'"

A flustered breath. "I . . . I can't right now. It's hard. It's hard to just say it," Stephen replied.

Disappointment drowned out my chest.

As it stood, I just couldn't return his feelings—even if we were so close, even if the line between friend and something more was often blurred. Even if we truly liked each other, I wasn't convinced those feelings were strong enough to face, and fight, the expectations my parents had for me. If we decided to be together, it would have to be for the intent of marriage, and my parents would laugh in my face at the very idea. He wasn't Muslim, the number-one requirement my parents had for my future husband. His being Black also meant racist family members would likely say things that would only tick me off. I never wanted him to be subjected to that.

In short, we couldn't be together. So what would be the point of accepting his confession? Especially if I was still afraid to bare the more intimate pieces of my heart.

But if Stephen *had* said it, in that moment—if I'd known whether he'd truly meant it . . .

Well, there was no point in dwelling on *what-ifs*.

For weeks, Stephen and I didn't talk. The whole thing had left me so discouraged, so confused. I hated moping, but I couldn't help myself; there was this horrible, knotted feeling in my chest, and I didn't know why.

Finally, I went home for a weekend and decided to do what most forlorn people do when they're sad: I got a cat, a white Siberian kitten I named Kisa. I sneaked her into my dorm room. Raised her with Kaya and Rach and Ally. Slowly forgot that horrible, knotted feeling in my chest.

A week later, the dorm cleaning crew found out about her. They knocked on my door and threatened to tell the administration about my crime, since nonservice pets weren't allowed on campus.

"Unless," one of the cleaning crew, Gloria, added with a wink, "you let us pet her whenever we want."

Meanwhile, Stephen was still texting me occasionally, just to check in, even if our conversations were still stiff and awkward.

I told him about Kisa, which was why I shouldn't have been surprised when Stephen showed up at my dorm room door.

"Hi?" I said, befuddled by his sudden appearance.

"Hi," Stephen replied. He was huffing, like he'd run. Behind me, Kisa was busying herself with scaling my bed, digging her claws into my comforter. The sounds of ripping fabric filled the silence.

"Look, I know things are weird between us," Stephen said finally, "but you have a freaking *cat* now."

A smile crept onto my face. "I do have a cat now."

"And I just think—I think I have visitation rights."

Stephen looked so serious saying something so ridiculous, his eyebrows furrowed in desperation, I started to laugh. "*Visitation rights?* I don't think that applies here."

"Fair enough. But—" His eyes trailed behind me, to Kisa. "Can I—can I meet her? Please?"

I opened the door wider. "Come. Meet Kisa."

Five minutes later, Kisa was smitten with him, the little traitor; she curled in his lap and fell asleep while Stephen and I caught up, like nothing ever happened.

We didn't talk about his confession again.

CHAPTER 8

Maybe This Time

My mother announcing that she had changed, that the therapy had done its job, felt the same as the shadiest person in the world telling me to *just trust them*. In my head, I couldn't help picturing her giving me the most sinister, villain-curling-his-mustache smile, something out of a cartoon. But despite the suspicions in the back of my mind, I was still too naive to understand that someone saying they've changed—so confidently, always so sure—often means that they are certain they can *convince* you of their growth. And perhaps they can, for a time. But real, meaningful change needs no announcement. Real change speaks for itself.

Unfortunately, in my sophomore year of college, when I got a text message from Kareem claiming he'd changed, I took him at his word.

Why did I believe Kareem had changed?

1. Because when you know someone for such a long time, when you've grown up with them, it becomes increasingly difficult to detangle them from your heart—and despite everything, Kareem was knotted in deeply.
2. Because I wanted to believe him. Because maybe that would make what happened hurt a little less somehow.

I didn't have any proof he'd changed, but that wasn't the point. I had to give Kareem the benefit of the doubt. Who was I to say he hadn't changed? Forgiveness was a good thing, right? *To err, human, to forgive, divine*, and all that.

"I'm sorry, are we just going to completely forget what he did to you?" Stephen asked when I told him about the text. We were in my dorm room at Bryn Mawr, like any other day; me glued to my desk with my laptop, him sitting on my bed.

Of course I hadn't forgotten. Nor had I forgotten how that relationship and its aftermath destroyed my seventeen-year-old sense of self. For months after the breakup, I'd stopped eating normally, minimizing my calorie count to the point of starving. I'd convinced myself that the relationship had fallen apart because I'd somehow *failed* to keep him—and if I couldn't control my relationship, then maybe I could at least control my body.

So I tracked everything I ate, wrote it down in a notebook, and calculated every calorie to ensure I ate no more than twelve hundred a day. At one point I weighed ninety-eight pounds, but my clothing was usually so baggy, no one noticed. When I could no longer even go up the stairs to my bedroom without heaving, breathless, I finally realized something was very wrong. It took me years to develop a healthy relationship with food again.

"But that was all over three years ago," I replied. "Maybe he really has changed."

"People who do things like that don't change. I'm sorry, I just—" Stephen squeezed at his skull and sighed. "I just don't want you to get hurt. Again."

"Nothing will happen. He said he wants to be like a big brother to me. He's not going to try anything with me."

Stephen stopped pacing. "A *big brother*? Really?"

I hesitated. "Yeah. I think that'd be healthier, too. Plus, it'd be nice. Having an older-brother figure."

Plus, there was something about cutting Kareem off entirely that hurt. The Muslim community I'd grown up with was like an extended family, for better or worse. And he was a part of that. He'd also been the one person in my life who understood who my mom really was. The only person I could really talk to about her.

"Sure. But I highly doubt that's what he's really planning," said Stephen. "That conniving piece of shit, suddenly reaching out to you out of the blue after—how many years? Yeah, there's *no way* he doesn't have an agenda."

I swallowed uncomfortably. Stephen had a habit of ripping out the thoughts I'd hidden away in some filing cabinet in the back of my brain.

"Look, I don't fully understand your relationship, and it's not my call." Stephen met my eyes, his expression gentle but determined. "But when you meet up with him, I'm coming with you, okay? Please."

I looked away. I've had an anxious habit of nail-biting since I was a child, and it was taking every ounce of my willpower not to chew my fingers down to the bone right now.

"All right," I answered. "Honestly, I was hoping you'd say that." Maybe deep down I knew it'd be safer to have Stephen around. Maybe he'd pick up on something I'd missed.

About a week later, I met Kareem in the parking lot at Haverford. He'd driven thirty minutes from his own campus at West Chester University to pick me up from class and drive me back to Bryn Mawr. *A nice gesture*, I'd thought.

Kareem looked exactly the same, despite it being three whole years since I'd last seen him. His style of clothing—a button-down shirt with dark jeans—hadn't changed, nor had the way he always kept eye contact with that pinning stare of his. But he'd gotten a haircut, and his curls looked a little more deflated than I remembered. His presence was disquieting. I felt on edge. The feeling of treading murky water, and knowing something—*something* lurked beneath.

Stephen was right behind me.

"Kareem!" I said, waving him over. He swept me in a hug. Despite my attempt to act casual, I stiffened.

I gestured behind me, shaking it off. "This is Stephen. I've told you about him before. He's my best friend. He wanted to meet you."

Kareem smiled. "Hi. I've heard a lot about you."

Stephen didn't respond. Instead, he took Kareem's hand, and the two of them shook. Unlike with my mom, Stephen wasn't nervous.

"I've heard a lot about you, too," Stephen said finally.

It was a threat. Kareem was wearing long sleeves, but I could see the muscles in Stephen's forearms, his veins bulging. Years of college tennis had sculpted his arms, and now he was putting them to use against Kareem. In a way, it was flattering. Like Stephen was warning Kareem not to mess with me, the way an actual older-brother figure might.

But it also filled me with embarrassment, and I had the urge to run away from them both.

"Okay, well! Now that you two have met," I said, breaking up their prolonged handshake, "how about you drive me over to Bryn Mawr and I show you around campus, Kareem?"

Kareem's expression was all cheer again. "Sounds good. I'll take you to my car."

I looked over my shoulder, to Stephen.

"We'll be *fine*," I said.

Stephen's mouth was in a tight line.

After I'd given Kareem a tour of Bryn Mawr, the two of us catching up, I showed him my dorm room. I was proud of it: I was a sophomore, and it was my first dorm room without a roommate. A veritable *room of one's own*. I'd decorated it with posters and vinyl I'd thrifted; I'd even gotten a tiny fridge for my birthday, which I'd filled with pints of gelato for late-night study sessions. Sometimes Stephen and I would go through my stash in a single night.

Kareem took in my room, saying nothing. Then without asking, he sat on my bed.

A voice inside my head screamed for him to get off. But I said nothing, instead choosing to stand a foot away, unsure of where to sit.

"So," he said, smirking.

"So . . . ?"

"I was thinking it earlier, but you look good. Beautiful."

I froze. Kareem was normally so ungenerous with compliments, and if this were three years ago, I'd be swooning. Now, I felt nothing.

"Feels like nothing's changed, huh?" he said.

The mood between us shifted. Like the air itself had gone viscous and sticky and wrong.

It happened in slow motion: Kareem reached for my arm and pulled me toward him. Toward my bed.

I yanked back, nearly stumbling into my desk.

"What are you doing?" I snapped.

He chuckled, amused. "What?"

"Oh God, did you—did you really think I would—"

Big brother, my ass. Stephen was right. Hell, *Kareem* was right: nothing had changed at all.

How stupid I'd been. How naive. I almost laughed. It was all so absurd. Kareem really thought he could just come here and hook up with me? That I'd *want* to? Did it even matter to him if I did?

Perhaps this is why we forgive people who don't deserve it: nostalgia is a hell of a drug. It blurred all the bad, brightened the scant good, and told you pretty lies.

Just like Kareem.

All the fury for the past three years, fury I'd locked away, came rushing out at once.

"Get away from me," I said, my voice shaking, "and *never* talk to me again. I mean it. Never."

Slowly, Kareem got to his feet. Looked at me with that intense gaze of his, the one that made me feel like we were the only two people in the world. Only this time, it was unsettling.

"Is that what you really want?" he asked. "Because I'll do it. I'll disappear. It'll be like I don't even exist. You will *never* hear from me again." It was a promise. It was a threat.

"Good."

Seconds passed in silence—until finally, unceremoniously, Kareem left.

This time, I didn't cry, like the first time he'd hurt me like this. Instead, I thought about how I wanted to shower. How I wanted to pray and ask for forgiveness I felt I didn't deserve. How Mom would kill me if she knew I'd almost let something happen again.

And I thought about how I owed Stephen a gelato.

When I'd caught my breath, I called Stephen. He picked up right away.

"Everything okay?" I could tell he was trying to sound calm, unaffected. Unlike Kareem, though, he was never a good actor.

"Yeah," I said. "He's gone. I kicked him out. Could you come hang out for a bit?" I needed to fill my room with other voices, anything to drown out the ghost of Kareem's presence. I needed a friend.

There were shuffling sounds on the other line. Stephen was already on the move.

"What happened?"

I began to laugh. "You were right!" It wasn't funny, of course. But saying it out loud, thinking about it, I couldn't stop the laughter. It was absurd. Everything about it was so damn absurd. "You were so, so right about him."

Stephen didn't laugh with me, didn't press, didn't say anything. No *I told you so.* No *You should have listened.*

All he said was that he'd be there soon, and a half hour later, he was.

I don't remember the first time Stephen and I hugged; I was never touchy-feely, and he knew that. But I remember his hug that day: the way his arms wrapped around me, but not too constricting, not too firm. He was giving me an easy way out, if I wanted—and I did not.

There was something particularly pained about the way he said *I'm really sorry* against my head, as if he'd failed me. As if somehow, in some impossible, incomprehensible way, this were all his fault.

I hugged him tighter.

CHAPTER 9

From Nothing Came Something

Later that year, Mom asked me to come home for a weekend dinner party.

Dinner parties in our Pakistani American Muslim community were a common occurrence. Some family would announce they were hosting a dinner; then on a Saturday or Sunday evening, other families living within an hour would descend upon their home, lured by the promise of vats of chicken biryani and haleem and fresh pakore, and more important, long-winded debates about politics. And while the adults were debating, loudly, in the living room, the kids would camp in the basement.

These dinner parties happened in an endless rotation between the same ten or so families, including mine, so we kids were well acquainted. Years of being forced to spend hours together at least once a month, all of us resorting to playing video games to pass the time.

Amina was one of the girls at the party. She was the one who, years ago, had concocted the short-lived plan to pose as secret agents and message Kareem on AIM. We'd grown distant, though, after I'd caught her trying to break into my email soon after I'd started dating him—and since then, she'd become a one-girl rumor mill.

"Did you hear Kareem's dating someone?" she told me, whispering conspiratorially. Her eyes gleamed, as if she was pleased to be the one sharing this juicy knowledge—knowledge she was certain I didn't know.

My body tensed. "Oh yeah?"

"It's that girl, Maha. The one that moved from Arkansas a few years ago."

I wasn't sure what Amina's intent was in telling me this, but it wasn't worth dwelling on it. I was worried about Maha. I hoped she was okay. Had she gotten caught by Kareem's honeyed words and promises, too? Had she already seen the signs, felt the manipulations? I only knew a little about her. She wasn't the girl Kareem had cheated on me with— that girl he'd moved on from. I wasn't sure what became of her, other than she now went to the same college as Maha and Kareem. What I did know was that Maha was from Arkansas, she was my age, and she was the eldest of three sisters.

"They met on campus; I guess 'cause they're both going to med school, they're in a lot of the same classes. She knows about you, though." Amina went on until something in my expression made her pause. "You probably don't want to talk about it."

I shrugged. "It's none of my business."

I'd long moved on in my own way. I was in a better place.

But I kept thinking about Maha. Back when I'd been recovering from our breakup, I'd often asked myself a question that kept me up at night: If I could go back in time, what would I have done differently with Kareem?

This time, the answer was obvious:

I'd warn myself to stay away.

That night, I found Maha on Facebook and wrote her a message, trying to sound as friendly and nonthreatening as I could. I knew, of course, there was a chance she wouldn't believe me. I knew there was a chance she might think I was a jealous ex. Their relationship, as I'd told Amina, was none of my business. But still.

This is going to sound weird, but we should talk sometime. ☺

If you want.

Her response came back within the hour:

We definitely should.

❦

After a few weeks of talking on Facebook—of Maha sharing all the insecurities and worries Kareem had dredged up, ones that once so closely mirrored mine—we had somehow become close friends. *I'd wanted to reach out to you sooner, but Kareem told me not to,* Maha confided, grinning.

I had learned that Kareem had refused to define his relationship with Maha, asking her, "Do we even need a label?" which had cornered her into never being able to tell him how she felt, how she wanted something serious.

Maha and I had quickly forged a bond of iron, built on trauma only we knew. It was comforting to feel the blossoming of a friendship from something so ugly. As if maybe, just maybe, experiencing all that pain wouldn't be meaningless.

Through me, Maha started to see the emotional abuse she'd been enduring, the holes she hadn't been able to acknowledge. Talking to someone who'd dealt with Kareem gave her the strength to second-guess him, and eventually pull away for good.

For me, talking to Maha felt like vindication. For so long I'd believed that everything that had happened with Kareem had been my fault on some level. And yet after talking with Maha, the patterns were clear: the way he'd isolated me, he'd isolated Maha. The way he'd bring us up, only to bring us spiraling down the next day. The way he'd get us to share our deepest fears and insecurities, only to use them against us.

Not long after Maha and I had gotten close, Kareem told Maha, with little explanation, that he wanted nothing to do with her anymore.

Maha called to fill me in. Her voice was swollen, punctuated with sniffling.

"I should have known something was wrong the moment he told me to stay away from you," she said. "There's only one reason a guy says that: because he's got shit to hide. If we became friends, he'd completely lose control, and God knows that guy *always* needs to be in control. The loser."

"I'm very glad we're friends," I told her.

"Me too. Now we can move on with our lives. Maybe occasionally talk shit about him and revel in the fact that there's nothing he can do about it." She chuckled before going quiet for a moment.

"You know, I wanted to tell my mom about him," she admitted. "She was the one who told me to be friends with him in the first place, so I reached out to him to ask for advice on med school."

She let out a miserable scoff, and it broke my heart.

"But I can't tell her about *this*. I could never tell her about *any* of this."

I smiled sadly.

"Yeah," I said. "I know the feeling."

CHAPTER 10

The Lost Year

Two years later I graduated from Bryn Mawr College with a degree in English and a general world-weariness that left me with the urge to retire early and become a recluse. Stephen had graduated the year before I did, and every waking moment of my senior year was spent, like everyone else in my year, working on my thesis.

I'd decided to take a year off before attending law school. This meant I had a whole year to study for the LSAT. I'd live with my parents in their home in Chadds Ford and work a part-time job while studying. But I had to live with my mom again.

I wouldn't have to worry about rent, at least, or being thrust into adult life so suddenly after graduation, like my other friends. Kaya had moved all the way to Japan to work as an English teacher—how she was managing all that on her own, I couldn't fathom. And Maha—who had become like a sister to me—had recently gotten engaged in a whole whirlwind affair and was busy preparing for her wedding in Chicago. We'd lost touch after that.

At the very least, Mom wasn't *completely* against my first-choice law school: Lewis & Clark in Portland, Oregon, which had the best environmental law program in the country. It was also far away from Pennsylvania, which made it perfect.

"It's no big-name school, that's for sure," Mom said, peering over my shoulder as I showed her their website. "And I don't like the idea of you moving across the country. It's too far."

"But it's still a *good* school." I scrolled through photos of the campus, which was close to an old-growth forest. "Plus, I've always wanted to try living on the West Coast."

"We'll discuss it more if you actually get in," she replied before leaving my room.

Meanwhile, Stephen was having a tough time. The years after college had not been kind to him; though he did well on the MCAT—he was an *amazing* test taker—he couldn't get into med school. It crushed him.

"Where the hell did I go wrong?" he'd begged me when I'd visited him at his apartment. Though his test results were fantastic, apparently they still weren't good enough.

There was nothing I could say. We were closer than ever, in some ways, but I couldn't help him. Not with this. It was one thing to watch your dream crash and burn, but what happened when it died before it could get off the ground? How could *anyone* help?

I was frustrated: with myself and my inability to help see him through this. With Stephen, for not seeing how talented he really was. Slowly, he pulled away from my life and retreated into himself. He rarely responded to my texts anymore.

I missed him.

My new part-time job was a needed distraction. Weeks after graduation, I began work as a legislative assistant at a Pennsylvania state senator's office. Constituents would walk in—some with appointments, but most did not—determined to speak with the senator about issues ranging from gun control to parking regulations. Once, someone came in to talk about the increasing cost of groceries before stealing a handful of pencils from the secretary's desk. It was my job to take down complaints and to assure the constituents that the senator definitely cared about these issues, that he would *definitely* get their message.

It was nice having a real job, where I could get out of the house. Living at home felt miserable. Mom constantly hovered. I had a curfew again. If I left the house, I had to explain where I was going, whom I'd be with, and when I'd be coming back. When I didn't leave the house, Mom would ask why I had no social life. Several times I'd caught her listening in on my phone calls, lingering by my bedroom door; she'd get angry if I locked it, saying locking the door meant I had something to hide.

The autonomy I'd had in college was now gone. It made the past four years of college feel like some kind of fever dream.

The only bright spots of being back home were being able to spend time with Shaz again, living in my parents' clean, spacious new home (especially when compared to my old apartment), and gardening with my dad.

I liked being in his garden. And Dad loved gardening because he believed it was an act of worship. Gardening reminded him that God exists, that God *must* exist, because how else could one plant a mere seed into the dirt and watch as the earth itself would *transform* it with only a little water and tiny bees to act as stewards? And soon that tiny, seemingly insignificant seed would be replaced by a flower, a tree, even fruit to eat. *And is that not amazing?* he'd say with all the passion of a Sufi poet. *Does it not make you believe in the beauty of the world?*

I'd nod, looking at the new dogwood tree we'd just planted together. His favorite, he'd shared, due to their adaptability and pretty flowers.

Yeah, I'd said. *It does.*

I also still daydreamed of becoming a writer. I even emailed a literary agent named Eric for publishing advice; he responded graciously, encouraged me to try for a publishing internship. Told me he would be there if I had any more questions. In the end, I chickened out and never wrote to him again.

Stephen's dream had died in the cruelest of ways, despite how hard he'd fought for it. Mine I'd rejected before even giving it a chance.

※

Mom came into my bedroom one day, and immediately I knew I wouldn't like what she had to say.

"What are you up to, sweet pea?" she asked in her *Other* voice.

The feeling intensified.

Recently she'd gotten a Brazilian blowout to straighten her hair. *My hair's always so frizzy,* she'd complained. *You should get one, too.* I missed her curls. She once had beautiful Julia Roberts–style hair: a long and thick mane of dark ringlets perfect for a nineties rom-com protagonist. After the treatment her hair was straight and silky, but . . . characterless.

"Just getting some studying done," I answered.

"Your dad and I have been talking," she started. "This is a good time to think about what you want for your future."

"That's what I'm doing . . . ?" Without Stephen and Kaya around, studying or going to work was pretty much all I was *ever* doing. I signed up for online LSAT classes with a tutor and spent hours every day doing LSAT homework. "Have you thought about marriage?" asked Mom.

I looked up from my LSAT study book. Downstairs, my brother was playing the piano, some piece he'd composed himself. Those days especially, his music was a comfort. A beckoning.

"What do you mean?" I asked.

Of course I'd *thought* about marriage. Lately I'd been staying up late at night playing weird romance games on my phone. It was entertaining, yes, but maybe it was also a cry for help. I wanted love—who didn't, in some capacity? And Mom knew I did.

Finding it, though, was another matter. I hadn't been with anyone since Kareem, and I felt wary of the whole endeavor.

"You're already twenty-two, in case you forgot," she said. "Knowing you, you're going to need at *least* a few years to get to know someone before you get married. It's the perfect time to find someone."

I stared, confused. After Mom had gone to therapy a few times, she'd stopped pressuring me to find someone, much to my relief. I'd hoped it had been the end of her insistence.

"I thought I was supposed to focus on the LSAT right now."

Mom laughed. "You can do *both*! It's not like finding someone is the same as studying, where you need to invest hours at a time." She leaned against the wall just beside my desk, which was covered in LSAT logic games. "You just have to keep your eyes peeled. If you want, your dad and I can help."

The whole idea was making me anxious. Since graduating from college, my skin had broken out into painful, cystic acne. In a bout of madness, I'd begun naming each pimple. What little, insignificant pride I'd had in my appearance had long disappeared, incinerated by benzoyl peroxide cream. The stress of trying to get into law school was doing its damage on my soul *and* skin barrier.

Plus, I wasn't sure I could trust that my preferences and my parents' preferences would mesh. Whereas my parents had a simple checklist for my future husband that they'd instilled in me since I was a kid—that he be Muslim, that he be a doctor/lawyer/engineer/someone filthy, dirty rich, and that he come from a good, respected family—I wanted to fall in love, naturally, organically, to experience a whole *falling-in-love* montage. I did want to marry a Muslim, and it wasn't like I disliked the idea of an arranged marriage. From a logical standpoint, my parents' checklist made sense. But I wanted to be 100 percent certain about the person I'd be meeting at the altar. I wanted to be 100 percent ready for it, for them. And whoever would agree to be dragged into *my* life, into *this* family, would have to be ready, too.

Maybe it was better I stuck to the romance games.

On the other hand—marriage would give me instant freedom. If I were married, this lack of autonomy that I, and many South Asian daughters experience throughout their twenties, would finally cease. There'd be no more questioning, no more having to hear passive-aggressive quips about the successes of other kids my age, no more being dragged to dinner parties hosted by relatives my parents didn't even like. I could finally become my own person, an adult—if and only if I attached myself to a man.

"I'd rather find someone on my own," I answered.

"I'm not against it," replied Mom. "You know the kind of man we'd want for you, though, so keep that in mind. But if you don't find someone soon, you'll be too busy for it in law school, and by the time you finish, you'll be almost *thirty*."

"I'll be twenty-six. And twenty-six isn't old."

"That's old when you're picky."

❧

Later that night I created an account on a dating website. I filled out a profile, indicating that I was looking for someone who was serious about relationships. Someone who was looking to marry. I filled out my preferences in a spouse, the way I knew Mom would want: that the person had a higher degree. That they were Muslim, didn't smoke or drink. That they were close to their family.

Briefly, I thought about what Stephen would think about this. I hadn't heard from him since he'd gotten the rejection letter. He'd probably be surprised my parents were rushing me. He'd probably hate the idea of me rushing into anything, especially something so important.

I shook the thought away.

"*Bismillah,*" I whispered as I pressed DONE. *Here goes.*

And a few weeks later, I met Yusuf.

CHAPTER 11

We Remain a Question

Per day, during the Christmas season—from November 12 to the first week of January, approximately—750,000 visitors come to gawk at the towering eighty-plus-foot Christmas tree in Rockefeller Center, a staggering number even by New York City's standards. In total, that adds up to over 40 million people.

At the tail end of 2012, I was one of them.

Most couples who'd come to visit the tree held hands, a desperate attempt not to lose each other in the suffocatingly dense crowd. Not Yusuf and I, though. We were hardly a couple; ever since we found each other through the dating app, we'd talked mostly through text messages and were still in the awkwardly painful process of trying to get to know each other—a process that neither of us seemed to enjoy, but understood we had to endure if we wanted things to move forward. As a result, our conversations tended to be straight to the point: questions would be asked, and answers would be given, in the same efficient manner you'd fill out forms at a doctor's office.

Yusuf was a Pakistani Muslim, like me; he was a year older and already wrapping up his first year of medical school in New York. He could hold a pleasant conversation, ask the right questions, and had a schedule that revolved entirely around his med school rotations. Yusuf and I also had similar values: We both prioritized education. We both valued our faith. We both tried to pray five times a day, though sometimes the day would get ahead of us, and we'd miss a prayer or two—and we both wanted to be better at that. We also wanted to find love in a halal way: find a marriage candidate, get to know them, and if things looked promising, get our families involved. The latter part would be easy for us, at least: in typical Pakistani American fashion, our families already distantly knew each other—some second cousin of mine had married one of his second cousins. Very convenient.

He was, well, *normal.* Painfully bland at times. But in my mind, this was a good thing. It meant he'd be predictable. Sensible.

And that, surely, meant he was a good match. Mom and Dad would have no complaints.

Yusuf and I also had similar tastes in books—though it might be more accurate to say that we both simply liked books in the general sense, which was good enough for me. Once, he'd lent me his copy of *Musashi* by Eiji Yoshikawa, one of his favorites. *It's a classic,* he asserted, *and it's about samurai! It doesn't get cooler than that!* Despite his valiant attempt at selling the premise, I was skeptical of the nine-hundred-page book. But I devoured it quickly. I was eager to show him I cared, to impress him, even though Musashi himself came across the page like an arrogant, misogynistic ass who reveled in murdering so thoroughly that, on one occasion, he masturbated after the deed. I'd been reading the book at a Starbucks when I got to that scene, and I ugly-gasped so loudly that others noticed. I slammed the cursed book closed and fled the store.

I didn't pick up the book again.

"So what'd you think?" Yusuf asked excitedly when I'd returned the tome. I'd just driven over two hours to visit him in New York and had been dreading this very question.

"I liked it," I said.

Yusuf grinned. "Told you it was amazing."

❧

Stephen, meanwhile, was still trying to find his own way. By then he'd gotten a job in a lab to pay for his own apartment in nearby King of Prussia, but he was, in his own words, miserable.

"It's where dreams go to die," he described the lab, laughing bitterly.

We hadn't stayed in touch the way we had in college; we didn't update each other on our lives often. I was taken aback when his mom had called me once, in a desperate move to reach him. Though Stephen talked about them sometimes—unlike me, he was close with his parents, who still lived in Jamaica—I'd never met them before. Now he'd been avoiding their calls for days, and they were worried.

"It's not like him to avoid us," his mom explained, her Jamaican accent light and musical despite her worry. "I'm sorry; normally I wouldn't bother you with this, but Stephen gave us your number a while ago in case of an emergency, and—"

"It's fine," I answered. His mom seemed so nice. Like she truly cared about her son's well-being. "It's good that you called. I'll see if I can reach him. He's probably just busy with work or something."

Afterward, I shot him a text, equally worried: Hey, your mom just called me. Give her a call or something? We just want to make sure you're okay.

His response didn't come for another thirty minutes.

Thanks. I will.

I think the feeling of not being where you were supposed to be— of watching the train of success leave you behind, while your friends ride it off into the sunset—was unbearable. Especially when his surroundings—the lab he worked at looked more like a warehouse with bare, concrete walls—were so bleak. *Everything* in his life looked gray. Colorless.

It was no wonder he didn't want to talk to his parents.

After a week and a long lecture from his mom, he eventually came to visit; since my parents didn't allow boys at the house, I met up with Stephen at the nearby Starbucks.

I finally told Stephen about Yusuf; in college, after the whole cherry blossom festival debacle, we'd promised to be honest with each other about everything. Which meant also telling Stephen that after our coffee catch-up, I'd be making the two-hour drive to visit Yusuf again.

"Are you sure you even like him?" Stephen asked.

"He's handsome," I answered, which was sort of true—Yusuf wasn't particularly tall, but he had a nice jaw, a pleasant mouth, a thick mop of black hair. "And he's a great guy. We'd make a good couple."

"That is not what I asked."

"I don't know." This was fully true. "But I think I could learn to."

The word *think* was doing some pretty heavy lifting, and Stephen could tell.

He gave me a somber look as he walked me to my car.

"I'm not saying you have to be one hundred percent certain," he said after a while, his voice gentle. "But I do think it might be good to take the time to think about it. This is your *life* we're talking about. If you love him, that's one thing, but are you one hundred percent certain that you're not doing this because it's what your parents would want? I just don't want you to have any regrets."

His earnestness stirred something in me. He was asking the questions I'd been avoiding myself. Stephen was the type of best friend who, instead of keeping the peace and watching me walk off a cliff's edge, would firmly—but lovingly—tug until I realized I was about to fall.

But I wasn't quite ready to hear this at all. It would mean admitting that I'd been disregarding my own feelings. That, in a way, I was about to repeat my mom's biggest mistake and rush into a marriage, a *lifelong freaking commitment!*—just to please my parents. Heck, I wasn't even sure they truly liked Yusuf, either—they hadn't even met him.

Then another, far uglier thought crept into my mind: What if—what if Stephen was jealous? Since I'd known him, he'd never dated anyone, always claiming to be too busy, but it felt like an excuse. I couldn't help thinking back to Stephen's confession in college. I'd moved past it. I had to: that type of noncommittal love wasn't worth going after for a guy my parents wouldn't approve of, and toppling my chances at a life they'd be proud of. Stephen respected that, of course. But had Stephen truly moved past it?

"I have to go," I said, reaching for my car door.

"Yeah. Okay."

I caught a glimpse of Stephen's face in the rearview mirror: heartbreakingly melancholy and troubled, his dark curls hanging over his forehead. It haunted me the entire drive to New York.

⁂

Later, when I met up with Yusuf, we talked about him meeting my parents. I'd already told Mom and Dad about Yusuf; Mom had in turn told her sisters and mom. This was it. This was becoming real.

I waited for him to say something. He'd been the one pushing for us to get married sooner, after two months of talking. Not that this was unusual, by Muslim standards. But now, though, his eyes had darkened, his earlier enthusiasm seemingly fizzling. Like there was something holding him back.

"Before we move forward, I need you to promise something," he said one night on the phone.

"What is it?"

"Your best friend," he said, and I went still. We never talked about Stephen, but Yusuf knew about him. Even in this conversation, Yusuf wouldn't say his name.

"Maybe it's a lot to ask," said Yusuf, "but I don't think I can feel comfortable if you're still talking to him."

"But he's just a friend—"

"I know. That's what you said. But it's hard to say what he's really thinking, right? If we're getting married, I wouldn't feel right if you were talking to other guys." Yusuf let out a breath. "Sorry."

I couldn't figure out what to say. I was too focused on the horrible sensation of a hundred pinpricks assaulting my chest, and now I felt a numb, pulpy mess.

Of course. Of *course* Yusuf didn't want me to talk to Stephen anymore. I couldn't exactly shame him for feeling insecure about his potential fiancée's best friend being another man. Asking to cut Stephen out—it's not like it was an unreasonable request. From a cultural standpoint, it was more unusual that I considered a guy to be one of my closest friends. And wasn't the willingness to sacrifice a cornerstone of love? Not talking to Stephen anymore would be my first sacrifice at the altar: proof that I would do what I could to make Yusuf and me work.

Stephen and I weren't as close as we used to be, anyway. It would be a clean break, even if it still hurt.

"Okay," I replied, choking on the word.

CHAPTER 12

Cold Hearts

Not talking to Stephen anymore wasn't the only request Yusuf asked of me.

He also admitted to disliking my plan to move to Portland for law school. "If we get married and then you move across the country, it's going to be hard for us," he complained. "We'll never see each other."

Never, I thought, was a bit of an exaggeration. It wasn't like there weren't breaks during the school year and I wouldn't *ever* be flying back home to visit. Law school would be only three years. After that I'd be done with school for good and could practice law wherever Yusuf eventually ended up for his future residency program. Even if I did attend a law school on the East Coast, Yusuf would be busy as well with another three years of med school in New York. Was I supposed to be at his beck and call?

I didn't understand. Yusuf kept stressing how pleased he was that I was going to grad school, that he imagined us in the future as some sort of enviable power couple: A doctor and lawyer, side by side. Now I was beginning to realize he only wanted me in grad school on his terms.

By then I'd already talked to Stephen about how Yusuf felt about us, and Stephen had only smiled sadly. "You have to do whatever you feel is right," he said, without complaint, and I felt as if my heart would break.

But now Yusuf wanted me to abandon my dream law school. None of this felt right.

I saw a future for myself where Yusuf would ask sacrifice after sacrifice of me until I no longer recognized myself in the mirror. This was not a relationship where compromise would be an option.

For days I researched my problem: "Should I sacrifice my education for love?" I scrolled through a Google search, as if somehow I'd find the answer to solve everything—and not, say, a link to a Quora page where some poor soul asked the same question only to get an incomprehensible response that only confused me more. I later read an article on a reputable site that affirmed *all* close relationships required sacrifice. This also confused me because I'd never felt like I'd sacrificed anything in my friendships with Kaya, with Maha, with Stephen. I'd never needed to.

I began to doubt my understanding of what *sacrifice* even meant.

Immigrant parents, my own included, made sacrifices for the future of their children—like leaving their countries behind to give their children more opportunity elsewhere. An act of sacrifice, done out of love.

Muslims believe the prophet Ibrahim (peace be upon him) sacrificed his son Ishmael at God's request—at least, until God intervened at the last moment and spared his son. But the prophet was willing to do so out of his love for God. In a similar vein, Christians believed that Jesus (peace be upon him) sacrificed his life to save his people, in another act of love. Sacrifice, clearly, was a common theme in faith—something considered laudable. Noble. But if to sacrifice, at least in the context of love, meant *to give up something precious in order to gain or maintain something*, as my dictionary put it, then what was I gaining here? What was I maintaining? It seemed strange to sacrifice so much for someone I barely knew when I had yet to do any grand gesture of love for myself.

Yusuf finally came to my family home to meet my parents. The visit was unenthusiastically lukewarm. He showed up empty handed, I noticed disappointingly when I let him in the house. Mom had cooked a few Pakistani dishes, and he ate lunch with Mom, Dad, and me; Shaz had already eaten, for which I was grateful, because lunch was painfully awkward. Mostly Yusuf politely talked to Dad, who in turn asked him a polite but disinterested series of questions. Yusuf met my brother briefly, talking to him for approximately two minutes in a strained attempt at small talk before making some excuse about needing to head back. He didn't stay for a tour of the house. He didn't even meet my two cats, Kisa, now three years old, and Binx, a black male cat I'd adopted during my senior year of college. This omission felt especially unforgiveable.

At first I chalked up Yusuf's behavior to nervousness. But as lunch progressed, it felt more like he simply didn't care enough to get to know my family.

Still, Mom was happy. Yusuf was brag worthy, which was everything she'd wanted in a future son-in-law. The prospect of a giant wedding excited her.

"I was getting worried," she told me, the light dancing in her eyes. "You were having such trouble finding someone, I thought maybe something was wrong with you."

Sometimes I wondered if something *was* wrong with me.

A few weeks later, Dad and I drove home together from a wedding—some distant cousin or cousin's cousin on my mom's side was getting married. Weddings, and any big gatherings, had become a sordid affair for me. Too many aunties and uncles would ask me about my postcollege plans—would I be attending grad school? *Yes.* Where? *I haven't heard back from any schools yet.* Where did you apply? *Everywhere I could.* What kind of law would you practice? *I don't know yet, but probably environmental law.*

After a few hours of answering invasive questions from people who had hardly acknowledged my existence until now, Dad and I decided we'd done our duty. It was time to make the long drive home. Shaz had managed to talk our parents out of his going (the lucky bastard), and

Mom stayed behind; she was enjoying herself too much to go home just yet. Mom and Dad had been doing that more and more lately: arriving at parties and dinners and even family's houses separately, then leaving separately. Mom had said it was just easier this way. No one would have to wait on anyone else.

I sensed there was more she wasn't saying.

In the car I stared at my phone, waiting for a check-in text from Yusuf that I knew probably wasn't coming; our already short conversations had puttered into little more than the occasional, obligatory *hello* and *hope you are well.*

Strangely, I felt relieved. I didn't want to text him, either.

Dad left the radio on; he'd grown fond of the Siriusly Sinatra channel on Sirius XM, and Sinatra's silky baritone filled Dad's Acura MDX. Dad loved jazz: Fitzgerald, Bennett, Martin, both the Sinatras. During long car rides, my brother and I would complain that we wanted to listen to our music, but Dad would shake his head and tell us that radio privileges belonged to whoever was in the driver's seat. A button press later, and it was Siriusly Sinatra time. Except it was hard to argue with jazz. It eventually drew us in, my brother and me—the spontaneity, the freedom, the self-indulgence of it. Secretly I appreciated that my otherwise seemingly taciturn dad loved jazz. It was like seeing a glimpse of who he truly was, some secret self that he hid behind a stern gaze.

Fly me to the moon; let me play among the stars . . .

"You never told me how you felt about Yusuf," I said softly. It was a question I'd been dreading asking, but it felt like the right moment.

Dad stayed quiet, but I heard him inhale.

"After you met him," I went on, "you just went back to your room. But I'm curious to know what you think. Especially if . . ." I trailed off. *If he and I get married.* I couldn't say it.

"He's okay. He has a good head on his shoulders."

Damn! I thought Dad might have felt tepid about Yusuf—Yusuf hadn't exactly gone out of his way to make an impression on anyone in my family—but this was infinitely worse. Dad felt nothing about him at all.

"Right. But do you think—do you think he's a good *fit* for me?" I pressed.

In other words, please be true
In other words, I love you . . .

"Why do you want to go to Lewis & Clark?" asked Dad suddenly.

I furrowed my brow, confused. "Well, it's the best school for what I want to do. It'll help me be an environmental lawyer. It's in a place I'd love to try living; I've always wanted to go to Portland. And based on everything I've seen, I just feel like it's the best fit for me."

The car came to a slow stop at a red light. Outside, it started drizzling.

Dad let out a long exhale and began to speak.

"The way you have put a lot of thought into which school you want to attend, what career you want—this is the kind of thought you need to put into who you're going to marry," he said. "More so, maybe. These are the most important choices you make in life; the same way your school and career will help you go where you want to go, your partner will help you become who you want to be.

"You're still so young," Dad went on. "You still have time. You can always focus on school until the right person comes along. Then you'll know."

I gripped my phone tightly.

I don't know what I expected Dad to say, but it wasn't this: not an answer that felt so much like a reflection on his own decisions in life. I wondered if this was some kind of admission about Mom. They'd married so young, maybe too young; Mom was only eighteen, and just starting college; Dad was only twenty-four. Did he regret not waiting a little longer?

And yet it was so very like my dad to give this kind of direct, unvarnished advice. It was so profoundly simple. But somehow I'd gotten so swept up in the rush, in building the infrastructure of what I thought my life should look like, that I'd forgotten this basic fact:

There was no need to hurry. Not with Yusuf or anyone. Not with anything.

I'd been wanting to open up to my dad more, ever since he'd stepped in with Mom and urged her to go to therapy. He'd proved himself to be someone I could talk to about my life. He'd been the one to give me the context I needed to understand where Mom was coming from—not to excuse her behavior, but to help me process it. It hadn't made me feel better, exactly, but it gave me the objectivity I needed to clear my head.

Here he was once again giving me the objectivity I needed.

Not long after my conversation with Dad, Yusuf and I talked on the phone and agreed to break things off. It was quick. Painless. We'd known each other for only six months. On New Year's, we hadn't even held hands or exchanged romantic looks when the ball dropped.

"Happy New Year," said Yusuf, with a small smile, then: "Damn, traffic out of New York is going to be hell. Look at this crowd."

In a way, it'd felt like it'd been over between us for a while.

When I told Mom, she was disappointed but quickly recovered.

"Well, you can always find someone in law school. Though, honestly, you should probably just focus on school from now on."

❧

"So how do you feel? Are you okay?" Stephen asked over the phone. We'd started talking again, not long after Yusuf and I broke things off.

"I want to dig a twenty-mile-long hole and jump in, but I don't have a shovel," I answered. "I don't know what I saw in him. I can't believe I thought we were good for each other. Why the hell was I *rushing?*"

"You do tend to do that," said Stephen, gently.

Meanwhile, while I'd been having an existential crisis, Stephen's had ended. He'd finally quit his soul-sucking lab job and begun looking into post-bacc programs to bolster his med school applications.

I never brought Stephen up around my parents, not since Mom had met him in college—to protect him, and myself. I knew they'd bristle at the thought of me having a guy best friend, or worse, they wouldn't believe we were just friends. But after my potential engagement with Yusuf fell through, my dad and I grew closer; between LSAT study sessions, I'd sit down at the kitchen table with him, and we'd talk about the news, politics, what I'd been learning for the LSAT. During one of these conversations, I finally told him about Stephen, this best friend who seemingly had a permanent place in my life.

We were talking about my birthday. Dad asked what I wanted as a present, and I saw my opportunity. "There's this guy named Stephen," I began, and explained our friendship. "And it'd be nice to have him over and hang out with me and Shaz."

I was surprised by my own boldness, but the one good thing that had come out of that experience with Yusuf was that I dared to ask for what I really wanted. I wanted to spoil myself a little.

It paid off. Though Dad's already permanently furrowed brows somehow nestled deeper into his face when I'd shared my request, a week later, on my birthday, Shaz, Stephen, and I were playing video games in the basement.

Mom remembered him; when I told her I'd been in touch with Stephen since college, she'd rolled her eyes. "I can't believe you're still friends," was all she said.

Soon Stephen was coming over every other weekend. Talking to my parents like he'd known them for years. He'd sit with Dad, ask him about his early days as a resident, about his experience with clinical trials. He'd talk to Mom about some paper she'd read about the health benefits of turmeric. But that was Stephen's special brand of magic, the kind he'd used on me when I'd first met him and on my friends back at

Bryn Mawr. He could get along with anyone, could make people feel at ease; he always seemed so unbothered by the world around him, so able to connect over shared interests. The moment he walked in through the front door of my family's house, it was as if he had always lived there.

He even effortlessly won over Shaz.

"I can't believe Stephen fell asleep while we played *Dark Souls*," said Shaz, after Stephen had left. "How do you even fall asleep like that? That game's scary as hell."

"Yeah, he does that. He fell asleep the first time we ever hung out." We both did, but that was beside the point.

"But he was snoring. *Peacefully.*" Shaz's gaze remained on the TV screen, but I could see the subtle tug of a smile. "He reminds me of a dog."

I snorted. Insults were our love language; insulting someone was the closest my brother would ever get to saying he liked them.

While I'd hopefully be starting my first year of law school, my brother would begin his first year at Franklin & Marshall College. He'd struggled with finishing high school: in part because of the bullying he'd faced, the isolation. With every passing year, it was like some invisible darkness was chewing through him, but I could see it. It was so deeply embedded in his bones, so seemingly ephemeral, he couldn't name it, let alone talk about it. One day he'd be his normal sarcastic but bright self—when we were in the basement playing video games, or when he'd sit at the piano, bringing Chopin back to life—but the next he'd tell me he no longer saw the point.

"Of what?" I'd ask. We'd been driving back from the grocery store to pick up a few things Mom had forgotten and were talking about the upcoming school year.

"Of anything," he replied.

I wanted to be free. I wanted to run away from my parents. I deserved to be a little selfish with my own life. But would it be worth it if it meant I'd leave my brother behind?

"Since your parents are cool with me hanging around, I can keep an eye on Shaz," Stephen promised me one night. "It'll be like you never left."

"That's assuming I get into Lewis & Clark," I said. "It might end up being a moot point."

"You'll get in," he replied, uncharacteristically confident. Then again, it felt like his confidence in many things was finally, steadily growing.

A few weeks later, in February 2013, I received an acceptance letter to Lewis & Clark Law School.

Stephen was right. I was moving to Portland.

PART II

We All Fall Down

CHAPTER 13

Its Music and Its Glass Cities

I settled in Portland relatively quickly.

The city itself was a mix of silver skyline against a dazzling, verdant green, with breathtaking views of Mount Hood's peak from almost every angle. I could breathe easier, too; I loved the crisp air hued by the faint smells of pine, concrete, salt, and, more importantly, the food carts I'd stalk on weekends like a tired, feral raccoon.

It was nothing like home back in Chester County. It was pretty, with its idyllic colonial landscapes straight out of an Andrew Wyeth landscape, but it carried a snobbish tension in the air, the anxious buzz almost emblematic of the East Coast. But Portland was a slow, languid city that did not care, seemingly, about *anything*. It was like I'd woken up in a world dressed as a Tame Impala song: all blissed out and psychedelic with a *what is will be* state of mind.

Portland, I learned, was not a place that would take itself seriously, and therefore, why should I?

People in Portland actually recycled, clung to their well-maintained bike lanes, and cared about where their food was sourced from—not enough to inquire about the names of the chickens they ate like I'd seen on *Portlandia*, but close enough. Some of my classmates brewed their own kombucha and craft beer (a popular coping mechanism for exam season). A man dressed as Darth Vader often rode a flaming bagpipe unicycle near a famous doughnut shop in the city; seeing him felt like a sign of good luck.

Portland was also very white, with nearly 74 percent of the population describing themselves as Caucasian (Philadelphia is 34 percent white). The law school was self-aware, at least, and provided a mentor network for students of color, which helped us find each other quickly; before classes had even officially begun, the program coordinators had even driven a bunch of us out to a lodge in the Willamette Valley for a weekend retreat in hopes that we'd all bond. It was also an attempt to get students to stay after graduation. I didn't know if I would stay; I hadn't thought that far ahead. At the very least, Portland would be my home for the next three years.

Best of all, Dad had offered to pay my tuition. It was part of our little unspoken agreement about my education: as long as I studied either medicine or law, Dad would cover my education costs. It meant I could focus. I was lucky.

Law school is supposed to be hard. Soul-crunchingly, heart-pulpingly difficult. It tests your mental and physical endurance. Not only must you sit in a lecture for hours on end, only to rush to another lecture for another several hours, all while sitting in the most uncomfortably hard chairs in human existence—designed, I think, to meld plastic into one's ass—but you also must do it while remaining on edge, awaiting the moment your professor calls on you to answer an impossible question about the reading you should have done.

It's three long years of peeling back the curtain on society and realizing that humans are capable of the most heinous acts. You learn things you wished you never did: *Dred Scott v. Sandford.* The Chinese Exclusion Act. The existence of animal crush videos, resulting in the Animal Crush Video Prohibition Act of 2010. But it was also the first time that I felt like I was really in charge of my life.

I paid close attention to the book publishing cases in my entertainment law class: on publisher obligations, on copyright protection. For the sake of pure curiosity, I justified.

I took an Islamic law class to grow closer to my faith on my own terms, and ask questions I'd been too afraid to ask—*What does the Quran say about the hijab? About interfaith marriage?*—but only now felt comfortable enough to talk to Dad about.

Law school made me realize that everything—everything—was far more complicated than I imagined. In a way, it was as if I'd been living my life in a fugue state until then; now I'd been slapped by adulthood and rudely awakened.

Living on my own brought a buffet of difficulties. I knew how to cook, thankfully—enjoyed it, even—and could do my laundry and clean just fine. I reveled in being able to sleep whenever I wanted, without Mom poking her head into my room, or being able to leave my apartment without her demanding to know where and why I was leaving. But learning how to sign up for a gym membership, lease a used car to get to school, sort out recycling, find a new primary care provider—this was new to me, and I loved the independence I felt.

On most days, after classes I'd do some work in the library, then head back to my apartment to my two cats. Then I would study and read. Make dinner. Do more work until I couldn't keep my eyes open anymore. Rinse and repeat.

Then, when the month of Ramadan rolled by—the holy month in which billions of Muslims around the world fast from sunrise to sunset—I fasted by myself. I'd wake up when it was still dark outside, stumble out of my bed to throw together some semblance of a meal, and pass out again until it was time to head to class. I'd pray alone, too. Ever since Yusuf and I broke things off, I'd started consistently praying five times a day. God, at least, was a familiar presence, and talking to an observer, even a silent one, was a comfort on those rare, lonely days. But I barely had time to feel lonely.

And hundreds of miles away, Stephen was fasting for Ramadan, too. "For the sake of solidarity," he'd said, which made me happy. He'd been learning about Islam; he'd gotten a sheikh to teach him, and even began visiting a mosque close to him. He'd never been particularly religious, even though he'd gone to a Catholic school in Jamaica, but lately he wanted to know more about what it meant to be Muslim, had been curious for years now It sort of tracked; I'd never seen him eat pork or drink alcohol. "Plus, I know your faith's important to you and your family," he'd said, so casually, and left it at that.

Once, by some incredible coincidence, Stephen accompanied his sheikh friend to a community interfaith event: the same interfaith event where my dad and Shaz happened to be volunteering (or more likely, Shaz had been dragged). As Stephen put it, the moment Shaz noticed him there, his mouth quite literally fell open. "Why are you everywhere?!" he demanded, to which Stephen only wheezed with laughter.

Stephen's reports from back home brought me comfort.

My only other respite was being at Powell's to find new books to read, and I'd recently discovered an author—we'll call her Anne Marie Karson—whose work I devoured. I loved Powell's. It felt like a labyrinth of books. It's the world's largest indie bookstore, and the moment you walk in, your nose is assaulted with that intoxicating paper smell. The rows of shelves go on forever. It was easy, too easy, to get lost in them, and forget about the world and all its problems. I'd go after classes during the week, when it wasn't so crowded, usually with people in Birkenstocks reading something by Cormac McCarthy, or books about home gardening or self-help.

Sometimes I would even write, masquerading as someone working on a book: an attempt at a young adult historical fantasy novel set in London during World War II. There were ghosts and orphans and murder, and in many ways, it was probably a cry for help.

But then I'd remember I was in law school. I couldn't waste time writing stories.

Between classes I got to know my classmates; most were easygoing, nothing like what I'd assume a "typical" law student would be. A woman named Pauline kept me company most days. She was my age, from New Orleans (she often wore colorful NOLA T-shirts beneath dresses she sewed herself), and had a rescued pet squirrel (who I was completely certain was still feral and at least a little murderous). In addition, she kept a chinchilla, a dog, a cat, a rabbit, and at least three or four other pets I've since forgotten. I got the sense she was the kind of person who would rescue *any* sad creature that happened to cross her path, whether it be rabid squirrels, alligators, or me.

"Oh, so you're doing animal law? Or maybe environmental law?" I asked her excitedly, after she'd listed her plethora of pets at orientation. This would mean we'd be in many classes together.

"Nah. I'm doing family law," she said matter-of-factly. "Animal law seems way too stressful to me."

Having eight-plus pets seemed pretty damn stressful, too, but I kept my mouth shut.

⋙⋘

As much as I loved Portland, though, it was hard being so far away.

Being away meant things were happening at home I had little control over, that there was no one to talk Mom through her arguments with Dad. Their already tenuous relationship was getting worse. She'd even called soon after I'd settled down, telling me she was thinking about divorcing him.

"That feels like a very big decision to make without trying couples therapy," I'd said.

"Your dad isn't the kind of guy who thinks therapy is necessary," she snapped. "He doesn't *want* to. He doesn't think we need it. You know him."

"Have you talked to him? Told him how you feel?"

"Like he'd listen." Mom let out a sigh. "This is exactly why I need this divorce. I thought you'd agree with me. You're in law school, for God's sake. Shaz is in college. I have a job." Though Mom had been a homemaker throughout my childhood, now that we were older, she had begun work as an accountant at JP Morgan. "I can live on my own, support myself. You are away, Shaz is in college. Now is the perfect time."

Since I was a child, Mom had always talked about being unhappy with Dad. This wasn't the first time she'd mentioned wanting to divorce him. But it had always been a passing thought without shape or substance, said aloud only after they'd had an argument and Mom was still buzzing with frustration.

"I don't think it's as easy as you're thinking." This time her threat seemed to have purpose and shape. It gave me this strange feeling in the pit of my stomach—a feeling so palpable it hurt. If Mom and Dad got divorced, I wasn't sure we'd ever see Mom again. I had enough sense to keep that part quiet, though.

The stress of that was bad enough, but homesickness was the worst of it—a casual gnawing at my chest most days. And sometimes, in the quiet of night, I could hardly breathe. I missed Shaz and watching him play games until I was soothed to sleep. I missed talking to Kaya and Maha. I missed Pakistani food: my dad's biryani, my mom's nihari.

And although I was happy that Stephen was acting as a conduit for home—he and my brother made regular trips to Philly for cheesesteaks—I missed him.

On one of our catch-up phone calls, I told him how I felt.

"I'm busy all the time. But I almost have to be, because the moment I let myself rest, I start missing the people back home, you know?"

Stephen went quiet for a moment.

"You know that day we had our class project, and I forgot your birthday?" he asked.

"Yeah?"

"I didn't forget. I lied."

"What?" I blinked. "Why would you lie about that?"

"I was a coward. When it came time to give you your birthday gift, I chickened out. I was scared you wouldn't like what I got you."

"Wait, you actually got me a *birthday gift*?"

Stephen laughed. "It was a pencil. Because you'd forgotten to bring a pencil for our first meeting. Wrapped it up in a little box and everything, like a dork."

I smiled. "I would have loved it."

"I know that, now," he said softly. "So, I decided. I need to stop doubting myself and start doing what I want." Before I could ask him what he meant, he went on: "I applied to a post-bacc program in Portland. At Portland State."

I sat bolt upright in my bed, scaring my cats. "*What?* And?!"

"I got in." I could practically hear his smile on the phone. "Want some company in Portland?"

CHAPTER 14

What You Wish For

Stephen moving to Portland was like having a piece of home with me.

He had his own apartment close to his campus at Portland State University, but he spent most of his time in mine. He was, for all purposes, my roommate. We set up a projector and watched movies together. If I ran out of milk or eggs, he'd grab them from the grocery store, no questions asked. On weekends, we'd go to Powell's together and work in comfortable silence.

Once we stayed up late while I practiced an oral argument for a competition—a 1L rite of passage. By some miracle—and more likely, thanks to Stephen's ruthless feedback and a reminder to treat it, as he put it, "like acting!"—I ended up winning the award for best argument.

It was like being together in college again, only we were older, wiser—and slightly more capable.

As soon as I realized Stephen was there to stay, my body began to unwind. I'd been on edge for so long, I hadn't even noticed how tense I'd been. Being alone wasn't a bad thing; I'd liked the quiet evenings by myself; somehow solitude brought out my creativity, my mental fortitude, my ability to focus on work. My inner voice was my closest companion, and I was growing to love her, flaws and all.

But with Stephen around, I no longer had to worry about the fact that if I choked on my food, I would likely die alone in my apartment, and my cats would probably eat my body. If I was sick, I'd have someone to care for me. If I needed to walk outside in the dark, there'd be someone to call if I felt unsafe. And if I saw something funny—some silly meme or video on my phone—I would no longer have to laugh alone. After a semester of law school, my best friend was there. Wilder still, I was in law school, and my best friend was living in the same city as me. It felt like the best gift he could have given me. Because that was the thing about Stephen: the world looked a little brighter when he was near.

"I missed you," I admitted one evening, when we'd come back from a snack haul at the grocery store for movie night.

"Oh yeah?" He smiled playfully before adding: "I really missed you, too."

❧

Come 2L year, emboldened by Stephen's presence—and in a state of delirium brought on by midterm exams—I adopted a dog: a small, anxious whippet mix with noodly legs. Stephen had been skeptical, at first. "Adopting a dog while still in law school feels like . . . a choice."

"A good choice?" I asked hopefully.

"An *interesting* choice."

But when Stephen was done with his post-bacc classes for the day, he'd be at my doorstep with a determined expression.

"I found a really good dog park nearby," he'd say, "and I need some exercise."

So we'd put Stellaluna—I'd named her after the eponymous fruit bat in my favorite children's book—in a harness, and we'd spend hours together in the park.

Like a weird little family, I'd thought.

I told Mom about Stella, but I had yet to tell Dad. How he would react to my dog, I genuinely had no clue. Mom seemed to think it wouldn't be good.

"Don't tell him until you come home for the summer," Mom said tiredly over the phone. "I'll keep it a secret until then. How does the saying go? Better to ask forgiveness than permission."

"Sorry," I said. "And thanks, Mom."

And I meant it.

Mom's sigh was her response.

Mom was unwinding, too. My relationship with her had changed since I'd left home—the serendipitous result of the new distance between us, and the comfort she'd gained in knowing that I was in law school. At parties, she could finally partake in the age-old South Asian custom of showing off her kids, her head held high.

Her check-ins were supportive in a way she'd never been. "If you're not certain about environmental law, you can always explore other options," she'd said over the phone when I'd told her I'd been undecided. "Whatever kind of law you want!"

I even told her I'd begun writing a book in my spare time.

"Oh, wow, can you imagine? My girl being a lawyer and an author on the side! Imagine your book signings!"

Then I told her that Stephen had moved to Portland. In retrospect, I should have kept my mouth shut, but I didn't want to hide it from her. And I was never a good liar.

"Sometimes I think you're too honest," Mom told me once, like it was a bad thing; she'd asked me what I thought about her newly straightened hair, and I'd admitted that I preferred her curls.

But Stephen—I wanted to be honest with Mom about Stephen. I wanted her to know that Stephen had helped me. I wanted her to accept that he was a part of my life.

Even if Mom didn't approve.

"So he's *living* with you?" she asked.

"No, he—he has his own place. He just hangs out here a lot."

"But eventually he's just going to move in. And then what? I'm paying for his rent, too?"

"Why would you assume that?"

"Because I know how these things go, Farah. Why is he even there? He's going to be a distraction."

"If anything, he's been helping me," I said.

"Whatever. It's your life, I guess." Mom groaned, tired. "Maybe it's a good thing you're across the country, so no one can find out. But you *cannot* tell your dad. He can't know. I'll have to keep this a secret from him. *Another* secret!"

Time had dragged its toes, Portland-style, but now that Stephen was there, it jogged at a steady, peaceful pace. Not long after I'd started my 2L year, Shaz came to visit. Reunited, the three of us spent a week blissfully doing nothing but eating at every favorite food cart and playing video games until we passed out in various spots around my apartment. Shaz met Stella, who quickly decided my brother was her new favorite person.

I was almost halfway done with law school. I'd survived so far—not without pain, tears, and a soul-shredding lack of sleep. During one of my final exams, I felt a searing pain in my abdomen so acute that after I finished, I had to rush to the hospital. It turned out I had an umbilical hernia, for which I needed surgery and a month of rest (which truthfully felt like a vacation after the hell of exams).

But at least I'd proved to myself I could do this whole law school thing.

It was almost anticlimactic.

It was a Sunday, and I'd been walking back from the grocery store when I found a baby crow on the road by my apartment. Crows, I had learned, were a common sight in downtown Portland. The sky above would sometimes become overcast with thousands of them, a swirling cacophony that darkened the sky. They were a part of the landscape of the city, a part I loved.

The baby crow was a tiny thing, with startling blue eyes and oil-slicked feathers that glistened under the sun. Its parents, and its nest, were in a tree above it; the parents dived into any passersby to get them away from their baby. When they noticed my approach, they dived into me, too, with such force that I stumbled back.

Were they trying to teach it how to fly? I was definitely no expert on crow behavior, but their caws sounded too frantic for that. The more likely scenario was that their baby had fallen out of the nest; it looked too young to fly, anyway.

I tried to call a local wildlife rescue, but they were closed. I paced nervously a few feet away until I noticed the baby crow hopping farther from the sidewalk and into a busy road.

I didn't think; I ran into the road and grabbed the baby. Carefully, I put it back under the tree, shielding my face from its parents' righteous assault. But not seconds later, the baby was hopping toward the road again.

Panicking, I called Stephen. He came running out minutes later, and after almost a dozen clumsy attempts, the two of us placed the baby crow back in the nest. To my surprise, the crow parents had, at some point, stopped cawing or attacking. Perhaps they understood what we'd been trying to do.

Stephen and I grinned and high-fived. My heart was racing, and it felt good to help in our own little way. We'd worked together, felt the same sense of urgency, were on the same page when it had really counted.

"It was so small," Stephen reflected later, in awe. "I could feel its heartbeat."

But the next morning, Stephen had come into my apartment look-ing solemn. I knew something was wrong.

"I saw the baby crow," he murmured. He wouldn't look at me. "It jumped back in the road and—" He swallowed the rest of his words. It was too difficult to say.

It was hard to explain, but that baby crow had felt like our respon-sibility. And with its death, we had somehow failed. We couldn't control what happened, no matter how good our intent was, no matter how hard we'd tried.

So what were we supposed to do? What should we have done to save it?

It almost felt like an omen.

❧

Then, during the last semester of my 2L year, my cat Binx suddenly died. He'd been running through the apartment, playing and warbling the way he did most evenings when I was at my kitchen table, study-ing. Then I heard a thud, followed by a bloodcurdling, childlike wail. I found Binx on the ground, lying on his side, taking shallow, desperate breaths. Stephen, miraculously, was visiting; he picked up Binx's body, and his dark-bright eyes, wet with tears, met mine. That look of hope-less dismay would be burned into my brain for the rest of my life. A look that mirrored mine.

Seconds later, Binx was gone. He'd died of a heart attack, despite being, as the vet had put it, "otherwise one of the healthiest cats" she'd ever seen.

I'd loved that cat. Binx was the reason, Mom joked, that I'd never find a husband. Binx had simply set the standard too high. When I had the umbilical hernia and had to get surgery, Binx never left my bedside during my recovery. Wherever I walked, he remained close behind, like my own little shadow. He gave soft, encouraging headbutts while I studied for exams. Carried his favorite toys in his mouth and brought them to me as offerings. He'd been a source of comfort on those lonelier days in Portland.

Shaz loved him. Even my parents adored him. A world without Binx felt wrong. Cracked, tainted by a profound sense of melancholy. I'd been so certain of my future, only to realize now how easily it could be taken away. It felt like I'd gotten a glimpse behind a curtain that I'd never asked for.

Life was so terribly delicate. Too delicate.

CHAPTER 15

Leaves Compared with Flowers

After finishing my 2L year, I spent the summer in DC, where I'd snagged a clerkship at the United States Justice Department, in the Environmental and Natural Resources Division. It was a blissfully uneventful summer; I shared an apartment with my cousin, Shaan, who'd gotten an internship at the Pentagon, and we ate our weight in halal kebabs from a local Afghani restaurant. And the clerkship itself was exactly what you'd expect: I got to work on cases against companies that dumped chemicals in protected water sources, and helped create legal presentations on the protection of elephants under CITES (the Convention on International Trade in Endangered Species of Wild Fauna and Flora, a name I never want to type out again) for international allied organizations. I learned a ton.

But it felt like no time had passed before I was back in Portland as a 3L.

The 3L year is known as "the year they bore you to death" by most law students. At that point, you're too busy thinking about post–law school life to care about classes anymore. Your brain's on the bar exam, the MPRE, getting a job.

On the bright side, though, it goes by *fast*. And everyone knows a quick death is far preferable.

Stephen, meanwhile, had already left Portland; he'd finished his post-bacc program and gotten a job at a hospital in New York City as a clinical research coordinator.

"You, in New York City. I still can't imagine it," I'd told him over the phone.

Stephen laughed. "Is it weird that I'm kind of excited?"

It was the first time I'd heard him sound excited about anything career-wise in years. He hadn't given up on med school, but working as a clinical research coordinator was a good fit—it was flexible, and he loved looking at data. I barely understood half of what he did, but from the sounds of it, he was already thriving.

It was a little lonely at first; now it was just me and my cat, Kisa, in a new apartment closer to campus but farther from downtown Portland. Having to leave Stella behind in Pennsylvania certainly didn't help.

As it turned out, my dad was not angry about the dog I'd secretly adopted. Just days before my flight back to the East Coast for the summer, I finally decided to tell him about Stella through a Skype call.

"There's someone I'd like you to meet," I said nervously.

Dad immediately stiffened.

"This"—I pulled Stella up to my laptop camera—"is Stella."

Seconds passed in silence as Dad narrowed his eyes. For a moment I wondered if the camera had frozen.

"Is that—is that a cat?" he asked. "That's a very ugly cat."

"What?" I blinked. "No. No, Stella's a dog. She's a whippet mix. I don't know what she's mixed with—I got her from a shelter—but she's definitely not a cat."

"Farah . . ." Dad made an exasperated noise. "Why would you— Is she at least potty-trained?"

"Yeah! She's great. I've had her for a while now. Binx didn't like Stella much, but Kisa gets along with her just fine."

"Okay." A pause. "Okay."

I could see the slow absorption behind his glasses. The look of resigned acceptance.

"You're bringing her then, right? When is your flight again?"

By the time we landed in Philadelphia, Dad had already bought my dog several sweaters, toys, and two kinds of organic dog food.

"Stella and I are going out in the garden," he'd cheerfully announce on a Saturday morning. "She likes the dogwoods, I think. Farah, you should leave Stella here with us. Having a dog is too distracting from school. Come, come, Stella!"

One evening, weeks into my first semester of 3L year, Mom called me without warning. This was unusual, since she normally texted first to see what I was up to, or if I was free to talk. Sometimes we wouldn't talk on the phone for weeks. Sometimes our calls would last only minutes.

"Shaz is having trouble with school," she told me. "He wants to drop out."

"What do you mean drop out?"

"What do you think? He doesn't want to finish college."

This wasn't going to be a five-minute conversation. I began to chew at my nails.

"Does he know what he wants to do instead . . . ?"

"He doesn't know. But he's stopped showing up to classes. He's at serious risk of academic probation. Dad's on his case. We'll drag him to class if we have to. In the meantime, I'm taking him to a therapist. Maybe they can knock some sense into him."

What the hell happened? He'd been struggling with school—Mom had even told me she thought Shaz might have depression—but this was huge. It sounded like he'd completely given up.

Mom was asking me about my next break, the next time I was planning on visiting home. I could hardly hear her.

"Why didn't he tell me?" I whispered.

"He didn't want you to find out, clearly."

Did he think I'd be disappointed? Was he ashamed? My stomach churned at the thought. Truthfully, I *was* a little disappointed—he'd worked so hard to get into Franklin & Marshall, had been so proud when he'd shown me the essay he wrote for his application. All that work, wasted. Instead of getting help, he was throwing it all away. And he *deserved* success, damn it.

If Shaz dropped out of school, his mental health would plummet. My brother was always sensitive; he felt things and he felt things deeply; it was what made him a brilliant musician. I *loved* that about him. But if he dropped out, our parents would make him feel a hundred times worse. The guilt alone, that feeling of failure, would be torture; and to pair that with the uncertainty of his own future—I didn't want to imagine what it would do to him.

"Talk to him," said Mom. "All he does these days is lock himself in the basement in the dark. I swear one of these nights I'm going to go down there and find him hanging upside down in the closet."

I'd have laughed if I didn't feel like crying.

❧

Shaz and Stephen came to visit me in Portland again not long after that—with Mom's encouragement, probably.

But it was a good opportunity to talk to Shaz, and to get him out into nature and moving. Fresh air would certainly be good for him—for all of us. I took the two of them to Washington, to hike Dog Mountain.

The six-mile trail would be doable for amateur hikers, or so I thought. It wasn't steep, and at the very least, it'd be a beautiful trek: the trail snaked through pristine meadows and dense forests straight out of a fairy tale.

But at some point Shaz began falling behind us.

He told us to go on ahead without him. "You freaks look like you're itching to go faster."

"Are you sure?" I asked. "We can slow down; it's fine."

"No, I prefer to be on my own anyway."

Stephen and I lingered for a moment. But I knew my brother; he wouldn't say he'd rather be alone unless he truly meant it. The trail was safe. He'd be fine.

We moved on without him.

After a half hour, Stephen and I decided to wait for my brother to catch up.

Minutes passed. Fifteen. Twenty.

At long last, Shaz lumbered over a hill toward us, mildly out of breath and a little sweatier than we'd left him. I jogged toward him.

"Where have you been?" I asked, worried. "We thought you died!"

"I saw someone coming down the trail wearing an *Assassin's Creed* T-shirt, so we got to talking."

I stared.

"How did you manage to make a hike involve video games?"

"It's a gift."

Half-concerned that my brother would get distracted again, Stephen and I decided to stick with Shaz for the rest of the trail. Just because he could be alone, we decided, didn't mean he should be.

An hour later, when we'd finally reached the peak of the mountain, the view stole what little breath I had left. It was dazzlingly verdant, an elysian view of the rolling hills of the Columbia River Gorge. A carpet of wildflowers, dappled by afternoon sunlight, gently swayed in the wind. The river itself was a glittering, pristine glassy blue—an exposed vein of lapis lazuli—snaking through the peaks.

The three of us said nothing, simply taking in the color. The raw beauty. The *life*. Here, we were untouchable, cradled by an earth so much bigger than ourselves.

It was like we'd found the heart of the world.

After a moment of humble, awed silence, we sat on soft grass to rest. As we planned our journey back, I glanced at my brother. It was a long shot, I knew, but did he understand what I was trying to say in bringing him here? Words would never be enough, but a view like this—could a view like this move him in a way I couldn't? Did he understand that the same world that had made him so jaded could also look like *this*?

I was distracted by something moving in the air—

It was a crow, gliding on the breeze.

"Is that crow *windsurfing*?" I pointed.

Stephen laughed. "Wow. What a life."

"Oh, to be a crow among the wildflowers," said Shaz, smiling fondly. His eyes trailed the crow's movements. Transfixed.

I grinned.

The crow continued to hover above us so expertly, it didn't have to flap its wings once. At one point, the three of us clapped as it pulled an effortless aerobatic loop. There was something so magical about watching an animal experience joy for joy's sake.

A few minutes later, the crow flew off, seemingly quite pleased with itself.

I remembered, then, the baby crow Stephen and I had failed to save. How we'd tucked it back into its nest and walked away, convinced it had escaped danger.

But this, I thought sadly—

This was how it should be.

❧

After a long, mildly sweat-spiced car ride, Stephen, my brother, and I were back in my apartment. While Stephen showered, Shaz and I were finally alone.

This was it. This was the time for me to be a Big Sister.

A hundred questions peppered my brain, and I struggled to find where to begin: *What was happening? Are you hiding something? Why haven't you said anything? Why won't you tell me?*

I had to say something. Mom would want me to pry something, anything, out of him. At the very least, I needed to get clarity on why he was dropping out of school.

But in the end, I didn't ask anything. I wasn't even fully sure if I had any right to interfere; if he wanted me to know, he would have told me, right?

Or maybe—maybe I was afraid of the answers.

"So," I asked instead, "any thoughts on dinner?"

CHAPTER 16

In the Midst of It All

I was *itching* to be done with law school.

At least Stephen was happily settled in New York City. He loved his job, loved the city itself; he taught himself how to cook and went on long runs through Central Park. On our phone calls, he sound winded, exhilarated. The city had breathed life into him.

Back home, though, my brother's need to drop out of school had become only more dire, and my parents were at their wits' end. So much so that when I returned for winter break, my dad demanded a family meeting. The agenda? Shaz's life.

Dad, Mom, Shaz, and I sat at the kitchen table while Dad presented the facts: Shaz was on academic probation at Franklin & Marshall. Shaz had been diagnosed with depression and was seeing a therapist who, my brother claimed, was not helping.

A few weeks ago, Shaz had also come out as bisexual; he'd told my parents while I was away at law school, and this, too, was affecting his mental health. I wish I'd been there. But, apparently, it had gone surprisingly well. The three of them had been sitting at the usual kitchen dining table to discuss Shaz's falling grades and his falling mental health when the truth had finally burst.

"I'm bi. I'm bisexual. I can't help it. And the stress of it all, on top of everything else, has been too much," he'd said.

Being gay was difficult enough, but being gay in the Muslim community was to lead an impossible life. His very existence would be deemed by some as a sin; others would consider him finding a partner—finding his happiness—a sin. There'd be no winning. Even if we were to keep quiet and shield him from those kinds of people, the weight of knowing how others viewed him would remain.

Mom and Dad, thankfully, remained oddly supportive.

But although the truth was finally out, Shaz's grades still suffered, and now Shaz didn't want to finish college anymore.

"The thing is, Shaz," Dad began, "even if you are gay or, or *bisexual*— it does not matter. To any of us. Okay? What matters is school."

"Uh," I piped in, "I wouldn't say it doesn't *matter*—"

"You know what I mean. The point is, being gay is no excuse."

Shaz's eyes were downcast. In the past year, he'd looked hollower than I remembered. Like the color had leached from his skin. "I don't want to talk about this."

Dad's eyebrows furrowed behind his glasses. "We have to talk about this. This is your life."

"There's nothing to talk about!" Shaz snapped. "I want to drop out. That's it. End of story."

"You're being ungrateful, Shaz," said Mom. "We're paying your tuition. You can't just drop out and sit around our house and do nothing with your life."

"I need some time. That's all I'm asking," retorted Shaz. "If you want, I'll get a job, pay you rent."

"So you get a job, and then what?" Mom folded her arms. "How much time do you need? How much time are you going to waste? The problem is, I don't think you've even thought this through."

I bit my lip.

On one hand, I could understand, at the very least, my parents' frustrations. But it was clear that something else was happening beneath the surface. Shaz was enduring a lot, emotions he couldn't quite grasp or articulate. Dropping out of college wasn't ideal, but it wasn't like it meant his life would be over. He still had his music. If he needed time to rest and sort things out, why shouldn't we give it to him?

But it was like my brother forgot how to hope. How to dream. I was afraid my brother would spend years locked away in a room, living in his own world, until he was just a shell of himself.

"I don't want to talk about this," Shaz repeated, pushing away from the table. He stormed out of the kitchen, and his footsteps faded; he'd gone up to his bedroom. Knowing him, he'd be in there for hours if we let him.

The silence he left behind made my ears ring.

Dad was the first to speak.

"What are we supposed to do?" Dad sat back in his chair. "We've been talking to his adviser. His therapist. We even gave him the option to take a year off. All we care about now is that he at least gets a college degree. It doesn't even matter what it is!" Dad, normally collected and frustratingly rational, looked at me with pleading eyes.

"What else are we supposed to do?"

❧

I gave my brother a solid hour before storming his bedroom.

"My darling baby brother," I said calmly. "What's going on?"

He was lounging in his bed with his laptop by his pillow. Discord was open, and on his screen, text flowed down in an endless stream. Clearly he had friends to talk to; that was good, at least.

Shaz's eyes remained glued to the screen, but I knew he was listening.

I sat on the edge of his bed.

"I feel like you're hiding something. I don't want to pressure you into telling me anything you're not ready to, but I feel like there's more to this then you're letting on." I patted his blanket. "Talk to me, seriously. Maybe I can help."

Slowly, Shaz sat up. His eyelashes fluttered in thought. He'd looked rough lately, but his infuriatingly long lashes remained. When he was a child—thanks to the round face he'd inherited from Mom and those long lashes—he'd looked like a doll. Once, when I was almost twelve and Shaz was six, there was a terrible thunderstorm, and the lights had gone out for hours. Our parents lit candles, and the four of us kept to the kitchen. Mom and Dad talked to pass the time in hushed, intimate tones; the dim light had a magic way of softening everything it touched. Meanwhile, I pulled out my hairbrush and every hair clip I owned, and gave my brother a ridiculous makeover. By the time I was done, he was sporting at least six different flower barrettes, two pigtails, and a shade of lipstick I'd borrowed from Mom that didn't suit him at all.

He didn't complain once, didn't say anything about it being "too girlie."

My brother and I rarely said "I love you," but with the way he'd often indulged me throughout his life, I knew he felt the same way I did.

I waited patiently for Shaz to speak, willing this feeling of love and support into the room in a way I'd hoped would reach him.

He took a breath.

"I have a boyfriend," he uttered.

My eyes went wide. "Oh. Oh! Shit. Really? How? Who?"

"I met him online. He's been helping me the past year with everything. You know how my freshman year, I had a shitty roommate?"

I nodded. Shaz's roommate had been a loud nightmare of a person who had no concept of a normal sleep schedule and often pretended Shaz didn't exist.

"I joined a Discord channel to just cope. That's how I met Keith."

"Okay," I said slowly. "Have you talked to him? Like actually *talked*? He's not, like, secretly a seventy-year-old predator or anything, right?"

"No! No, I've talked to him on the phone. I've seen him on webcam. He's my age."

"So what's the problem? Why won't you tell Mom and Dad? They said they're okay with you being bi—their priority right now is that you stay in school."

"Keith's engaged to someone else."

I felt the blood drain from my face. Everything went blurry. For a moment I couldn't recognize the boy in front of me.

"He's—what? Engaged?" I swallowed. "Does the person he's engaged to know that you're dating him? How does that even—"

"Everyone knows. His fiancée doesn't love it, obviously, but she knows."

"So it's a poly thing?" I asked, ignorant.

"Not exactly. It's more that he likes me, but he also likes her. He's trying to figure out what he wants to do."

My face darkened.

"So he's stringing you along."

I was angry. Was this jackass making my brother hold on to empty hope? It reminded me of Kareem, the way he'd cheated on me.

"It's fine."

"How is that *fine*?"

"I'm okay with it. If he can't decide between us, then he doesn't have to. As long as I still get to talk to him . . ." Shaz trailed off. "I'll wait."

I felt a vise grip on my heart. My brother looked so lonely.

Even if I didn't like this, he was an adult, capable of his own decisions. As his big sister, I could give him advice, but I also had to give him the opportunity to learn, to make mistakes, even if it meant doing things I disagreed with. Mom had never let me make mistakes, and that deep-set bitterness chewed at me constantly.

I wanted my brother to respect himself more. I wanted him to be loved by the one he loved, without question or hesitation. This clearly wasn't it.

"Is this why you want to drop out of school?"

"Sort of." Shaz shifted uncomfortably. "It feels connected, maybe, but I don't know. I just . . . feel lost, I guess. About a lot of things."

"Why?" I asked softly.

"If I knew that . . ."

I wish I understood him better. My whole life, I'd internalized a very clear road map instilled by Mom, one that I'd mechanically followed. I'd never once questioned it. I never felt I had a reason to. It was just the way it was.

But Shaz had forgotten how to imagine a future to work toward, let alone plan for. Now this sense of failure was keeping him paralyzed. His mind was filled with doubts: *What was the point? What if I work hard, but nothing comes of it? What if I fail no matter what I do?*

I wondered if the person he loved feeling uncertain about him was also keeping Shaz in limbo. In the same way he was waiting for Keith to make a choice, Shaz was also waiting for life to extend a hand, a sign of what to do.

Drifting with no purpose felt easier: drifting meant no expectation, and thus, no disappointment.

"Are you ever going to tell Mom and Dad?" I asked.

"And give them more reason to be disappointed?" Shaz let out a short, bitter laugh.

In truth, they would be disappointed. Maybe more than disappointed. I'd learned in Sunday school, and even in my Islamic studies classes in college and law school, that several Islamic scholars—citing the story of Lot—believed that homosexuality was a sin. Other scholars believed homosexuality itself was not a sin, per se, but acting on it was. Either way, homosexuality, it was believed, was a test from God, and only by resisting your urges would you pass the test. As if gayness was simply a craving to be fended off, like a late-night desire for chocolate cake when you're supposed to be on a diet.

But Shaz had a boyfriend. A boyfriend who already had someone. "Fuck."

"Yeah," said Shaz. "This sucks. You know I'm supposed to be getting my wisdom teeth out tomorrow?"

"At least it means you *literally* can't talk to Mom and Dad?" I offered.

That won me a smirk.

CHAPTER 17

Sakinah

When I was around fourteen years old, I dreamed my dad had died. I couldn't remember the details, only that Dad had died from some mysterious illness related to his poor health. The dream took place at his funeral. I couldn't see his body; it'd been covered with a white cloth, per Islamic tradition.

I woke up crying.

I rolled out of bed and stormed into the kitchen, where Mom and Dad were sitting at the kitchen table.

"You need to take better care of your health," I announced to Dad.

"Eh?" said Dad.

"I had a dream you died. Because you don't take care of yourself." I wiped at my eyes, still wet. "You're going to die at this rate. You should—you should eat more veggies, exercise more!"

Dad's mouth scrunched in thought. "Maybe I should exercise more, but that doesn't mean I'm unhealthy."

"You don't know that! What if you have a disease? And taking better care of yourself is the only way to prevent it?" I know I sounded ridiculous, but my fear was getting the better of me. "Remember I had that dream about Nana Jan dying? We need to take it seriously!"

Mom and Dad shared a look. Like I'd grown a second head and now spoke from both. They were rarely on the same wavelength. Of course *now* was one of those times.

Finally, Mom sighed. "Farah, you have dreams about *everyone* dying. You're not a psychic. You're just, I don't know, anxious."

Maybe she was right, but that wasn't the point.

One year before this dream, when I was thirteen, I had a dream about a funeral. Everything was in black and white. I recognized my mom, surrounded by her two sisters and Nani. I tried to speak to them, but they couldn't hear me. Then I noticed the grave, still open. I peered over the corner to get a glimpse of the body—but I was ripped away, and the dream faded.

When I woke up, Mom and Dad were, strangely, out of the house. Instead, my dad's younger sister, who'd been staying with us at the time, greeted me in the kitchen, unable to look me in the eye when I asked where my parents were. Apparently my Nana Jan had died in the early hours of the morning. He'd had a heart attack, and Mom and Dad had rushed to Virginia to help Nani Jan with funeral preparations.

My dream was like a sign.

And now I'd had a dream about Dad dying. Dad, the voice of reason in our home. If something ever happened to him, our family would fall apart. I'd do anything to keep him from dying.

"But that dream I had before Nana Jan—"

"A broken clock is right twice a day. That dream you had about Nana Jan was just a coincidence. And look, your dad is perfectly fine," interrupted Mom. "Though I should start cutting down on the oil in the karahi chicken."

"You need oil for it to taste good," Dad retorted. "Farah, I'm healthy. I just had my yearly physical. You're being silly."

Embarrassed and defeated, I went back upstairs. I wouldn't tell them about my dreams anymore. They were just dreams, after all, and over the years, I must have had a hundred dreams where I died, or my friends died. When I first got my cat, Kisa, I dreamed she died (I suppose this wasn't far off the mark). Once, I even dreamed my dad had cooked and eaten my pet rabbit, Elvis. Obviously this was a thing with me—I had this unexplainable fear that death would take everyone I cared about away from me, that death was this unstoppable force that could pounce at any moment.

I never told my parents about those death dreams again. Over time I stopped having them altogether, and eventually I forgot about them entirely. Everything was fine, after all. It was a bad habit of mine to envision the worst-case scenario, an almost compulsive need to prepare myself for the worst possibilities.

By the time I was sitting on Shaz's bed, learning about his boyfriend and cracking jokes about his wisdom teeth, the only evidence that I'd had those dreams at all was Mom's cooking.

It had become a little less oily.

✿

After New Year's at my parents' house, Shaz's secret safe with me, I flew back to Portland with Kisa in tow.

Immediately, I hurled myself into work. My days consisted of frantic note-taking in my final classes, hunkering in the library with Pauline and my friend Loren who was studying Native American Law, and going to meetings with my adviser for a capstone paper I'd need to finish to graduate. I was worried about Shaz, but I knew it was time to focus more than ever.

But when I wasn't writing my capstone, I was writing stories. More snippets. I hadn't given up on that ridiculous young adult ghost book I'd started. I'd found other aspiring writers on Twitter; we'd talk about what we were writing and cheer each other on. Through them, I learned about writing workshops: retreats that lasted several weeks, where aspiring writers learned how to write alongside their peers.

Maybe after law school I'd try writing on the side. One day, maybe I'd publish a book. Mom and Dad would never let me throw away my law degree to be a full-time author, but if I published a book someday . . . Well, it was nice to dream a little.

⁂

Toward the end of January, a snowstorm hit the Philadelphia area. Dad texted me pictures of Stella, enjoying the snow in a new jacket he'd bought for her.

I'm jealous, I texted back. Portland doesn't get much snow.

A few moments later, a reply popped up on my screen.

Can you talk?

I called immediately.

Dad, always straight to the point, told me he had pancreatic cancer. Stage four. He'd been having stomach pains for months. His first round of chemo would start next week. It was bad, but he would fight it, he assured me. He would win.

"How long—" I swallowed. "How long have you known?"

"Ah . . ." There was some shuffling on the other end. "A few weeks? We found out right after you left. I wanted to wait until the end of the month, but . . ."

He wanted to wait until after my birthday to tell me. Someone must have convinced him otherwise—Shaz? Mom?

"You should have told me the moment you knew," I said.

"We were worried it would distract you. You need to focus, Farah. You're in your last semester."

He was right about that, at least. No amount of worrying was going to change the circumstances.

Still, though—I imagined my parents coming back from the hospital. I imagined them telling Shaz the news. How had they all reacted? How had they all felt?

On the phone Dad told me he loved me—something he rarely said—and I told him the same before we hung up.

I sat on my couch in a daze, a news ticker of half-formed thoughts running behind my eyes. I thought, for one bizarre second, about that dream I'd had when I was fourteen. About the white shroud that covered his body, his face I couldn't see.

Pancreatic cancer. After we hung up, I pulled my laptop close and researched it.

Pancreatic, I learned, was one of the worst, if not the worst, kinds of cancer to have, with the highest mortality rate. It was almost impossible to detect early. It spread quickly, rapidly, and had a poor prognosis; only one out of one hundred people survived their cancer for three or more years after diagnosis.

Dad was going to die. He was going to die soon.

And I was stuck in Portland.

I took a deep breath. My hands shook as I called Stephen.

"Hey," came his voice. "Everything okay?"

I burst into tears.

CHAPTER 18

The Slow Hours

I felt like I was losing my mind.

Every day I woke up in my bed in Portland, I'd be hit with a low-grade bitterness that coursed through my chest. I sat in the back of my classes, boring holes in the back of my classmates' heads, wondering how it felt to be them. Most had family close by, family to head home to after class. Families that probably weren't made of glass, waiting at the edge of their seats for that final second, that final, tiniest pressure that would make the whole thing fall apart. I was jealous of them. I felt marooned. It was unfair, I thought, for everyone around me to lead their relatively normal, stable lives, untainted by death, while I bore the weight of Dad's illness.

God, I wanted to go *home*. I hadn't even celebrated my birthday; I'd stayed at my apartment and eaten my body weight in Reese's Puffs, then spent the rest of the night researching bar exam study programs. A birthday seemed so insignificant in the wake of everything.

"What do you need from us?" asked the associate dean for student affairs, a woman named Laura.

I'd seen her around campus before; she was almost always in a black suit, which made her flaming red hair even more effulgent. This was the first time I'd ever spoken to her one-on-one, though. We'd been sitting in her office, me across from her, on a plush couch, while she looked at me with concern.

I'd told her about Dad.

"I don't know," I replied. "Just understanding, I guess. I'm not asking for any slack or to be treated any differently, exactly. But it'd be nice if my professors knew, in case . . ."

Just in case of what, I wasn't sure, either. Maybe I just wanted them to know. Maybe I wanted a little—just a little—more softness.

"Of course. If you need to take any mental health days off, you'll have permission. Whatever you need," she said gently. "What about exams?"

We were already halfway through the semester. Thankfully my capstone paper was almost done; I'd long finished editing my first draft for my adviser. But I'd have to start preparing for final exams soon.

More bitterness. I'd have to sit in a classroom, taking a test like everyone else—all while my dad was dying at home.

My eyes stung. The fact that I was even having this conversation was absurd.

"No, I'll be fine."

Laura nodded, gave me a stiff smile that didn't quite reach her eyes. We both knew I was lying, but the nicest thing she could do for me was pretend I wasn't.

Shaz knew being so far away was hard for me. Almost every week he'd send me music, a curated list of songs he'd found—sometimes just a single song, which he'd text me with no context. He introduced me to neo soul and lo-fi hip-hop, genres I'd never heard before. He'd prescribe songs like medicine:

Listen to this while driving. Preferably on a highway.

Listen to this one when watching the sunrise—yes, the sunrise.

He'd also send old songs I'd long forgotten, songs from childhood that we used to listen to in the car on long drives to Virginia, where Mom's youngest sister lived. Shaz and I would share headphones as I played through several early Daft Punk albums. A lot of early Coldplay. Coldplay was one of the reasons he'd been interested in learning piano.

Shaz never had the right words—and, really, what could we say?—but he always had music. And his musician brain always seemed to know what I needed to listen to most.

Stephen, too, helped. He'd been recommending different video games to try. If anything could keep my mind off Dad's diagnosis, he'd said, it'd be games.

"So there's *Mass Effect*," he suggested over the phone. "You remember *Mass Effect*—I played when we were in college."

I made a face. "I don't want to play some male-centric space game."

"You can make your own character. You can be a woman."

"Huh." I spread myself across my IKEA couch, slightly torn thanks to my cats. "Okay, that's more intriguing. I'm not really into sci-fi, though."

"But the story is amazing. I think you'll like it."

He explained that you play as Commander Shepard, a Special Forces soldier tasked with organizing a team of both humans and aliens to save the galaxy from an ancient, monstrous AI race called the Reapers.

"Not gonna lie; it sounds a little like military propaganda."

"Oh, absolutely. But it's well written."

I bought the game, downloaded it on the computer on which I was supposed to be doing my law school work. It felt sacrilegious, but I figured I'd uninstall it the next day.

An hour into the game, I was a goner.

I didn't sleep. I raced through the first game like a woman possessed. I was no longer a law student in desperate need of a shower; I was Commander Shepard. I was saving the galaxy.

Weeks went by like this; I'd wake up, go to classes. I'd rush home, do my reading for school in a haphazard scramble. And then I'd play until the morning horizon peeked its orangey head through my window.

"I beat the game," I told Stephen, my throat dry from lack of sleep.

"Just wait until you get to the second one. It's even better."

"Shit. Right. It's a trilogy." I sighed. "Off I go then."

I was having *fun*. It was like a part of me had woken up, something that had been dormant and lying in wait. Now I could finally see it with such clarity: the truth. What I wanted, more than anything. The story of the game was what got me hooked.

I wanted to write stories. And as the credits began to roll for the third and final game in the series, I laughed, a body-shaking belly laugh while tears began to soak my T-shirt. Everything had changed. For the first time in my life, I realized, I really *wanted* something. *Needed* it.

"I can't be a lawyer anymore," I told Stephen over the phone. I was pacing the room, my thoughts coming in a mad stream of consciousness.

"I want to write. I want to make stories that move people, that make them feel the way this made me feel. Stories like this—this is what makes me want to live. But law . . . my soul is being sucked out. I want to save animals, but no one gives a shit. How am I supposed to do this for the rest of my life? How am I supposed to be studying for the bar right now? How do I make people care about something they can't or won't? The world sucks, and all being a lawyer does is remind me of that. So what's the point?"

I sighed. "Dad's going to die. And life is so fucking short. I can't waste it doing something I don't love. I just, I can't do this. I can't do law, not after feeling this. I can't. I *won't*."

I could hear Stephen's smile on the other line.

"Then do it. Be a writer."

I scoffed. "Mom and Dad aren't going to let me. *Especially* now."

Truly, it made no sense. I was just about to finish law school. At my dream law school. Hell, I'd given up a potential marriage for this. I'd put myself through an election to be copresident of my Student Animal

Law Society, fought tooth and nail for an externship at the Department of Justice. And I was just going to throw all that away?

My parents could barely handle my brother. The news about me giving up being a lawyer would make them lose their damn minds.

"Maybe. But they can't exactly stop you from writing," Stephen said, his voice alight with a conspiratorial playfulness. "So *write*."

❧

The last song Shaz had sent me before the end of law school was called "To Build a Home" by the Cinematic Orchestra.

When I asked him for more song suggestions, he refused.

I have some, came his text. But you'll have to wait till you get here.

❧

I managed to finish my final exams by the skin of my teeth. After I'd turned in my last exam, the next day, I tossed all my belongings that could fit into boxes and said my goodbyes. Then Kisa and I left Portland for Pennsylvania.

I didn't even attend my law school graduation. I couldn't have cared less.

CHAPTER 19

The Way It Should Be

Dad looked different.

After several chemo treatments, he'd lost his already sparse tufts of black hair and was left with wisps of white that had aged him twenty years. The impressive weight he'd carried for as long as I'd known him had long vanished; now his shirts were loose by several sizes.

Most days he still went to work, but only for a few hours. The rest of the day he spent on walks with Stella, or in the garden.

On weekends he would drag me into the kitchen.

"You should learn how to make biryani. Do you know how to make biryani?"

"Follow the instructions on the Shan masala box?" I offered.

He clicked his tongue. "I'll show you."

Dad walked me through the steps to making seafood biryani—the frying of oil and onions called tadka, the careful layering of basmati rice and shrimp and scallops as the familiar smell of cloves and cumin permeated the kitchen. Smells of home that I'd missed.

"Make sure you write this all down," said Dad, scooping ample portions into a bowl.

I took my serving and nodded. "I will."

But I never did. Writing it down felt like acceptance that Dad would die soon, and I would never be able to ask him questions again. If I forgot, I'd just ask him how to make his "famous"—he always called it famous—seafood biryani. And he'd once again walk me through all the steps, happy for the chance to teach. He would teach me a hundred times until I finally committed it to memory and didn't need to use cooking as an excuse to talk to him.

Those days the house often smelled like cumin.

I was thrilled when Stephen got to try Dad's cooking for the first time.

Stephen was coming over every other weekend from New York; he'd take the Chinatown bus after work on Friday, and by eight he'd be with us.

Dad allowing Stephen to eat dinner with us was a huge win. It felt like Dad finally understood that Stephen was a fixture in my life. Stephen, in turn, would gratefully eat every portion given to him, then inquire about Dad's preferred cooking techniques—"So how much time did you grill this for?"—which would instantly lower Dad's defenses and open the conversation to bigger, more important things: like Stephen's plans for the future, or religion. For the past year, Stephen had been studying Islam with one of Dad's acquaintances, had even gone to a mosque to take the shahada and convert.

The rest of the night Stephen would be in the basement with me and Shaz, where we'd watch Shaz play his video game of choice. Not long afterward, Stephen would fall asleep.

"Yeah, he does that," Shaz would say before turning back to the screen. He'd grown used to it while I'd been away, and Mom, who'd occasionally come down to check on us, would merely sigh. "Let the boy sleep," she said once. "He can just crash here."

I stared in disbelief. "I'm sorry, you're actually letting him sleep over?"

"I'd rather not make a habit of this, but I think we can make an exception. I don't want him taking a bus back to New York this late. It's not safe."

"Wow, Mom." It was a miracle. All the times Stephen had visited my family's home—even while I was away at law school—my parents hadn't allowed Stephen to sleep over. As if Stephen sleeping over was some all-important decorum threshold they couldn't let him cross.

But lots had changed. In the two years before Dad got cancer, and while I'd been away, he'd been cheating on Mom. He'd been exchanging emails and texts with a woman he'd worked with on volunteer campaigns in Syria. When Mom found out, Dad's defense was that he'd been lonely, that Mom didn't love him the way he needed to be loved. If there'd ever been a chance they could work things out, that they would go to couples therapy, it was dead and gone.

But not long after, Dad's stomach pains began, and they tabled all talk of divorce. Mom's disdain remained, though. I wondered if going against his wishes, letting Stephen stay the night like this, was her subtle way of getting back at him. Small, meaningless jabs.

I'd been furious about the affair, too, how Dad could ruin the already-fragile relationship they had. It was a coward's way out, to cheat instead of putting in the work to fix their marriage. Dad was a flawed man, just like any other, but I'd always respected his seemingly strong sense of morality. But he'd faltered, and now he was reliant on the very woman he'd cheated on.

Worse, it felt like it was my fault; I'd been the one to talk Mom out of divorcing him. And I knew Mom blamed me, too. Once I overheard her on the phone talking to a friend about it. *I was going to divorce him years ago,* she'd said, voice harsh, acrid. *But Farah told me not to.*

Sometimes I wondered if she'd wanted me to hear it.

"What about Dad?" I asked.

"What's he going to do?" Mom scoffed. "*I* said it's fine. If your dad's going to be stubborn about this, I'll pay for a hotel for Stephen myself."

Since I'd come home from Portland, my parents had grown slightly more lenient; I wasn't sure if it was because I'd graduated from law school and could finally be viewed as a (semi)functional adult in the eyes of my parents, or if it was that Dad's illness had made rules about propriety seem meaningless. The question "What will people say?" haunts many South Asian families, but who the hell would dare say anything when Dad was dying? The promise of death, it seemed, had an uncanny way of rendering all other problems too small to care about.

In this case, no longer was Stephen a young bachelor whom they barely knew hanging around their unmarried daughter. Now Stephen was a friend, a *family* friend, who'd enthusiastically clap when Shaz played piano, who brought us food from New York, who helped Dad grill kebabs. Who made the weekends a little livelier and brought a lightness we so desperately needed.

Not long after Mom's pronouncement, Stephen woke up from his nap in the basement. I told him he was allowed to spend the night, if he wanted.

"Nah, I'll head home," he said, smiling. "I don't want to add any unnecessary tension, you know?"

"It's almost midnight."

Stephen stretched out his arms, putting on a good show of being rejuvenated from his nap, though I knew better. "Great. So buses are still running."

I insisted on paying for a train ticket, which again he refused, and just like that, he left. The house always felt a little colder after he did.

Some expectations, though, my parents hadn't changed, and that included the bar exam. I hadn't told Dad yet about how I'd given up on being a lawyer, even though he'd cleared out his office for me to use for studying. Instead, I pretended I needed more time.

"I'm not sure I want to take it right now," I told him one night when he checked in on me. I'd been in the office, researching—not bar study programs, but writing workshops. There was one called, aptly, Odyssey: it was a six-week workshop in New Hampshire that would provide feedback and guidance to writers of all levels, from beginners to successful professionals. A six-week writing *boot camp*. There I could learn how to write, properly. I could finally immerse myself in my writing, surrounded by my peers. Best of all, the workshop had guest teachers, including none other than Anne Marie Karson, whom I'd discovered at Powell's and had inspired my writing while I was in law school. It was almost too much of a coincidence.

Become the writer you've always known you could be, the website touted.

"Then when?" Dad asked. "You can't put off the bar for too long."

I swallowed. Dad had been so proud about my graduating from law school; he'd been talking about it with anyone who'd listen. He'd posted about it on Facebook. I'd even heard him telling his physician colleagues over the phone, even though they'd probably called to ask him a work question.

Now she's back home with us, he'd say, pleased. *It's good to have her home.*

"Studying for the bar isn't just some casual thing I can dip my toes in every now and then," I replied. "If I study for the bar, my schedule will be completely packed and I just . . . I can't. I can't focus like that, not right now."

Dad shook his head. "No, Farah, you should study. It's important that you take the bar; otherwise, what was the point of these last three years? It's okay if you fail the first time. You can live here at home and keep taking it until you pass. I'll pay for any study classes you need. You don't have to focus on anything else."

I felt myself wavering.

Dad was a flawed man, but I couldn't deny he'd been, for the most part, a good father. It was the only real way he'd known how to show his love for me and my brother: by providing whatever he could to ensure his children's success. And he would do *anything* to make it happen, even if it meant we hated him for it. It reminded me of how whenever I was sick as a child, Dad would bring me soup and Gatorade—unless we were out of Gatorade, in which case he'd create a disgusting concoction of water, too much sugar, too much salt, and too much lemon juice. "Drink all of it," he'd command sternly, and he'd watch to make sure I did, even as I whined and took infuriatingly tiny sips.

But without fail it would make me feel better.

Taking the bar was like medicine, too. More than that, it was a privilege. I should have been grateful, and I *was*. Several of my former classmates would be studying for the bar while balancing full-time jobs, caring for their families and their kids. Taking the bar was all Dad was asking of me.

Becoming an attorney and being able to officially practice law would give me job security. Stability. Peace of mind. It was what our family needed. Mom had recently quit her job at the bank to take care of him, while Shaz had dropped out of college; the only job he could get on short notice was as a pizza delivery driver. Dad needed to know that at least one of us would have something stable.

Plus, Dad had been kind enough to let Stephen into our home.

It didn't matter if I didn't want to take the bar; listening to my dad was an understandable obligation. After all, he was only trying to secure my future.

"That's nice of you, Dad," I said quietly. "I'll look into it."

"Mm. Good." Dad got to his feet. His expression was the same as always, but I could tell he was relieved.

"I need to sleep. Shabukhair, Farah. Don't stay up too late."

"Yeah. Shabukhair, Dad."

I should have told him. The thought was like a low keening in my chest. *I should have told him the truth.*

I took a deep breath. Chewed at my nails. Turned back to my computer. On my screen, the page for "How to Apply to Odyssey" stared at me, beckoning. To apply for the workshop, I'd only need a four-thousand-word writing sample, which I had; I'd been working on that story in law school. I'd also need references, which I could get.

I decided to apply to Odyssey. I wouldn't get in, but at least I'd have tried, and I could move forward knowing that I simply wasn't cut out to be a writer. And in the meantime, I'd study for the bar, like a good daughter. That had always been the plan, after all.

Anything else, well—

It wasn't meant to be.

CHAPTER 20

That Thing with Wings

Weeks went by. Over a month. The deadline to hear back from Odyssey came and went. But I didn't feel disappointed. I'd given up on the idea of going the moment I'd applied.

Bar study had already begun to consume my life. To give myself a sense of normalcy, I treated it like a full-time job. I'd walk into Dad's office around 9:00 a.m. and hole up in there until 5:00 p.m. Sometimes Dad would walk in, bringing me a bowl of cut-up fruit. Sometimes it'd be Mom, asking if I could run an errand for her. By evening I'd be in the basement with my brother, playing video games.

I was on a break, standing in the kitchen and eating lunch by the fridge, when I got a call from an unknown number. Convinced it was a telemarketer, I picked up to request they remove me from their list, demand to know how they got my number, and, for some reason, thank them because I couldn't help myself. (This was 2016, a simpler time when we still believed we could make meaningful requests of telemarketers, and they'd listen.)

"Hello?" a voice on the other end croaked. "Is this"—a pause—"Farah?"

"Who's this?"

"This is Jeanne Cavelos. I'm the director of the Odyssey Writing Workshop."

I nearly dropped my phone.

"What is it?" asked Mom, who was in the kitchen with me.

"Oh. Hi! Hi, Jeanne. How—how are you?"

"I'm good. Listen, I've been waiting on your response. I sent out the acceptance letters a few weeks ago, but I haven't heard back from you. I just wanted to check in."

"I got in?"

"Did you not get your letter?"

I did not, I informed her, receive any sort of letter, let alone an acceptance letter. It must have gotten lost in the mail. Jeanne apologized and said that I had been accepted, but she needed to know if I was planning to attend. The workshop would be starting in a month, so there wasn't much time to confirm the slot.

After I hung up, I told Mom the details: that I'd be living in New Hampshire, that I'd be away for six weeks. But it was just six weeks of my life, and it suddenly felt like it could potentially change everything. I didn't want to pass up the chance.

"I don't know. The timing isn't good." Mom looked away in thought. "You'll have to convince your dad. And something tells me he's not going to be on board."

I chewed at my nails.

Maybe I shouldn't have applied, after all. Dad was dying. We didn't know how long he'd have. This was the time for our family to stay together. This was time I could never get back. How could I abandon my family again?

"Yeah, you're right. I'll ask Dad, but . . ."

But I knew what he'd say.

I would have to tell Jeanne I couldn't go.

"Uh, no," said Stephen over the phone, "you're going. You have to go."

"What?" I'd been so sure he'd agree that Odyssey wasn't a good idea. Plus, me going to New Hampshire would mean I'd basically be unreachable; if the workshop was anywhere near as vigorous as the website seemed to suggest, I'd hardly have the time to talk to anyone on the outside while I was there.

"First of all, you got in! Let's just take a moment and celebrate that you got in!" He sounded ecstatic. "You did that. And now—now you can actually go. You *should* go. When else are you going to get this opportunity?"

But I wasn't sure. I told him a hundred excuses, a hundred reasons why it wasn't a good idea. Patiently, Stephen listened to them all.

"Try, then," he said. "At least try. If not for you, then for me. Okay?"

༜

Stephen had a point. I decided to talk to Dad. I needed to try.

Dad was sitting at the kitchen table—the same table where Stephen sat with us for dinners on weekends, the same table where Shaz had come out—reading his usual newspaper. I sat across from him and told him about Odyssey, pitching it with the enthusiasm of a new lawyer.

Dad sniffed loudly. "How long would you be gone?"

"Six weeks."

He set down his newspaper as his thick eyebrows knitted together. "Farah, that's too long."

"It's not even two months. And then I'll be right back. This could be a great opportunity, Dad. I'll learn how to write. It's something I've always wanted."

"We just talked about this." He wasn't meeting my gaze, but his voice began to rise. "You're supposed to be studying for the bar."

"I can always study for the bar when I'm back. It's not going any-where." I exhaled. "I don't want to waste time when I have a chance to do something I've always dreamed of."

This time, Dad shook his head. The worst part was that he was smiling now, as if I was a petulant child asking for something com-pletely unreasonable. As if I must know I was pushing my luck.

"Writing is something you do on the side," he said. I got a sudden sense of déjà vu: of when I'd first told my parents I liked writing back in high school, of when they'd said something similar to Shaz when he'd first told my parents he wanted to be a pianist.

"Well, what if I don't just want it to be on the side? What if—what if I want to do more . . . ?"

This set Dad off.

"You can do all the writing you want after you pass the bar and become an attorney," he yelled suddenly. "But now you want to leave? You need to stay here. You're being immature, Farah. This idea is immature!"

I shrank back, confused. I'd expected him to not want me to go, but I hadn't expected him to *shame* me for asking. I'd *never* seen him lose his temper in this way, not even when Shaz wanted to drop out of college. Now, though, Dad's nostrils flared, and his usually thoughtful gaze had curled hot, transformed to one of pure fury directed entirely at me. On the table, his fists were clenched, trembling like he was barely holding them back. Like he wanted to *hit* me.

In my entire life, my dad had hit me once; it'd been years ago, when I was a senior in high school and I'd interrupted him on a phone call. We'd taken a family beach trip at his urging, and when Sunday afternoon rolled around, Dad had held us all up to pull over the car and take a phone call from a friend. But I was in a rush to get home. I had school the next day.

"Dad, just call him later," I'd said, gently tugging at his sleeve. When I got no response, I tugged again, like a child. "Dad, can we please just g—"

The slap had come so fast, it took seconds for me to even register the pain. Gone was the gentle father who loved to garden among the dogwoods, who spoiled my dog, Stella, with new sweaters. In that moment, Dad was a stranger, and I was afraid of him.

It had taken a while for me to move forward. To forgive what I'd thought was a one-time loss of reason. But there he was, furious, wanting to hit me again—even though I was twenty-six years old, a grown adult who, all things considered, didn't need to ask for his permission.

"I'm sorry, how is asking to go to a *writing workshop* immature?" I asked.

"Life isn't a game! And being a writer—it's too risky. You have one life, and you can't just do whatever you want, whenever you want. Law should be your only focus right now. Have I not told you this a thousand times? Have I not given you everything you've ever needed for your education. Haven't I? And you want to *waste* it?"

That hurt. "And I'm grateful for that, I really am. But I didn't realize you supporting me financially meant you could hold it over me if I ever did something you didn't agree with. How is that fair?"

"Writing isn't going to put food on the table, Farah! It's a *hobby*, not something you throw your life away for," he spat before getting to his feet. "I'm disappointed in you. You're supposed to know better."

Dad left the kitchen, leaving me at the table in a daze. My fingertips were trembling.

"What the hell just happened?" I asked out loud.

Mom had been in the kitchen the entire time, quiet. Watchful.

"I'll talk to him," she said softly.

The sudden role reversal was dizzying. Dad was supposed to be the reasonable one who smoothed things over.

Then again, this wasn't the first time he'd hurt me like this.

Once, when I was around eleven, Mom took me and Shaz to visit her family in Virginia. Since Dad was staying home, I'd left him in charge of babysitting Elvis, my pet rabbit. But over the weekend, he forgot to close the cage door, and Elvis escaped. Dad realized his mistake and drove to the pet store for a replacement—only they were out of dwarf bunnies. I came home to a large brown lop-eared rabbit three times the size of Elvis, sitting in Elvis's cage. Dad had hoped I wouldn't notice the change. Dad was the only one of my parents to talk to me like I was an adult, but in the end, he was no different from Mom. To him, I was still just a child who wouldn't know better.

At the time I couldn't even formulate a response. I was so, so angry, so *disappointed*. Eyes flooding with tears, I ran to my room.

And here I was, years later, crying all over again. Except this disappointment hurt so much more.

"He's acting like I just told him I'm becoming a serial killer or something," I said, wiping my nose.

"Chemo messes with your head," Mom explained. "Makes you have mood swings. It's called Chemo Brain. That's probably what this is."

Chemo Brain—was that really all this was? I knew Dad was afraid for the future. Dad had grown up in a family of sixteen brothers and sisters; his siblings would always call *him* for help. He'd chosen pathology because it would give him more flexible hours to spend at home. He rarely ever bought himself anything nice; most of his paychecks went into our education. He had always encouraged Mom to work, to have her own income that he wouldn't touch.

Stability, stability, stability. That was the only thing that mattered to Dad. He could plan around the unpredictable cancer that had so brutally interrupted his life, but that was assuming everything else would remain the same.

Me being a writer—Dad had never planned for that. Maybe Chemo Brain was just bringing out fears that had been there all along.

Once I'd finally stopped shaking, I went to my room. I locked myself in there for almost two days, leaving only to grab food before scurrying back. I didn't want to see Dad. Didn't want him to look at me with those disappointed eyes.

It was evening on the second day when Mom strolled into my room without a word and leaned against the wall.

She looked smug.

"I talked to your dad," she said. "Go for it."

"What . . . ?" I set down my phone. "Mom? Seriously . . . ?"

Heat rose to my face. I was so overwhelmed I couldn't even think straight; too many emotions threatened to spill over. I felt a pretty disorienting amount of gratitude. For Mom.

She'd done the impossible. She'd gotten Dad to (very reluctantly) let me go. Mom had actually done something for me—something incredible. For the first time in my life, she was acting like a mom. Someone who'd look out for me. Someone who would fight for the dreams I couldn't.

Mom smiled.

"You owe me. Now go—go be famous or something."

PART III

Dizzy with Heaven

CHAPTER 21

Djerba

And so, on Stephen's and Mom's urging, I accepted the spot at Odyssey.

It took place during the summer at Saint Anselm College in Goffstown, New Hampshire, and workshop attendants were to live in the dorms. I was paired to room with a delightfully fascinating Chinese American girl named Rebecca. A few weeks before our move-in date, she emailed me to inform me that she would be bringing the following: "a pot, and a dishrag, and also maybe a spoon." Like me, she had never taken a writing class before and was excited to meet other aspiring writers. "I love reading military fantasy and gruesome dark Chinese lore—what about you?" she'd asked, again over email. I could feel the beaming smile behind her question.

I never responded. She made me nervous, at first. Over email, she sounded mildly unhinged and far too energetic for someone as bone weary as I was.

By the time a month had passed, and I was ready to leave, Dad was deteriorating fast. He was over halfway through his chemo treatments, and what little weight he'd been holding on to had fallen off. Most of us will outlive our parents; we accept this. But watching your parents' bodies be whittled down by disease is unsettling in ways that will haunt you for life. It was brutal to watch, brutal to leave.

But when I arrived, the whole thing was like visiting a sacred place, a six-week test of wills and passion. It's hard to put into words, mostly because I'm pretty sure we had to sign an NDA.

⁂

But at Odyssey I learned how to write. Jeanne, the director, was a tiny woman clad in black—she always wore black—with metal-rimmed glasses that often slid down her nose. Her silver hair was always tamed in a tight, no-nonsense ponytail. She was a sage at her craft.

My favorite thing about her was her voice. She spoke with a delightful crickle-crackle texture, like she was a wise raven who'd not only learned to talk, but could take on a human form—and chose to teach a workshop, for some reason.

In Homer's *Odyssey*, the grieving Helen receives a potion to quell all sorrows with forgetfulness. The potion is called *nepenthe*, literally "that which chases away sorrow." The writing workshop was my nepenthe. It gave me a break from watching Dad's body fall apart.

Every day I was at that workshop, I felt transported to another realm entirely, where time no longer existed. I felt untouchable by former real-world worries, and focused only on absorbing as much knowledge as I could. We'd often write so late into the night that even the summer cicadas would grow quiet.

"The artist deals with what cannot be said in words," said Jeanne, quoting Ursula K. Le Guin on our first day of class. "The novelist says in words what cannot be said in words."

So as I understood it, we were there to learn the impossible. And we had only six weeks to do it.

⁂

It turned out I wasn't fully wrong about Rebecca. Thanks to a series of delayed flights, she didn't arrive at Odyssey until around midnight on the first day. But as soon as she walked through our door—petite stature, her thick black hair barely tamed by the scrunchie she'd thrown it in—I noticed it straightaway: Rebecca was like a toothy puppy, with sharp, limpid eyes and unbridled hunger. She was eager to learn, and nothing could escape her. Even if on the very off chance some information did, she'd tear after it not with a sense of fear or frustration, but only the excitement for the hunt. She was a scholar, through and through.

As I sat next to her, day after day—watched her diagnose and eviscerate any short story that crossed her desk with razor-sharp precision, even her own writing—I began to wonder if this girl could take on the entire publishing world. When I read her work, watched her skills bloom at an almost frightening rate, I decided she actually would.

She'd already sold books. I found her incredible; she was only twenty years old, but she'd poured her heart and soul and interests into an entire trilogy of books and signed with a reputable agent who, in turn, sold the books to a reputable publisher. It was dizzying, imagining that this was reality for some: that they could not only write books but have their books be read and engaged with and adored by others.

"So how is it?" Stephen called me for an update, excited.

"It's good." I sighed. "It's good, but I'm starting to realize that I've got a long, long way to go. There are so many talented people here. Their writing is ridiculously good, and I'm nowhere close."

Despite that, though, I couldn't stop writing even if I wanted. How astonishing it was that I could create whole worlds I could then escape to. Writing felt like a gift.

"But you've only just started. And that means you have loads of room to grow."

I smiled. "True."

"And you're having fun?"

I thought of Rebecca in the other room, who was cackling at her laptop; she'd begun playing a video game I'd recommended. *I want to try playing the games you said made you want to write,* she'd said.

"I'm having fun," I said.

"Then that's the only thing that matters."

Halfway through Odyssey, Rebecca, our adviser, Jeremy, and I had gone to a sushi place near Nashua. Where Rebecca was all infectious, frenetic energy and eagerness to learn, Jeremy was a soothing presence who spoke with intention, as if he couldn't afford to waste a single word. The three of us talked about favorite video games and books. We talked about our goals for the future.

"Just three Asians, getting our Asian food on," Rebecca joked.

Thirty minutes after we'd eaten, my stomach began to roil and froth. I drank lots of water and told myself to ignore it.

An hour later I began reaching critical levels of discomfort.

"Um, so I think I'm going to shit myself," I announced meekly on the car ride back to campus.

Jeremy, maintaining his usual air of calm, drove faster.

By the time we got back to campus, my stomach was ready to explode. I ran back to our dorm room and took over the bathroom while Rebecca and Jeremy ran to find medicine.

Nothing bonds people more, I think, than being forced to take violently loud bathroom trips while the others worriedly stand guard on the other side of the door.

By the time I had nothing left in my stomach to throw up, I was a shell of my former self, curled up in a ball in my bed. I wanted to take a bath. Death was also an option, but at that point I was almost too exhausted to feel ashamed.

"I got some more Gatorade," said Jeremy at my side. "Drink all of it, okay?"

I laughed weakly, reminded of how my dad would take care of my brother and me when we were little.

Meanwhile, Rebecca sat by my feet, fidgeting.

"Farah Naz—" She insisted on calling me by my full name, which I liked. "Oh, Farah Naz. Who did this to you? Who did this to you?!"

"I'm never eating tuna again," I whimpered.

❧

Anne Marie Karson had finally arrived at Odyssey to teach us for a week. Anne Marie, who'd won the Nebula, the Hugo, and the Locus Awards (among others) for her writing. A legend in the science fiction and fantasy space. And she would read our work—short stories or snippets of novels we'd been working on—and critique it herself in one-on-one meetings.

We were already several weeks into the workshop, and by now what little self-esteem the class possessed had been beaten out of us. We were drained. Hollow. Everything I wrote, I wanted to throw in the trash and chastise myself for even trying. I was incapable of writing anything prolific, much less unique; I was only regurgitating what I'd read before, what I knew worked.

"What do you want to get out of this workshop?" Anne Marie asked me in our first one-on-one meeting, in her warm, subtle North Carolina accent. "What do you really want? And what's holding you back?"

I looked down at my hands and thought.

"Me," I answered, talking slowly. "I think . . . I'm scared. I've never written before. Never really put myself out there like this. And now that I'm doing it for the first time, I'm scared."

Anne Marie watched me, patiently waiting for my thoughts to come.

"Being a writer feels so vulnerable. And your job is to think about characters, understand how they're feeling. You're trained to care about what other people think. But now I find myself wondering what other people are thinking all the time. Questions that haunt me at night. Like, what if people hate my work? What if—what if I write what I want to write, but other Muslims call me sinful? What if I'm just not good enough, no matter what I do? I'm so freaking *terrified*."

Anne Marie asked if she could hug me. I nodded, embarrassed, and she held me until I cried like a child. I cried until my eyes swelled and my stomach hurt all over again. I cried out all my fears at once, more than just the fear of being here instead of at home, more than just the fear of writing, or losing my father. I let out a baptism of tears.

When I was done, I felt different. I felt unbound. As if giving voice to my deepest fears had allowed me to face them, to see that they were nothing but that: *fears*. Not real, if I didn't want them to be.

I had to change. I couldn't hold back anymore. If I wanted something, I would do it. Even if it meant letting those three years of law school go to waste. Even if I didn't take the bar exam and hurtled head-first into writing. Even if Dad was disappointed in me. He'd understand one day. He, of all people, would eventually.

Life was too short to care about things that didn't matter.

❧

"One day, when we're all published, we're going to have our own cinematic universe," Rebecca announced late one night, when it was just the two of us working. "Our characters will show up in each other's books. Some of them might even be related. Maybe we just pop up as characters, make fun little appearances, little easter eggs."

"Yeah? A whole cinematic universe."

"Don't laugh! It'll happen!" Rebecca said indignantly. "It'll *happen*."

CHAPTER 22

Where I Can't Reach

I was back home in early August of 2016, and I sensed something had changed.

The house had always felt quiet—my parents had trained my brother and me in the value of keeping our voices down, mostly by yelling at us—but now it felt like our house had taken on the somber silence of a museum. A kind of purgatory, frozen in time—a slice of what once was and what would never be again.

It was still. It was unnerving. But every so often, Mom and Dad would crack, and all their stress would leak out in quick, frantic bursts. These were the moments where death would show itself and make them remember just how unprepared they were. Which meant, they soon realized, how unprepared their kids were. They began taking turns teaching me things, in an erratic, desperate sort of way.

When Dad's stomach pain began to worsen and he had to be rushed for an overnight ER visit, Mom dragged me into the office. "This is where we keep important documents," Mom said, avoiding my gaze. "You should know, in case—in case anything happens. You need to remember, okay? Just in case."

Later when Dad had been discharged, he called me into the garden, Stella at his side. Either he'd forgiven me for leaving for Odyssey, or he was so distracted by his deteriorating health, he couldn't care anymore.

He took a seat on the stone bench in the garden, too tired, lately, to stand for long periods of time. "You need to be watering the plants twice a week," he said, slightly out of breath. "Twice—any more and you'll drown them. Write that down somewhere. I just planted this lilac—look how beautiful it is—and I don't want it to die."

Dad had lost even more weight, I'd noticed.

I looked up how to care for dogwood trees. I learned about anthracnose, a fungal blight that had decimated dogwood trees throughout the country; once infected, the only chance for treatment involved cutting away most of its branches, dumping fungicide, and hoping for the best.

I was in over my head. There'd be a high chance Dad's dogwood tree wouldn't survive after his death. Already I felt Dad's coming absence like a black hole, like salt on the earth. His loss would be inevitable; maybe I could accept that. But the collapse of everything around him shouldn't have to be. It didn't seem fair.

Soon the shape of our family would forever change. I'd already begun mourning him. Mourning the empty place at the dinner table. Our long conversations about politics and history. The career advice, unwarranted or not. His garden.

Everything—everything we were about to lose.

Still, I prayed. At the end of every prayer, Muslims make a dua, a prayer within a prayer. But a dua is whispered into one's own hands, like a secret. An intimate conversation between human and God. My duas have always sounded the same since I was a child: *Allah (SWT), please bless me and my family, and keep us on the straight path, and protect us from any harm or danger.* This was the basic template dua my dad recommended I try when I was a child and he'd first taught me how to pray.

But then my dua would veer off into something different, depending on what I was going through at the time: *Also, Allah (SWT), if you*

can make me not fail my law school exams, that would be great. Please. Or
*Please, Allah (SWT), if you could make me a good writer, that would be
highly appreciated—thank you!*

This time, halfway through my dua, I stopped.

So many times, I had asked God to protect us. Was God really
protecting us now? Dad was in so much pain—couldn't God cure Dad's
cancer? Dad wasn't perfect, but he prayed five times a day. He'd performed hajj. Went to Al-Aqsa Mosque in Jerusalem after his diagnosis.
All things considered, he was one of God's most loyal subjects.

And yet.

I couldn't handle that train of thought. I stopped my dua; I didn't
want to ask God for anything, let alone wait for a response I was never
going to get.

Instead, I got up and went for a run. I went on many runs those
days, blasting music Shaz had recommended. Music felt like proof that
I was alive, the way it brought goose bumps to my skin, the way it made
my heart beat even faster. I was alive, because despite everything, music
still made me *feel.* Sometimes I'd run so hard my lungs felt like someone
had shoved them through a shredder, but I'd push past it because that
pain was better than anything else that was waiting for me at home. And
the weaker that Dad got, I'd tell myself I had to get stronger—as if to
make up for the muscle mass and strength my family had lost.

Dad was still using the time he had left to push for me to be a
lawyer.

"There was an article in the *Inquirer,*" Dad told me. We were in
the kitchen; I was putting together a fruit trifle, one of his favorites, to
entice him to eat.

"The starting salary for many entry-level lawyers is six figures. Some
of these young lawyers are making $180,000!"

"That's great, Dad," I replied, not meeting his hopeful stare.

I felt guilty. For giving my dad more reason to worry about the
future. For squandering an opportunity so rarely afforded to other marginalized kids. I was a South Asian Muslim—I could be using my law

degree to give back to the community, but I was turning my back on it all, and for what? To write books?

But I also didn't want to sabotage my own happiness when there was so little of it to be had. And I was tired of carrying obligations to my family like stones in my pocket. I wanted so badly to make my parents proud of me, but what about me? For once I wanted to fight for these tiny, fluttering dreams of mine, the ones my younger self had shoved in a closet to be forgotten.

Since coming back from Odyssey, I'd begun writing a new book: a young adult science fiction story about the end of the world. A book-packaging company had scouted me to write the book; they were offering a small fee compared to most other book offers, but they would walk me through the process of publishing a book from start to finish. It seemed like a good deal for a nobody writer with no experience.

If I could write the first fifty pages on my own and I felt good about it, I'd sign the contract: an act that felt like I'd officially be giving up my career as a lawyer.

It's like I feel this draw to writing that's impossible to ignore. I want to be a lawyer like my dad wants, but writing . . . I can't stop, I texted my friend Jeremy one night. My friends from Odyssey had been checking on me frequently through texts. But Jeremy always had the best advice.

Considering everything you're going through, doesn't that make sense? he replied.

What do you mean?

Think of it this way. We live in a dark, chaotic world, so we build structures through art to feel safe in it. The same way people build houses so they wouldn't be at the mercy of the weather. Things like stories, games—these are emotional houses from the random crap that happens in our lives. Like getting sick.

People dying. Reaping bad luck when you don't deserve it. Art is a safe house, he said. Your writing—that's your safe house.

❧

"Dad," I said, as calmly as I could, "I don't think I'm going to take the bar anymore."

I'd found my dad sitting at the kitchen table with a half-finished cup of Tetley and a newspaper he hadn't yet started. He rarely finished his daily cup of Tetley anymore; it hurt his stomach too much. I'd often have to make him peppermint tea instead, one of the few things that soothed the near-constant inflammation in his gut, if only for a precious minute.

Dad said nothing at first. Licked his lips. Took a shaky inhale.

"What do you mean, you're not taking the bar?" he asked.

"I don't want to waste time studying for it when I don't even want to practice law."

"I paid your tuition because you *wanted* to practice law. It'll only take a few more months of study. You're at the finish line. I don't understand—there's no reason not to."

God, the *guilt*. The problem was, I could see where he was coming from. I sounded like a selfish, ungrateful daughter. I was so lucky to have a parent who'd cover my tuition. And he was *right*—I was at the finish line.

But I couldn't lie to him anymore. That aching fear of not living the way I wanted was maddening, especially when my own father was dying. That's the thing about death. It gives you perspective. A painful reminder of your own fleeting mortality.

"I'd rather spend my time writing," I said. "Writing is what I really want to do. I just didn't know until now."

Dad's austere face warped into one of palpable disappointment. His eyes narrowed at me, like he were looking at a stranger. It was like that awful Odyssey conversation all over again.

"How could you do this, Farah?" he said, his voice shaking. "I let you write, even when I disagreed. You went to that workshop. Just take the bar! You just have to practice law for a few years, get some financial stability, and then you can write on the side. And down the line, if you happen to get successful, you can even think about writing full-time. But it makes no sense right now. No sense!"

Everything in my skull went white with frustration. Dad said it like it was so easy. I just had to hop a dozen stepping stones before I could even *touch* my dreams. Get into a good college. Get into a good law school. Pass the bar, practice law, make money. Get settled. Then, and only then, would it make any sense to write.

I know he was only saying it from a place of worry. But how many years would that all take? How much energy, how much of my soul?

"I'm sorry. I'm sorry, I know, but I want to write, Dad. Please. If I fail, then I fail. I can always come back to law. But I'll never forgive myself if I don't at least try."

Dad got to his feet, and I shrank back. For a moment he just stared, his eyes boring holes.

"I'm disappointed in you, Farah," he finally replied. "I can't stop you. But I'm very disappointed in you."

He may as well have stabbed me in the stomach. It'd probably hurt less.

He left the room, leaving behind a choking silence in his wake. I leaned back in my chair, trying not to cry. My whole body was so tightly wound, I felt like I'd never relax again.

But at least I'd done it. I'd said it, and now it was over.

Now the hard work could begin.

Stephen continued coming over every other weekend, but Dad stopped joining us at dinner. Eating, he said, had become difficult; he no longer had much of an appetite. Or maybe he was still mad at me.

"I can cook something he'll like," Stephen offered. "Not to brag, but I've gotten pretty good at it."

But Mom shrugged her shoulders sadly. "It doesn't matter. He can't really stomach anything these days."

Stephen had already been doing so much for us. He'd travel to Philadelphia on weekends and spend each day at our beck and call. He'd rush to the pharmacy to get prescriptions, or anything else Dad needed to stay comfortable. He'd take Stella on walks. He'd fill up the gas in Mom's car. As soon as he'd step through the doorway—"I'm here! What can I do?"—Mom and I would let out a sigh of relief.

With news that Dad's condition was deteriorating, dozens of family members and Dad's old friends came to visit from every part of the world. They'd stare at Stephen, confused by this out-of-place young man who practically seemed to live with us.

"Oh, this is Stephen," Mom and I would tell them. "He's a friend."

No other context was given. We didn't feel like explaining; there was nothing to explain. Ten minutes later, Stephen would be talking to our guests like he'd known them for years.

I watched him closely for a moment when the mask would slip. If I just looked long enough, behind all his eagerness to be helpful, I'd find some darker reason, some secret, ugly intention Stephen had kept hidden all this time. It was just a matter of time, I told myself. It was just a matter of time before he became fed up with all of this and left us, never to return.

Except not once did Stephen complain. If there was any secret thing he wanted—if he even wanted anything—it was simply to be here with us.

I remembered Stephen's clumsy confession so many years ago. How I doubted he'd loved me, with such certainty.

Watching him now, I'd be a fool to doubt he loved me, at least as best friends. What else would explain how much he cared, how he was always there for me? How he was the only consistent thing in my life that made sense?

But it's hard to recognize love and all its forms when you've never seen it before. I was so sure that there was only one kind of "real love," and that real love would be some big dramatic, storybook moment, a sudden flare of passion that would make itself known.

What if it wasn't that at all? What if love was a patient thing that simply stood at your side, offering you a hand? What if it was all the best of friendships—a partnership, a promise to face the unfeeling world and all its follies together? Or simply the quiet, intimate details of a person, like how their lips part when they sleep, how they take their coffee, their preferences in tea?

That was so much more precious than any storybook moment.

He was my best friend in the world, and in that sense, I loved him, too. He was practically family. And that was more than good enough for me. Could our love become romantic? I wasn't ready to find out. Exploring the depths of the love we shared, even acknowledging its existence—it was a terrifying prospect. Even if I was sure of him in my life, I was wildly uncertain about the concept of *us*. It all felt too big, too much. It could change everything, in a way that I couldn't control.

After all, Stephen was my one constant—and with Dad's illness, with everything going on, I couldn't even consider the risk of losing that, too.

❧

One evening, my dad needed help moving to his bed; he'd been sitting in an armchair, but even sitting exhausted him those days. Stephen was there in an instant, putting himself beneath my dad's arm and gently hoisting him onto his pillows.

Dad, out of breath, closed his eyes and sank into his bed. When he opened his eyes again, he looked at Stephen.

"Thank you," he said. "Thank you, Stephen. For everything."

Stephen smiled. It was the first time any of us had heard my dad call him by name.

Though he and Dad had talked several times at the kitchen table, when Dad first allowed him to start coming over, it was clear Dad was still unsure about his presence in my life. He also didn't like that Stephen hadn't gotten into medical school; he'd told me as much, after one of Stephen's visits a few months ago.

"It points to instability," Dad had said. "He's a smart boy, but he's given up too quickly. And if he gives up on this, who knows what else he will give up?"

But maybe Dad had begun to see something in Stephen that changed his mind. It made me happy. Like Dad had given our friendship his blessing.

Afterward, Stephen had to go, so I let him out of the house and watched him drive off into the dark.

Those days, every so often, I caught myself staring at Stephen's brow, and imagining myself pressing my lips against it. Not that I'd ever tell him, of course.

❧

By the end of August, Dad's skin was becoming slightly jaundiced. He'd taken several trips to the hospital to get a stent. A stent, Stephen explained to me—his research job at Mount Sinai Hospital was proving very helpful—would help with blood flow. Dad's bilirubin levels were too high and the stent was no longer working. The end, it seemed, was nearing. We all knew it but wouldn't say it.

One of the times Dad was hospitalized, Mom came home briefly just to shower and grab a change of clothes before rushing back to the hospital. I found her in the kitchen, leaning over the counter, her head in her hands.

"You okay?" I asked softly.

Shaz and I had visited the hospital earlier, but Dad was having trouble speaking. When he finally could, he told us to go home, waved us away.

He doesn't want you to see him like this, Mom had explained.

Now Mom looked up at me, the weariness casting her face in a lifeless gray. I'd never seen her look so tired.

"Today was hard," she said. "Your dad is angry. At God. He kept going on about how there was so much he still wanted to do, all these things he still wanted to accomplish. But every time people come to visit him, they tell him that it's God's will, a test from God. Who the hell wants to hear that when they're dying?"

I clenched my jaw. *Allah is the best of planners.* Hadn't Dad always believed this? Hadn't I? And despite everything, I still wanted to. It was a singular source of comfort when trying to search for patterns of meaning, to make sense of a horrible situation. But it felt cruel to tell someone to look for the light, for the silver lining, when they were fumbling through an endless, swallowing dark.

The fact was, Dad had been robbed of his light. Divine plan or not, it still, simply put, *sucked.*

Mom sighed. Rubbed at her eyes behind her glasses. "Even though he cheated, your dad was still one of the best Muslims I know. But if your dad is angry at God, then what hope is there for the rest of us? How am I not supposed to feel angry, too?"

I wish I knew. Grief, I thought, was supposed to be beautiful in its own way. Like shards of ice on skin: a stingingly cold, delicate yet razor-edged proof of the love left behind.

Instead, grief had obliterated me, leaving me so empty, so broken, I could hardly feel anything at all.

❧

A week later, Dad was finally discharged back home.

But the buildup of bilirubin in Dad's blood had turned his skin completely yellow. It also meant that his stomach pain was becoming too much to bear; now he needed morphine injections. We did what we could to distract him from the pain, sometimes playing board games in his bedroom so he could watch. Sometimes we'd watch TV, Mom on the bed, Dad in his armchair, me and Stephen on the carpet.

The 2016 election season was in full swing, and Dad, despite his health, was determined to watch the debate between Hillary Clinton and Donald Trump. I'd been watching the election coverage closely, at first to have something to talk to Dad about, but then out of anxiety. I couldn't look away. Trump was polling well, all things considered. He actually had a chance of winning. And with his rise came the rise of anti-Muslim language, with talk of curbing immigration, a "Muslim Ban." The 2015 Chapel Hill shooting was still fresh on my mind, when three Arab American Muslim college students had been killed in their home by a disgruntled, deeply disturbed neighbor. It felt like the world was transforming—or maybe it was that a long-standing infection had finally begun to fester and show itself.

I was scared.

"I think Trump's going to win," I said. "I don't think people are taking it seriously enough."

Dad shook his head in a rare moment of lucidity. "No. Of course he won't win. People aren't stupid. We have to trust that voters will see through him. He's running on a whim; even he doesn't expect to win, anyone can see that, but Hillary—she has experience."

"People are going to vote for Trump just to see what happens, Dad. They're talking about it like it's a game on social media."

"Social media is no indication of reality," said Dad. "I've been in this country for a long time. You just have to trust."

Law school and the history it taught me had left me with a far less positive attitude when it came to politics. This thing in the air, this coming storm, was tangible, real. You only had to look out the window.

My dad had so much faith in this country—and why shouldn't he? He was the poster child for the American dream. He'd never received any support from his parents; he'd immigrated to America from Pakistan with hardly a penny to his name, and through hard work and perseverance became a pathologist with his own practice. Dad trusted this country because it'd allowed him to achieve what he thought he never otherwise could.

If others didn't make it, maybe they hadn't worked hard enough. Look: he was a brown Muslim man, yes, but through his own hard work, he'd proved himself.

And yet, at airports, we'd be delayed before nearly every flight; I can't remember a time when TSA agents hadn't pulled Dad aside to do a background check on him.

"I'm in the military," Dad would say, indignant, while a steel-faced agent would type away at their computer. "Please, I'm in a hurry. I'm a colonel in the air force."

I'm one of you! I'm American! I'm one of the good ones! We put up an American flag on our door after 9/11!

They ignored him every time.

Dad, with his accent and brownness, could walk around the airport carrying his citizenship and wearing his uniform. They could look him up on Google and see that all his life he'd organized interfaith events in his community, sometimes even bringing his daughter to local churches and synagogues, to make pretty little speeches. *Muslims! We're just like you!* Dad would still never be accepted. And now he was going to die believing in a country that didn't believe in him.

"I hope you're right," I said.

It was the last conversation we had.

Later that night, Stephen asked if I wanted him to stay another couple of nights. There was the unspoken truth in his offer: Dad wasn't looking good. He might not last much longer.

"It'll be all right," I replied. "Mom says his doctors think he's got another couple weeks, at least."

"Are you sure?" he asked. "I can always call work. They'll understand." He held my hand and gave it a gentle squeeze. I'd chewed my nails down to tiny stubs; I didn't want him to notice how bad they'd gotten.

"Seriously, it'll be fine," I said, and nudged him through the door.

The next day, Dad's brain began shutting down, and the morphine stopped helping. He could hardly speak; instead, he trembled and writhed in his gurney as if the cancer was scalding him from the inside and his body could no longer contain the pain. Sometimes it felt like he was begging someone, pleading incomprehensibly with some unseen force. He didn't want to die. It wasn't fair that he had to die, and yet, in a slow and cruel unraveling, his very cells were dying, one by one.

All we could do was watch, and wait.

In the final days of his time on earth, my dad—the man who'd taught me how to throw a ball and fly a kite and grow a tree, whose powerful voice could command a room—would leave it whimpering.

CHAPTER 23
Al-Baqarah 2:286

Dad died on a Tuesday, which, in my opinion, is the worst day of the week to die.

Monday, at least, is the start of the workweek, a new beginning. You may be already missing the carefree bliss of the weekend, sure, but you're still full of *hope*. After all, the rest of the week hasn't yet gone to shit (yet). If it's Wednesday, you're already halfway done: the top of the mountain. Thursday is just Friday lite, when you can taste the coming freedom, the buzz on your tongue. And Friday is, well, Friday: the day that signals the coming weekend, heralding in Saturday and Sunday—i.e., salvation.

Tuesday is (usually) forgettable.

Tuesday is (usually) uneventful.

Tuesday is (always) the slog.

On that particular Tuesday, while my dad was upstairs in his bedroom, taking his final breaths of life, I was sitting in the basement guest room, completely oblivious.

The basement was like a portal, a place to forget the goings-on in the rest of the world. It was where Shaz and I escaped our parents to play video games so often.

Recently, we'd begun playing the newest iteration of the Legend of Zelda, *Breath of the Wild*; I'd be the one with the controller, and my brother would lie beside me, curled beneath an old NASCAR comforter he'd used since he was five years old, when he developed an inexplicable obsession with cars. Like always, Shaz would watch me play and offer helpful hints. Or simply laugh, hard, whenever I led poor elf-like Link to his demise—which happened often.

But Shaz wasn't with me in the guest room that Tuesday. He'd left the house earlier, likely fleeing the maddening silence of a house holding its breath. The rest of my family—my mom, my aunt Amber, my uncle, and a small handful of cousins who'd been staying with us for the past few days—was upstairs in the kitchen, nibbling on whatever could be scrounged from the fridge. They talked quietly about anything and everything, as if Dad's impending death wasn't looming over them like an uninvited guest.

This meant that my only company was Link, crouched in tall grass up on the TV screen, and Stellaluna, made especially anxious by all the visitors we'd been having.

On my screen, Link was hiding from a mob of bokoblins in some tall grass when someone burst into the guest room, startling me and Stella. It wasn't Mom, like I'd expected, but one of my dad's cousins, breathless, her pink hijab disheveled.

At least, I think she was Dad's cousin. I'd met dozens of people in the previous weeks, people who'd claimed to know and love my father, though I'd never seen them before. They each insisted that if anyone could fight pancreatic cancer, he could. I tried to remind myself exactly *who* this woman in pink was, but I couldn't remember her name. She had arrived a few days before and told me she'd known me when I was a toddler, and didn't I remember?

I'd simply nodded, unsure how to explain that I had no memory of her whatsoever.

Dad's cousin's jaw was taut, her mouth pressed into a thin line. She looked at me with a blend of pity and dread—the kind of expression someone makes when they carry bad news and the burden of sharing it.

I paused the game and stood. The faint sounds of background music, of violin plucks and soft piano melodies, filled the room.

"Farah," Dad's cousin said, her downturned eyes rimmed with red. Before I could say anything, she swept me in a bone-crushing hug. She was an older woman who smelled like mothballs and saunf, a South Asian snack made of sugarcoated fennel seeds thought to help digestion.

"You have to be strong now, okay?" she whispered into my shoulder.

The room spun as the true meaning of her words settled in.

Dad was gone.

I think about that moment a lot, in part because of how strangely *calm* I'd felt. In truth, I thought that when Dad did die, I'd feel an uncontrollable rush of emotion and burst into tears: the obvious, natural reaction to a parent dying of cancer. It'd be something out of a Pakistani drama: I'd fall to my knees and bang the floor with my fist as the tears streamed down hollowed cheeks. *My dad is dead. My dad is dead!* I'd sob. *What are we going to do?*

I'd been doing that a lot lately: imagining hypothetical scenarios and what-ifs consisting of the worst possible situations. *What will I do the moment Dad dies? What will I do when I miss him, when I have a question only he can answer? What will I do at his funeral, when I watch them lower his body into the earth and I know I will never see his face again?* I'd walk myself through each god-awful hypothetical in what was a (perhaps weird) morbid attempt at mentally preparing myself, just in case. Just in case.

Maybe the mental preparation had worked, after all.

I could feel my dad's cousin searching my face, awaiting a reaction. "Okay," I said.

Her expression faltered.

Wordlessly, I brushed past her and walked upstairs, Stella at my heels. The world around me felt blurry. From somewhere in the house, I could hear someone's muffled crying. Hushed phone calls being made. Whispers of a prayer for the dead: *Inna lillahi wa inallah-e-raji'oon.* Verily, to God we belong and to God we shall return.

But what was the prayer for the people left behind?

❧

Unnoticed, I slipped into my bedroom and closed the door.

Moments later, the entire house erupted into chaos. EMTs rushed down the hall. Someone yelled—my mom's sister, maybe—*"Where the hell is Shaz?"* The house filled with people flocking to my mom: Family and friends from the local mosque. People my dad had worked with. Strangers who'd come to say they'd *been there* when Colonel Mazhar Rishi, MD, had died; gossip was always juicier when plucked firsthand.

I could hear it all through the walls. It was the most lively the house had sounded in weeks, even if it was just the sounds of a community in disarray. I vaguely wondered what happened to a bee colony when their queen dies. I wondered if it felt like this.

From the silent refuge of my bedroom, I shot out a text message to Stephen.

Dad is gone, I wrote simply. I felt my dog's anxious gaze as I waited for Stephen's response. The words on my phone screen looked strange, like they were written in a language I couldn't understand.

Stephen had been such an anchor for me these past few months, a reminder that I wasn't alone. He'd *always* been there, visiting every weekend, holding my hand through it all: A solid, familiar constant. An extension of myself. Except now he was back in New York City, over two hours away.

His text came back almost immediately.

I love you. Got my train ticket. I'll be there soon.

I put down my phone.

Time had started moving again, but it was moving so fast I could hardly keep track. Already fifteen minutes had passed. I'd been living in a world without Dad for nearly fifteen minutes.

My brain was flooding with questions.

Did someone tell Shaz?

Was he home?

Was Dad finally at peace? Who was with him when he died?

What about Mom—was she okay? Shouldn't I be by her side?

She'd be fine, I realized. Right now she'd be surrounded by people, just the way she'd want. Dad's death was a spectacle, after all, and the best seats would be by her side. There'd be no space for me.

Over fifteen minutes had passed, and no one had even thought to check on me.

In that moment, the curse of being the eldest daughter in a brown family was more apparent than ever. You are trained since birth to put others before you, to put family first, while you remain an afterthought even to yourself. All the while, you are also a translator and therapist, advocate and secretary. You are a punching bag and a guinea pig.

And you are Atlas. Forced to carry the weight of the world, watching life unfold around you and without you, as you slowly crumble beneath the burden—lonely and weary and forgotten.

I looked at Stella, her big liquid-brown pools for eyes trained on me, and gently scratched her head.

"It's okay, sweet pea," I told her.

Her eyes reminded me of Stephen's. Worried. Unconvinced.

Then I walked into my closet and tucked myself into a tiny ball in the far back corner. In a rare moment of privacy, I cried so hard I left a snot trail down my T-shirt.

I don't know how long I spent in that closet, cramped into a ball, weeping. Only once the sobs had subsided did I let myself unfurl. I sat among my clothes, knees curled to my chest. I didn't want to leave, didn't want to face the world. This closet felt like a sacred, liminal space, just mine alone.

Then the closet door swung open.

It was Mom.

"Hi . . . ?" I said, giving her a sad little wave. I felt embarrassed at being caught—by her of all people. But still, she'd found me. She'd thought to look for me, in the midst of her husband's death, waded through the crowd to get to me. That counted for something.

Strangely, Mom seemed . . . fine. Behind her glasses, her eyes weren't red-rimmed and glazed over, like mine. If anything, she looked lighter somehow—like someone who'd been choking for days but could finally breathe again.

"Ah, I thought I'd find you in here," she said, amused. She joined me in the closet, closing the door behind her.

I stiffened. My mom was never one for pep talks.

"I want to hide, too. So many people are here already." Mom sighed, stared up at the ceiling. "I'm exhausted."

For weeks, she, Shaz, and I had been running back and forth from the hospital, the pharmacy, the airport, to pick people up who wanted to say their goodbyes. Now it was almost over.

"Things are going to change a lot, aren't they?" Mom said quietly, reaching out a hand to pet Stella.

I nodded.

⁕

Not long after Mom left my room, a pair of arms wrapped around me and held me close. I was certain it was Stephen. Or maybe Mom again. I was wrong.

"Hi, baby," came a familiar voice at my ear.

"Oh my God. Maha?" I blinked away tears. "How did you— Why—"

Maha gave me another squeeze before sitting beside me. "I heard. The whole community knows already."

I'd been in my bedroom for a little over an hour. The house had burst into life. I wondered who else had heard. I wondered who else had shown up.

Kareem had probably heard about it already, I realized.

"News spreads fast, huh."

Maha seemed to know what I was thinking. She always could. "You know who else is here? Shameen aunty. She's been sobbing hysterically since she got here. You'd think *she's* the widow."

I groaned. Shameen aunty had been a teacher at our Sunday school, made infamous for teaching kids that singing in the shower would, without a doubt, invite djinn to possess them. It scared the crap out of the kids; my dad had to talk to her about it to get her to stop.

I'd heard someone keening like a banshee outside for the past five minutes. Suddenly it made sense.

"Oh God, wait. Does that mean Amina's here?"

Amina, the girl who many years ago had discovered Kareem's AIM username, was Shameen aunty's daughter. Apparently, she had gotten hardcore into new age spirituality, and according to Mom, had texted my parents that they didn't need to worry anymore because she would *pray the cancer away*.

"Yeah, let's not think about that right now," said Maha. "If she says anything to you, I'll fight her. Come, you look tense. Lie down."

Maha didn't wait for me to move; she forced me down onto my bed and gently spread out my limbs. "You're in luck. I know *everything* there is to know about fascia and muscle work."

I could tell she was trying to change the subject, to get me to think about anything but Dad. For a moment it felt like college again, when we'd just hang out and banter about nothing. It was nice.

"What is fascia?"

"Connective tissue. It's where your tension is. Now shush and relax."

"Right. You're a *doctor* now," I said, dazed. It'd been almost four years since I'd last seen her; she'd gotten married to some guy I didn't know, then went off to medical school—she'd been living a completely different life. Our paths had diverged, the way they often do in long friendships.

And now here she was in my bedroom, like nothing had changed. She'd come back into my life when it really mattered, acting like the kind of big sister who looked out for the ones she loved. Only now Maha had an air of maturity about her, like life had carved out wisdom from within. She was still Maha, but clearer, more self-assured.

"Yeah, you know." Maha smirked. "Okay, this will feel weird, but just bear with me." A second later she tugged on my leg, and I felt a pop in my hips, an instant release. I hadn't even realized how much my body hurt until then.

"What . . . ? What did you *do*?"

"Don't worry about it."

Maha quickly went to work on my shoulders, and seconds later they were already starting to feel looser.

My eyes started watering again. "I missed you."

She kissed my head. "I missed you, too."

Then I sat up, realizing I'd forgotten something very important.

"I need to find Shaz."

A few weeks before Dad died, he'd called me and my brother into his room.

We sat on either side of the gurney where he'd spend his final days. Dad held each of our hands. It was The Talk we'd been waiting for, the one we dreaded.

"I need you to promise me to look after your mom," said Dad weakly. Talking was painful, and every word took precious energy.

"There are people who will try to take advantage of her. People she thinks she can trust. Friends. Even her family."

He was talking about Nani Jan, Mom's mom. Who else, though—I suppose I'd find out soon enough.

Dad took a shaky breath. Shaz and I waited.

"Your mom will be alone; she will be vulnerable," he continued. "And I'm worried she won't be able to see people's intentions. But I know you can." He looked at me. "You have to look out for her. Both of you."

"We will, Dad," I whispered.

"And look out for each other. It'll just be the three of you. You're all you have now."

I wanted to keep that promise I made to Dad.

"You okay to go out there?" Maha asked. "I won't lie, it's kind of a madhouse."

I licked my dry lips. "I think so." Based on the sound outside, though, I wouldn't be. Even the wooden floor in my bedroom trembled with all the movement of people out in the hall. So many people had come. So many people would give the same speech I'd already heard a hundred times all week.

Your dad was a great man.

His death is such a loss for the community.

He was proud of you, you know. He talked about you going to law school all the time.

But just before we were going to step outside, Stephen burst through the door, looking frazzled, *panicked*. Our eyes met.

And without a word, he swept me in a hug.

The next day was the janazah prayer at the mosque. The janazah is a funeral prayer performed by the entirety of the congregation to ask for forgiveness on behalf of the deceased. Dad's body was there, placed by the front of the imam leading the prayer; open caskets are rarely done in the Muslim community, but because of Dad's work and his prominence as a leader at the mosque, Mom thought it made sense.

Hundreds of people showed up to the janazah. There wasn't enough space inside, and a crowd had already formed to pray out on the grass. It was humbling, knowing that they were all here for Dad.

I'm related to him, I repeated in my head, a reminder to myself. *This is my father. This is for Dad.* But it didn't feel real. None of it did.

In his wooden casket—cardboard thin to ensure it was biodegradable, as is required in Islam—Dad looked so frail, so skeletal. He'd been cleaned and clothed in a white shroud, which brought out the yellow in his skin. It was strange, seeing Dad at the front of the same mosque where he had led prayers so long ago.

Even more people came to the burial: Dad's coworkers from the hospital. Stephen's parents, who flew in from Florida to show their support. A soft-spoken rabbi from a local synagogue that I'd met for one of Dad's interfaith talks years ago.

It was a sea of black, all watching Dad's body as it was slowly lowered into the grave. His loved ones would now grab fistfuls of dirt and toss it onto his casket three times, a symbolic acknowledgment that Dad would return to the earth from which he came: *We belong to Allah, and to Him we return.*

Mom was the first; she plucked tiny handfuls of dirt and dusted it over Dad, her mouth in a tight line. Shaz and I went next, simultaneously. I took as much as I could in each fist, tossing the dirt toward Dad's head. I thought about how in Islam, when Cain kneeled by his brother Abel's lifeless body, God sent him a crow. The crow pecked at the earth beside Abel, teaching him how to dig the first-ever grave—and so, perhaps riddled with guilt, Abel buried his brother in a last attempt to humanize him, one last time. To provide a moment of sanctity, even among such moral depravity.

Soon Dad would become part of that same earth: a single cell in countless rows of gray stone. But Dad, I think, would have liked to become a garden.

"Bye, Dad," I whispered.

My brother and I went to my mom, stood on either side of her. I realized it was the first time in days that the three of us had had a moment alone together. She wrapped her arms around us as I swallowed back the implication, all the hidden meanings of what Dad had said about it just being the three of us now.

Dad had been worried.

I was worried.

"The people at the cemetery said they can put flowers on your dad's gravestone," Mom said to my brother and me after the funeral. "What should we tell them? Dogwood?"

"Definitely dogwood," said Shaz. "He's mentioned loving dogwood a dozen times."

"Dogwood," I agreed.

❧

A few weeks after the funeral, my brother and I were driving back from the grocery store. Since I'd gotten back from Portland, drives together were something I'd looked forward to; I'd be behind the wheel while my brother would DJ. We'd catch up, or talk about nothing and everything.

We were listening to his playlist on the drive home when "Cough Syrup" by Young the Giant began playing.

> Life's too short to even care at all, whoa-oh-oh
> I'm losing my mind, losing my mind, losing con-
> trol . . .

Singer Sameer Gadhia's melancholy, honey-soft murmuring filled my little blue Mazda, and my heart clenched.

"It's such a beautiful song," I said, "but it's so sad! I swear I get depressed every time I hear it."

There was a pause. Shaz was looking out the window.

"When I kill myself," he said finally, "this is the song I'll play."

I slammed on the brakes.

"Hey. That's not funny!" I yelled, looking at him. "Don't joke about that. What the hell is wrong with you? Why would you say that?"

Shaz stared back at me, his face unreadable.

My brother and I had always had a dark sense of humor, but something about the way he'd said it—so casually, so vacantly—struck a chord; I couldn't let it go. He was just kidding. Maybe I was being dramatic. But hearing him talk about his own death, especially when I knew he wasn't in a good place in his life, rattled me. Maybe the song, and Shaz's words, had hit too close.

I was barely holding on in the face of Dad's death, still a raw, fresh wound. But a life without Shaz—I *never* wanted to imagine it.

"I swear to God, Shaz, don't *ever* joke about that again." I gripped the steering wheel, my eyes growing full. "If you ever killed yourself, I *swear*, I'll bring you back to life just to kill you myself."

Shaz looked ahead again at the road, silent. Uncomfortable.

I unplugged his phone from the car, fumbled to plug in my own.

"I'm putting on a different song," I said. "Something *happy*. Just to spite you."

CHAPTER 24

Banshee

The time after Dad's death was a blur.

The first week, my friends from Odyssey coordinated to send me a gift every day, a plan spearheaded by Rebecca. We also received dozens of flower deliveries; the house got so full of them, our dining room could have been its own flower shop.

But eventually the flowers wilted. October grew colder, and we felt autumn's absence like a beloved friend disappearing into the night.

I threw myself into writing my book. The book-packaging company was excited by what I'd written so far, and the contract came swiftly. As soon as I'd finished the draft, they'd sent the book out on submission—but they were fairly confident, they informed me, that the book would be picked up.

According to the contract, I wouldn't be paid much, and I wouldn't get royalties—a standard for book-packaging-company contracts, I'd learn later—but I was still reeling from Dad's death, and the contract was a life buoy. At least now I could say I was an author. I'd be paid to write. It felt like I could prove to my dad that being an author wasn't a pipe dream. It was something within reach. It was something already here.

Shaz had also enrolled in a local community college; he was ready, he'd said, to wade back into life. He'd begun attending therapy in earnest, and even started making music again, which he'd post on SoundCloud: incredible piano compositions with such lightness, such a delicate hesitancy, that listening to them brought me to tears. It was proof he was trying to hope again.

On his own initiative, Shaz had made flyers and posted them at the mosque:

PIANO LESSONS with SHAZ RISHI: Pianist and Composer with over 15 years of experience. First lesson FREE! Snacks provided ☺

"This is the cutest thing I've ever seen," I exclaimed, grabbing one of the flyers he'd printed to show me. He'd even included little tabs with his phone number on the bottom. "And free snacks?! Can I sign up?"

"Please shut up," he replied, biting back a smile.

But where Shaz had changed for the better, Mom had decided on a different approach. She'd begun going to a nearby gym religiously, and there had met two men named Anthony and Malik—brothers—who worked as trainers. They'd always wanted to open their own gym together but had struggled to find an investor, a business partner. Mom, who'd been looking for a new career direction after Dad's death, was ecstatic about the idea.

"You don't really know them that well, though," I'd said. On a late evening, when I'd been holed up in the office to write, she'd popped in to tell me her plans to invest.

Mom pouted. "I know that they're good guys, and they have nothing to hide, and that's the important thing. They didn't have to tell me about their background, but they told me."

"What do you mean, their background?"

"They were in jail for a few years," she answered, looking away.

"What are their full names?"

Mom told me, and I did a quick Google search. Sure enough, their names popped up.

"Mom, they literally have a criminal record. For selling cocaine."

"They did their time! I thought you were better than to judge people for drug records, come on now."

"This isn't about that. Look, I get that people make mistakes. I won't judge them for that, especially when we don't know the situation. But just because we shouldn't judge people for their mistakes doesn't mean you start a business with them. You've known them for like, two months."

Mom's face reddened, and her jaw grew taut. "You think I won't do my due diligence? I'm not an idiot, Farah. This is a chance for me to do something I want—I thought you of all people would understand that."

"And I do! I just think maybe there's a reason why they haven't been able to find an investor."

"You sound like your dad."

I bit my lip. She meant it as an insult. She meant it to say that I was holding her back, the way she felt Dad had all her life. I'd met Anthony and Malik—they were nice enough—but I didn't like the way they looked at Mom, the way they circled her with their eyes. They knew she was a recent widow. They knew Dad had left her some money.

This was exactly the kind of thing Dad had warned me about.

Mom was right about one thing, though; with Dad gone, this *was* a chance for her to explore her options, to find something she could be passionate about. She needed to move on, and I wanted her to have that chance.

I just wished she wouldn't throw her lot in at the very first opportunity.

Mom started leaving the house more and more: not just to go to the gym, but to go out with her friends Zaina and Usman, both physicians working at the hospital where Dad had been admitted. They'd recently moved to the area, and Mom had relied on them for treatment advice.

"We're going to a Roaring Twenties–themed party in New York!" she'd told me one night, wearing a blue sequined dress. She looked lovely. But she didn't look like herself.

Mom was in mourning, I told myself. Everyone mourns differently, and that was valid. She finally had the freedom to explore the things she wanted, without being questioned, without having to justify it to Dad.

Once Mom came home from one of her outings with a black eye. She'd gotten a little too clumsy and crashed into a door, she'd explained. I pressed her, worried.

"I tried something I maybe shouldn't have. But it's not a big deal." She laughed as she stumbled back to her bedroom.

The silence was stifling.

"You don't—you don't think she's on drugs, do you?" I asked my brother in the kitchen.

My brother said nothing, but I could see the thoughts swirling in his dark eyes. Thoughts he was probably too tired to voice.

"Want to go in the basement?" came my follow-up.

"Yeah."

The one good thing to come from Mom's change in behavior was that it had emboldened my job search; the book-packaging company wouldn't be paying anytime soon, and even then, it wouldn't be enough to live on.

I didn't take the bar, had officially moved on from law, but I needed a job. I needed health care.

More than that, though, I wanted to move out.

The past few months, I'd been applying for jobs in publishing as an editorial assistant. I'd even had an interview with a big-name children's publisher. I barely had any publishing experience and didn't even live in New York, where the job was based, so my hopes weren't high.

But the interview went well. Stupidly well. I'd taken a train to the city to meet with the editor who would be my potential boss. Charles was a fresh-faced (quite literally—his luminous skin made mine look like a dune buggy track) middle-aged man with a perfectly fitted gray suit. Energy radiated out of his nonexistent pores.

"The thing is, I'm a new hire. New blood," said Charles, sitting cross-legged in a crisp white, brand-new office chair. We were in his office at the publishing house; to our left was a dazzling view of the city that I couldn't stop trying to peek at. "And I have a *lot* of changes I want to make. This place needs an overhaul, but no one likes the new guy bringing in whole new ways of thinking. So I need someone in my corner. Someone smart, savvy, who can read me. Someone who wants to help restructure this whole thing over from the ground up and help champion diverse writers. Does that make sense?"

I had no idea what he was talking about, but that last part, especially, sounded great.

I nodded. "I'm at a place in my life where that sounds exactly like what I'm looking for. And I pride myself on reading people—it kind of comes with the territory of being a writer."

He smiled, revealing pristine white teeth; I had the sense he was the kind of man who used one of those fancy Braun toothbrushes after every meal. "True. I can already tell we share similar values. Even your outfit—my assistant has to be an extension of me, right? You dress well, and let's be real, how a person dresses tells you a lot about them. And I think your legal background will be an asset."

I nodded blankly again; at the very least, he was doing most of the talking. But he seemed, for whatever reason, excited.

At the end of the interview, we shook hands. "You'll be hearing from me soon," he said, flashing another smile.

Charles reached out again to ask me to do an editorial test; he sent me a manuscript to read, and I was to write a ten-page edit letter, as if I were an editor. With the advice of friends from Odyssey, learning from Jeremy's incisive writing skills, I finished the letter in three days and sent it back.

I'd loved doing it: reading a fresh manuscript, thinking about all the ways I could bring the story out. I wanted this, I realized. I really wanted this job.

But weeks turned into a month, and still I heard nothing back.

❧

Tensions continued to rise in the house. It started off with seemingly small things. Mom had realized, much to her horror, that with the coming colder months, we were having a field mouse problem. She'd found mouse droppings in the basement, left by mice trying to find a warm space to camp out in for the winter.

Mom hated mice.

"I'm getting traps."

"Don't use glue traps," I warned her. "They're cruel. They have cruelty-free traps you can set up. Or just call someone who'll catch them without killing them."

"Yeah, sure, sure," she said.

She didn't listen.

When I came home for the weekend, I found my brother coming up from the basement, a secret smile playing on his face.

"Why are you smiling like that?" I asked. Shaz rarely smiled like that without good reason.

"I found a mouse."

"What? Where?"

"Mom's apparently still been using the glue traps. There was one stuck in the basement closet. Kisa told me."

My face fell. Of course Mom was still using the fucking glue traps. Then: "Wait, what do you mean *Kisa* told you?"

"She was sitting by the storage room in the basement, scratching at the door. When she saw me coming, she started meowing, trying to get me to open it. So I did. And that's when I saw the mouse. It was squeaking and making all these horrible noises. Kisa didn't even *do* anything; she just sat next to it and gave me this look like she wanted me to get it to stop."

"Kisa is an embarrassment to all cats," I said, shaking my head. "What did you do? How's the mouse?"

"I looked up a video on how to safely free mice from glue traps, so I put on some of Dad's old gardening gloves and used some canola oil. Took me forever, but I eventually freed it. Kisa just watched the entire time."

I imagined my baby brother, crouched on the concrete, with painstaking care and precision, peeling the poor mouse from the trap's death grip. Mice are tiny. Delicate. Any wrong movement could have hurt it. But Shaz had succeeded.

It reminded me of a story my dad once told our class in Sunday school. In Islam, there is a hadith about a sex worker who found a stray dog. The day was unbearably hot, and the dog was dying of thirst. The sex worker had been on her way somewhere—perhaps she was in a hurry—but still, she took the time to fill her shoe with water from a well and give it to the dog.

For this one simple act of kindness, God forgave her for her sins, and she was admitted into heaven.

I laughed. "*Wow.* So where is the mouse now?"

"I let it go. In the house." Shaz smirked, pleased with himself. "Kisa didn't even chase it."

"You dork. You absolute dork."

I love you, I thought. *I love that we're related. I love that you trusted me enough to tell me. I love that you took the time to help.*

I loved that in a world that worked so desperately to cut us at every angle, my brother had chosen to hold on to his softness.

A few days later, my brother and I were startled when we heard our mom let out a scream that reverberated through the house.

"I saw a mouse! I swear I just saw a fucking mouse!"

Shaz grinned.

※

When the end of December rolled around—just before Christmas—I received an email from the HR department of the children's book publisher. Would you be able to start in the first week of January? they asked.

I'd gotten the job.

I let out a scream; Mom, who was home for once, asked what happened.

"I'm moving to New York!" I yelled. I was moving to New York to start a job in publishing. I'd have my own salary. Health care. I'd get to live the life I'd paused since Dad's diagnosis.

And I'd get to live in the same city as Stephen.

My new boss's email came an hour later:

We're going to do great things together.

CHAPTER 25

The Lives I Want

New York City thrums with an electric life force that makes the hair on your arms stand on end with anticipation. A city where steel and scuzz come to a crossroads. It's a city of overwhelming impossibility at every turn: with too many bodies, too much noise—too much of so *much.* The city will eat you and spit you out, and if you don't learn how to dance in the stomach of the beast, you won't make it out alive.

There are those who say the city is overrated, romanticized: people with suitcases and preconceived expectations of grandeur. There are, admittedly, parts of the city that feel like you've made a wrong turn and ended up in hell's armpit.

But those people haven't had life-altering conversations with strangers at a bodega, knowing they would never meet again. Been mesmerized by how the evening light hits the pond in Central Park just right, setting it ablaze in fiery shades of orange. Been lifted by the way a busker's music echoes in a subway—music in the city's veins—infusing a shitty, dying day with just a touch of magic.

It is these surreal, fleeting moments that make New York something special, if you're lucky enough to find them.

My mom helped me move into my new apartment on Ninety-First Street. My new home was in a prewar building that had to be entered through the basement and the rumbling boiler room, sticky humid even in winter.

Mom's friend Nyla had come with us, promising to help position the furniture to best utilize space even, as she put it, "in a tiny box like this."

I liked Nyla; she was the only one of Mom's friends I trusted, mostly because she was one of those people born without a filter. She would always be honest; she couldn't be anything but—much to my mom's dismay.

Nyla was also an interior designer with big hair and a chiseled, Pathani jawline. She spoke with a posh Lahori accent, wouldn't be caught dead outside without a designer handbag, and unironically called everyone, even complete strangers, *darling*.

I stood in the doorway of my new apartment, hesitating.

"It looks smaller than I remember." Stephen and I had spent the last week of December running through the city to dozens of apartment viewings; in the end, I'd settled on this one mostly out of desperation and exhaustion. This particular apartment had one bedroom—although it was generous to even call it that, as a bed would barely fit. The whole thing felt a little cramped for two people, plus a dog and a cat.

"It just needs a rug," said Nyla. "You'd be surprised at how much you can improve a room with a rug."

"A rug isn't going to fix this," my mom chimed in.

Nyla clicked her tongue. "Uff, ulloo ka patha! I'm trying to comfort your daughter, not point out that she's living in a *hovel*."

I laughed weakly.

Nyla turned to me. "Come now, darling, chin up. At least I haven't seen a single cockroach. You'd be surprised at how many of my clients, even the rich ones, find cockroaches on move-in day."

"Your stove doesn't work!" Mom suddenly called from the kitchen. "Welcome to New York, huh?"

Stephen and I would be living together.

It'd been Mom's idea. "You'll save rent, and it'll be good to be with someone who knows the city. I don't want you living alone out there. And it'd be a pain in the ass to find good roommates, right?"

I still wasn't convinced it was real. Normally the idea of living with a guy was something my mom would have disowned me for even considering. Not that I had many options; I couldn't live with Kaya, who was still in Japan, or Maha, who was finishing med school at Lake Erie. And Dad had vetoed any notion of living with roommates we didn't know ahead of time. *It's a safety issue,* he'd said. *You never know how dangerous someone could be.*

I wondered if watching Stephen help around the house while Dad was sick had changed Mom's mind about him. Maybe it was a testament to how much she trusted him now. Stephen had also recently taken the shahada; he was a Muslim now, which in Mom's mind meant that he'd be safe. But part of me also wondered if she was in a rush to get me out of the house.

Either way, I wasn't about to complain about the chance to live with my best friend, and neither was Stephen.

And Stephen was the perfect roommate. His cut of the rent was never late; he kept his space tidy—at least, far tidier than he had kept his dorm room in college. Our lives fell into a natural rhythm. He'd wait for me to get home to eat dinner—I always came home later, around seven—and we'd throw on a TV show to decompress under some faux Sherpa throw blankets. When I'd finally lean back into the couch, mildly more relaxed, Stephen would listen to me complain about work, all nods and polite *mm-hmm*s at the right places, sometimes even getting angry on my behalf. Then on weekends he would politely, but firmly, pull me and Stellaluna out of the apartment to go to the park. *You look like you could use some fresh air,* he'd say, and he'd be right.

At some point Stephen joined a recreational soccer league, and while he'd be gone, I'd write or grab coffee with friends from work or catch up with Shaz.

"So? Have you met anyone?" I'd asked suggestively, when Stephen would come back from soccer.

He'd smile, the way one does when they're holding on to a secret. "Nah. I'm too old for that anyway."

"You're *twenty-seven.*"

"Exactly."

It was clear Stephen had no interest in dating anyone. For as long as I'd known him, he never had. And if I ever asked, he'd come up with a different excuse: *I'm too old. Too tired. It's too stressful.*

I don't think it'd be fair to them.

So I'd drop it. After all, I was the same. I was too busy with work, and my mistake with Yusuf had made me overly cautious with love.

Still, it felt like something unspoken was slowly changing between us.

I slept in the bedroom, and Stephen in the living room, where he slept on the couch pull-out bed. But a few times, when I couldn't sleep and my brain was too tightly coiled from stress, Stephen would put me to bed the way one would a child. He'd lean over my bedside and play with my hair, his hands soft and delicate on my scalp, until my eyelids went heavy.

I'd wondered if this was a normal thing for best friends to do. I wondered that a lot lately, about a lot of things we did: how often we spent time together, how we were basically coparenting a dog together. How Stephen had moved to Portland to be closer. Even the topic of why he'd become a Muslim had been tabled, as if we were both afraid to touch it. Of what it could mean.

I wondered if it even mattered, what normal best friends did—if there was such a thing.

But something about him gently touching my hair made me feel a little embarrassed. Shy, even. Something I'd never felt around him before.

"You have work, too," I'd complain softly. "You're spoiling me."

Stephen would smile. "Shh. Just sleep."

And, eventually, I would.

⁂

Being an editorial assistant, I'd thought, would mean becoming Charles's mentee. He would take me under his wing and teach me how to edit stories with scalpel-sharp precision. I would watch him as he worked his editorial magic, like a sculptor carving away the excess. Of course, I would perform administrative tasks, like ensuring a manuscript was sailing through the publication process on time and other basic clerical tasks.

Instead, from the start, Charles decided to pull his best impression of Miranda Priestly from *The Devil Wears Prada*.

I managed his calendar (every appointment, every meeting, every midday facial at Heyday), made reservations at restaurants for his clients and editor friends ("Someplace fancy, but not pretentious fancy, you know?"), wrote back apologetic emails to his anxious authors awaiting his feedback. I would also get his morning coffee, his lunch, which he often made me deliver in the middle of his board meetings—which I'd interrupt with a hundred *sorry*s as I carefully placed his lunch in front of him, trying to ignore the pitying looks of the other editors. I'd get him snacks during the day, too, which is why I will never look at a yogurt parfait with anything but disdain. If he was in a good mood, he'd inform me to "get myself a little something" during those yogurt parfait runs. But I'd always feel too nervous to take him up on his offer.

Once, he had me hunt down the janitors to ask if they could hang some paintings in his office.

"We don't really do that," one of the janitors said.

"I'm sorry. Could you make this one exception? He only has two. It shouldn't take more than ten minutes of your time," I pleaded.

The janitor sighed and, to my relief, agreed to do it. I didn't dare imagine Charles's disappointment if I'd failed.

I'd already screwed up once when I'd forgotten to make copies of a form he'd needed for an acquisitions meeting. He'd torn into me afterward, telling me he didn't believe I was serious about this job, that he'd expected more of me.

But I just couldn't keep up.

"I'm so sorry. I won't make that mistake again," I said, biting back tears.

"Don't be sorry. I want you to be better. Okay?" he'd say, smiling like a murderous, poreless porcelain doll, before looking back at his computer like I no longer existed. Silently, I left his office.

Those smiles always brought chills down my spine.

My already packed schedule began falling apart when my first book was sold by the packager to HarperCollins. It was incredible, knowing I'd finally done it. I wondered if somewhere in the universe, Dad could see me.

But I didn't even have time to revel in the joy of finally being able to call myself an author; as soon as I'd get back from work, I'd sit down at my computer to work on edits for my manuscript well into the night. I was an editorial assistant, but I was also on deadline. I barely had time to keep in touch with Shaz, either; our text-message check-ins were brief, mostly just to share funny videos or vent about how the baristas at Starbucks always spelled our names wrong. I missed him.

I missed being able to breathe.

Sometimes, when I'd look away from my monitor for a moment, I'd find a cup of tea I hadn't made sitting by my hand. Chamomile, to help relax me.

And just like that, the long, late nights felt a little more bearable.

⁂

One day, Charles finally gave me my first big editorial assignment: to write an edit letter for a monster romance novel he'd recently acquired, which had big names attached to the project despite not being published yet. I was *thrilled.* I'd finally learn editorial skills! It felt like he was finally, nearly six months into the job, acknowledging that I'd grown, that I was ready to move a bit forward in my career instead of being a not-so-glorified personal gofer.

He gave me a week to read the full manuscript and write the edit letter.

I poured myself into it, taking every minute I could spare during work, and every spare minute I had when I got home to write out ways I thought the book could be stronger, more effective: things like, *This description is strong, but maybe you could cut this for pacing;* or *I'm not sure the protagonist's feelings are coming through here—what if we tried refocusing on this one core feeling?* The edit letter ended up being over fifteen pages, but I knew I had to thoroughly impress Charles if I wanted more of this work.

When the end of the week rolled by, I printed out my edit letter and handed it to him, beaming. I couldn't wait to hear his feedback, to learn to be a better editor. And how lucky I was to be able to learn all this from such a wonderful book.

In the end, he never gave me feedback. Later, he told me he had written his own edit letter, which I never got to see, and had already emailed it to the author.

I'm not sure he even read my letter.

But the final straw came when Charles asked me to build him a new chair he'd bought for himself.

I glanced at my clothes; I was wearing a skirt and heels that day. Just my luck.

"I can try," I said, breathless. I was always breathless. "I'm not really good with building things, so it might take a bit, but I'll definitely try."

"I'm sure you can. It's just a chair." He grabbed his leather-bound binder off his desk and moved past me. "I have a meeting now. You'll have it done by the time I get back?"

I nodded. He'd been disappointed the last time, when he'd asked me to organize his computer wires. I'd even bought several kinds of wire-organizing tools on Amazon with my own money, but he hadn't liked my attempt. This time, though, I'd build the chair perfectly and be at my desk working by the time he got back.

He smiled, amused. "Funny how life works, huh? You came out of law school and now here you are, building a chair."

"Yeah," I said.

On my hands and knees in his office, I got to work on building his new desk chair, cursing under my breath. The instructions, of course, were unintelligible, and already my arms were aching from having to lift and move it on my own.

I'd gotten halfway through when I noticed someone stopping by Charles's doorway; I'd forgotten to close the door.

It was the director of the children's publishing department: not Charles's boss, but Charles's boss's boss. I'd met him a few times: a friendly, relaxed guy, but a straight shooter. For him to see me like that—sweaty, heels off, crouched on the floor—was a special kind of humiliation I wouldn't wish on anyone.

"You're—you're building a chair?" he asked, wearing a bemused expression.

"Attempting to."

"Huh. Wow," he replied, blinking. "Wow."

"I have to quit," I later cried to another editor named Amy. "I'm sorry, but I just—I hate the thought of quitting after only six months, but I seriously can't stay here anymore."

Amy—or Amelia—was a beloved editor in the industry, and Charles had recruited her from another publisher. *I need more people in my corner,* he'd said when he'd first told me about her.

Amy was East Asian and a champion for marginalized authors. She and I had similar taste in books, in food, in everything—she was so easy to talk to. I had taken on work as her assistant, too, but working with her felt like an escape. Amy would carefully talk me through what she needed and why, how it played into the publication process. She cared enough to teach me. She was a balm on all my aches, one I so desperately needed.

But I had to leave. There wasn't a week that passed when I hadn't cried at work. Charles could be so unflinchingly cruel. And yet I found myself desperate to be praised: I'd wake up three hours before work to dress in the most fashionable clothes I owned, to put on makeup and do my hair—all because I knew he valued appearance. I'd run myself ragged at work to fulfill his every whim, even begging restaurants for last-minute reservations. I wanted to make my boss happy. I wanted to stay in publishing.

But that was just the thing. This was children's publishing. And I felt my already exhausted soul being torn apart.

I decided to email Charles, asked him to talk. I felt pathetic. I'd lasted in publishing barely six months. But here I was, already giving up.

"When you finally tell Charles you're quitting, when you walk into his office, remember you have *nothing* to be afraid of," Stephen said. "And no matter what you might think right now, you do deserve better."

"So walk the runway, not the plank?" I asked.

Stephen grinned. "Exactly."

When I told Charles I was quitting, his reaction wasn't what I expected.

"I see," he replied stiffly. "Well, all right." He paused. He seemed bored by the conversation already.

I stared, feeling deflated. I'd come into his office, bracing myself for him to yell, for him to tell me how disappointed he was.

Somehow his lack of care was even worse.

"So when will your last week be?" he asked, eyes glued to his computer. "Just make sure you put it on my calendar."

❧

Meanwhile, Mom had called to tell me she was planning on changing her name. She wanted to take back the maiden name she'd given up when she'd gotten married.

"And Samia Khan sounds so much better than Samia Rishi. It sounds more natural. Doesn't it?" she'd asked.

I wanted to encourage her; it was only fair that she change her name if she wanted. Hell, I'd decided to never change my last name if I ever got married. I liked my last name. I liked that it connected me to family, to ancestors I'd never met. I didn't want to give that up.

But the timing of wanting to change her name—it worried me. Already our family was so fractured. Already we shared so little. Now Mom wouldn't even share a name with her kids.

I bit my bottom lip hard; with all the stress of the editorial assistant job, I'd begun chewing at my lip so much that a blood blister had formed, which I'd hide clumsily with lip balm.

I could feel Mom waiting on the other line. She wanted my opinion. But she wanted the *right* opinion. *Her* opinion. Sometimes I felt like she said these things to test me, to see if I was still on her side, to see how much of Dad I still carried.

"Of course. Makes sense. Whatever you want," I answered.

But the further Mom pulled away from us, the more I wondered if Dad wasn't the only parent we were in danger of losing.

PART IV

Someone That Loves You

CHAPTER 26

I Carried You for Nine Months

A month after I quit my job, I started losing my hair, clumps of it, in the shower. Even touching it would cause several strands to slide off my head like dead leaves. In the coming months, I'd lost almost half the hair on my head. My muscles, too, had grown tight and stiff, to the point where moving felt painful. I was sick all the time, and I had no idea why. I'd fall asleep around 11:00 p.m. and be in bed until 10:00 a.m., feeling like I'd never slept at all. What little energy I had during the day, I used only to sit and write.

Worse, when I reached for a pencil that had fallen off my bed, I stretched my stomach and somehow reopened my umbilical hernia.

It was as if my body had aged thirty years.

"You've been on high alert for the past six months. This is probably the aftermath of all that pent-up stress and anxiety," Stephen suggested. "You need to rest. Let yourself rest."

Since Dad died, I'd become unreasonably terrified of being sick. Even with symptoms of a cold, my brain would immediately jump to the worst-case scenario. *Dad had pancreatic cancer. What if the cancer was genetic? What if I inherited the gene, too? What if cancer was ravaging me and it was too late to treat?*

I'd also become terrified of my loved ones getting sick, or worse. One night, only months ago, Stephen had called me from the ER; he'd gotten hurt at soccer when someone kneed him in the spine. It didn't matter that Stephen was perfectly calm over the phone; I'd panicked and sprinted all the way to the hospital because I'd forgotten that cabs existed. I'd just lost Dad. My heart couldn't take the thought of losing him, too.

In the end, Stephen's x-rays were clear, but it took hours for the panic to fade.

"I don't get it," I replied, frustrated. "Law school never made me feel this sick. So why now? Why is my body acting like this *now*?"

Stephen rubbed my back to help calm me. "Maybe law school was just the start. I mean, you had to rush back home. Your dad died, you moved to a completely new place, and then started a new job with a terrible boss. You've had a lot of big stressors piling up since then."

Everything Stephen said made sense. He had an ability to calmly rationalize his train of thought without condescension. It was like he'd become the physical manifestation of the logic part of my brain, the one that had been temporarily shut down by the panic.

I didn't like being touched, and Stephen had always been careful to respect that. But, lately, whenever he placed his hand on my back—*warm, always so warm*—the rumble of frantic thoughts, the screaming in my skull, would be lulled to stillness.

We concluded that I needed to see a doctor. That maybe I should also consider genetic testing. All of this, Stephen believed, would help settle my mind. The advice I'd gotten from my new therapist, whom I'd started seeing in the past few months, was similar. I had put off processing the events of the past year, and the strange, aching heart pains would keep me up all night. My therapist, a grizzly bear of a man with tiny glasses and a soft voice, had explained that grief disorders or PTSD could manifest after the death of a parent, and it could coincide with physical symptoms like the ones I was experiencing. I needed to see a psychiatrist for anxiety medication, and a cardiologist to ensure my difficulty breathing wasn't the result of something more dire.

"I know it sounds ridiculous, but it's like my feelings are too *big*," I told Stephen one night, after a panic attack. "And my heart feels far too small to hold them all."

But I'd lost my health care benefits from my publishing job. I could have signed up for Obamacare, but I had no substantial income; I was living off the advance from my book deal, which was a fraction of the deal after the book-packaging company had taken their share. And if I didn't sign up for health care soon, under the 2017 health coverage laws, I'd have to pay a tax penalty. I shared my concerns with my mom.

"I think you should marry Stephen," said Mom on the phone. "That would solve everything."

". . . What?"

"It's not right that you both are living together, anyway." *It was your idea,* I thought. But I was used to my mom's revisionist history, and her opinions fluctuating with the wind. Mom went on: "If people were to find out I let my daughter live with a boy, I'd never hear the end of it. You two shouldn't be living under the same roof. I don't know what I was thinking."

"Okay. Um." I closed my eyes, willing myself to remain calm. "So, I hear what you're saying, but Stephen and I aren't in a relationship. Just because we're living together doesn't mean we're having sex like a couple of bunnies."

"Don't be crude."

"I'm just saying, I get that you're worried, but do we really have to get married just because of what other people might think? Isn't it more important that we know the truth?"

Of course I'd always known that Stephen and I living together was considered unconventional. But God had already taken my dad away; if He was going to deem me a sinner for living with Stephen after everything we'd been through, well—

My relationship with God these days was shaky at best.

"*Do* we know the truth?" asked Mom.

"What do you mean?"

"For all I know, you've been doing God-knows-what together."

I sighed. "Please don't start that again. Believe me or don't believe me, it doesn't matter."

"I don't know why you're so against it. Getting married makes *sense*. Stephen is a good guy." I didn't point out that she'd practically insulted him a second ago when she'd insinuated we might be hiding our relationship from her. "He has a stable job at a hospital. More importantly, he has health care, and you don't. And I don't know how you're going to get another job anytime soon."

I felt my skin prickle. I'd already felt like shit after quitting my job, though Mom had, at the time, told me she'd supported my decision. She'd even offered to call Charles herself just to tell him off. But lately I couldn't shake the terrible thought that she supported me only when it suited her.

Was Mom really looking out for me? Or was she pushing me to marry Stephen because she didn't want people to know she'd let us live together in sin? The hypocrisy of it, too. All my life, Mom had strict conditions for the kind of guy she wanted to marry, but now she was cool with me being with Stephen?

"What's your point?" I asked.

"If you married him, you wouldn't have to worry about health care."

"So you want me *to use him* for *health care*?"

"Yes. Yes, actually. I think you should." She huffed. "Have you even thought about what happens if you're truly sick? Or your hernia gets worse? You have money from the book contract, but what happens when that runs out? If you marry him, you'll have someone supporting you. Then you could focus on writing. It could be a—what's it called—a marriage of convenience."

"Or it's called using my best friend for health care."

"He'd do it, Farah. You know he'd do it for you."

"And that's the problem. He *would* do it." I wasn't certain if he still had feelings for me; we hadn't talked about it since college. But still. He would do it because he was Stephen, and this was how he showed up for me. He'd proved as much during Dad's illness. But this was *marriage* we were talking about, convenient or not. To ask him to marry me when I wasn't sure how I felt—what a horrible thing to put him through. "And I can't feel comfortable with taking advantage of him like that, only to toss him when I don't need him anymore."

Mom let out a weary breath.

"Don't be dramatic. Just talk to him about it, that's all I ask."

Except it felt cruel to even ask him. I relied on Stephen too much. My family had already taken advantage of Stephen's kindness. Asking for more felt like pure greed.

But Stephen and my friendship had always operated on 100 percent honesty, never hiding anything. The good. The bad. The ugly. If he found out I'd had that conversation with Mom and never told him, he'd be hurt.

"Mom wants us to get married," I blurted.

We'd been sitting on the couch together. We'd been watching reruns of *The Office*, but I couldn't focus. I kept replaying that conversation with Mom over and over, until finally it burst.

Stephen looked at me.

"That's . . . random. Did she finally give up on trying to set up an arranged marriage?"

"I don't know. In short, she wants us married so I have health care."

We fell silent.

I slumped over on the couch, burying myself deeper in my hoodie. This whole situation was my fault. If I'd just put up with Charles, I could have still had a job and my own health care. I wouldn't need to talk to Stephen about something like *this*.

"How messed up is that, though? You know how many people actually get married for health care?" I said, changing the subject. "I swear to God, this country is—"

"I'll do it," he said, resolute.

"You'll— Wait." I sat up. "No. *No.*"

"Why not?"

"Because it's not an option. I wasn't asking you. I was simply *telling* you—and this is important—about a *ridiculous, absurd* idea my mom had, in which you were supposed to respond with *Ha ha, that's so funny,* and then we'd laugh about it and move on with our lives. This isn't something I told you because I wanted you to *actually consider it.*"

"Again, why the hell not?"

I let out a breath. "Okay, in normal circumstances, I would say that's the most unromantic way to respond to a question about marriage. But we *cannot marry for health care.* Do you know how dystopian that sounds?"

"Here's the way I see it," Stephen responded calmly. "I'm in a situation where I can help. And I am asking you, as someone who loves you, to use me. I *want* to help. I want—" He took a breath. "Look, it's really not a big deal. There will be no strings attached, no pressure. We can just do a legal marriage, put it to paper. Nothing will have to change. And down the road, when we need to end it, we can. Just like that."

He made it sound so simple. I could be overthinking it (it wouldn't be the first time). We were adults, two consenting adults, who could define marriage as whatever we wanted.

But this also felt too important *not* to completely think through. There was the issue of his parents, for one thing. What would they say to their son entering a deeply inconvenient marriage of convenience? Or what if, down the road, Stephen grew to resent me for it?

God, I couldn't *bear* the thought.

"But this is *marriage* we're talking about! What happens if you meet someone you actually want to marry? How are you going to explain this?"

How many times had I wondered why Stephen never dated anyone, and how many times had he sidestepped? It almost felt like a waste. He was cute, very cute. He could *pull*, if he wanted. But when I'd encouraged him, back in Portland, to create an account on a dating app, he deleted the app off his phone two hours later. He didn't feel the need to date anyone, he'd explained with a shrug, and left it at that.

But if, in the future, he met someone he actually fell in love with, but was trapped in a marriage of convenience . . .

I didn't want to be the reason why it wouldn't work out for him.

"I don't have to explain myself to anyone," he said. "And I wouldn't need to explain it."

"What do you mean you wouldn't *need*—"

"You know I've always loved you. Right?"

The room went still.

My eyes prickled. Since Dad's diagnosis, I'd made it a point to say *I love you* more to my friends, to my brother. That included Stephen, too: almost every conversation we had ended with a casual, unconditional *I love you*. I meant it, with a deep, rich affection. But for now I strongly suspected that the love we felt for each other took on different shapes; my love for Stephen was still frustratingly amorphous and unclear to me.

Stephen's love, though—this was proof, as good as any, that his was the real deal. There were no empty words with him. He'd shown me, again and again, how much he cared for me. He seemingly had an endless capacity for it.

Of *course* I knew he loved me, damn it. And that was why this was so painful. I wanted only the best for him. And I—I couldn't entangle him, *drag* him any deeper into my messy life more than I already had.

When I didn't respond, Stephen went on softly.

"If this is how I can help you, then this is what I want. I'm *happy* to finally have the chance. And at the end of the day, marriage—it's just paper. If the only thing holding you back is that you're worried about me, then this is me telling you it's okay. You wouldn't be forcing me into anything. The only thing that matters is what *you* want to do."

He looked at me, familiar eyes alight in shades of warm, rich brown. But there was an intensity there I didn't know—a silent, tender promise he'd kept hidden from me so well, for so long. I felt my face flush.

In our little apartment in New York City, the world stood still, suspended in a delicate balance between friendship and something deeper, unnamed. Unexplored. Feelings that had been idling in my heart flickered with life.

God, he always did this. Made sure I never put my own feelings second. He was too good, too kind. I needed to figure out how I felt about him. I owed that to him, and myself.

I knew that his quiet tenderness cloaked me like a warm blanket. I felt safest with him. I felt affection for him, ripe and bursting. Being with him felt like home, tasted like chamomile tea, comforting and familiar. I wanted him close. I wanted to see him happy, to make him stop doubting himself. I wanted him to see himself the way I did. I wanted for nothing else. "You swear?" I asked, finally. "You swear you're truly okay with this? Zero reservations?"

"I swear." Stephen smiled. "But seriously, no pressure either way. Let this just be an option on the table."

In other words, he was offering himself—his life—as the option on the table. To take or leave, as I saw fit.

I bit my lip. The more this feeling in my chest threatened to spill, the more frustrated I felt. None of it made any sense. Why would he do this? Who in their right mind would agree to something so stupid? Worse, why was I stupid enough to consider it? Was it because I felt vulnerable and alone, still mourning Dad's loss?

Or was there something deeper here?

I wanted to know. But I was also afraid to find out.

"I'll think about it some more," I answered, looking away.

༄

Mom's sudden desire for a name change was the first sign of a coming storm.

"Mom bought a G-Wagon," Shaz reported during our weekly catch-up call.

"I'm assuming that's a car?"

"It's a very expensive car. She got it used, but still."

"Weird time to buy a new car," I said. "What was wrong with the MDX?"

"She said she'd dealt with it for six years and that it was a 'Mom car.' Apparently the G-Wagon was always a dream of hers."

The last time I'd visited home, she'd been showing off several new pairs of designer shoes she'd bought ("These are Manolo Blahniks—I wish you could afford a pair of your own!") and a vintage Chanel necklace. As much as I believed a woman grieving should be allowed to indulge in luxuries, it felt a little harsh to rely on money she'd inherited from Dad, then scold Shaz for not working, or tell me to marry Stephen so I could afford to see a doctor.

"We need to stop spoiling your brother," Mom had told me over the phone just days earlier. "He needs to get a real job—he's twenty-two already! He can get a job, get his own apartment. I don't understand why he has no drive."

"He has *depression*," I retorted. "He's already making great progress, but things are delicate. I don't think we should push him to do anything right now. He needs time."

"I can't put my life on pause. I want to sell the house. I want to travel to Europe. I can't do that if Shaz is like this."

"Sell the house?" If Mom sold the house, where would Shaz go? He was still taking classes at the nearby community college. "You can't just spring that on him. Later, maybe, but not now. It hasn't even been a year since Dad died."

Mom let out an exasperated breath, but said nothing.

The more Dad's absence sank in, the more Mom grew erratic, clinging to the freedoms and vanities and vices she'd been denied all her life. For once she was allowed to make mistakes, and she made those mistakes in the name of independence. She was becoming her own person. But in doing so, she seemed to regress to a young teen told to watch over the house while her parents were gone.

She'd even pulled away from her own family. *They don't understand,* she'd told me. She even cut off several of her closest friends, including Nyla.

She also still hadn't shown us Dad's will. *It's not like you need the money right now, anyway,* she'd said, when asked, then changed the subject.

❧

Sometimes I felt like Mom didn't view my brother and me as our own people.

I'm sure she wasn't the only parent to think this about their children. She didn't really see us as fully realized beings, with thoughts and agency of our own—her children were an extension of herself: all her unrealized ambitions and aspirations, given a second chance in a new form. *Her* second chance. And if we were simply tools for her to use, control, possess, and manipulate as she saw fit, it was her right. She said it herself right after I was born: now she had something totally her own.

Mom named me Farah—"joy"—in hopes that I would be such for her.

But in the darkest pits of my mind, I don't think I ever made her happy. I don't think I could.

And now, disappointed by both her children, Mom was pushing us away. She was becoming someone I no longer recognized. I came home one weekend for a visit and found a lighter, plus several bottles of alcohol under her sink—most of them open, half-empty. Sometimes she'd come to the basement, where my brother and I would be playing video games, and fling out-of-the-blue insults about how *boring* we were, how *pathetic* it was that we never went out. Shaz and I would stare at each other, baffled.

In the meantime, Mom, despite the advice of me, Nyla, and her own sisters, had decided to move forward with investing in the gym with Anthony and Malik as business partners. Anything they asked for, she'd give, reveling in the feeling of being needed: "I give them money, they make a gym for the community—it's practically charity!"

When I told Stephen, he ran his hands down his face. "I'm not a fan of talking badly about our parents, but . . . I don't think your mom knows how charity works."

"No."

Stephen hugged me tightly. "I'm so sorry," he said. He had seen it firsthand, my mom's two sides. I'd watched, my whole life, people adore my mom and her infectious friendliness—the mom other kids wished they had.

The mom I'd so desperately wished would follow us home.

But with Stephen, someone else knew. Someone else saw what my brother and I did.

❧

My therapist had me try a little exercise, and it made me realize how, lately, the voice inside my head was a mimicry of my mother's. So often I spoke to myself as she spoke to me: jagged words and sharp rebukes. I'd look in the mirror and focus only on my flaws. Even my compliments were conditional. I'd tell my reflection that even if she looked nice that day, tomorrow she'd have new pimples and lose more hair and grow more bloated, so what did today's prettiness matter? My own inner voice filled my head with reminders I would never be good enough, that I wasn't worthy of love.

But what if, my therapist said, I was face-to-face with my younger self? What if I'd traveled to the past, to my bedroom in my child-hood home in Kennett Square, and met my seventeen-year-old self, the insecure, brokenhearted girl who'd begun starving herself in hopes she might see in her reflection a body she actually liked? Would I tell her she wasn't worthy of love? Or would I embrace her tightly and tell her to stop being a crybaby, to go eat a peanut-butter-and-jelly sandwich or cake or whatever else she secretly wanted to eat, and that the key—the *key* to everything that would make her happy again—is in books? In *stories*.

In the sanctity of my therapist's office, I'd imagine all of this. Except I'd also imagine Stephen, as I know him now, standing guard outside my childhood bedroom door as my two selves caught up. Probably making a corny joke so bad, the two of us would laugh.

Stephen and I were legally married at the city clerk's office in New York City. Shaz acted as our witness. I wore a wrinkled sundress from H&M I found in the back of my closet. Stephen wore his best button-down and trousers, none of which fit him well. It was a sweltering day in July, and we arrived in the clerk's office sweaty and exhausted. When it came time to kiss the bride, Stephen and I stared at each other, embarrassed. Finally, he kissed my cheek so tenderly my blood began to rush.

Afterward, the three of us went to a nearby Japanese café, laughed, and ate matcha ice cream like nothing had happened.

"In my mind," Stephen told me the night before, "marriage is a partnership. And it feels—I don't know, it feels like we've been partners for years."

"Yeah," I replied. "It really does."

CHAPTER 27

Your Hand, a Doorway

"Hypothetically," said Mom on the phone, "if I wanted to get remarried—what would you think?"

I was stunned into silence. Dad had been dead for ten months.

I hadn't said anything when she began drinking and dabbling in pot, when she disappeared at night to go to parties in New York City with Zaina and Usman, when she came home with a black eye. This time, though—this time, I had to say something.

"Farah?"

"Hypothetically?" I answered. "I hate it."

"Wow, that's a strong word."

"Who are you even thinking about marrying?" I asked.

"Again, it's hypothetical—"

"Bullshit. No one brings up hypotheticals unless they're thinking about something. So *who* are you thinking about marrying?"

"Zaina and Usman introduced me to a man named Joe," said Mom stiffly. "He's been helping me around the house. I want you to meet him."

"Zaina and Usman—the people you *party* with? Did you meet him at one of these parties?"

I'd met Zaina and Usman only once or twice before, when Mom had brought them to her house on the weekends I was visiting, but they hardly seemed interested in talking to me. Zaina, especially, treated me coldly. As for the parties, I didn't know much about them, either—it seemed like they were big dance parties at venues throughout the city. One of them was the Roaring Twenties–themed dance party that Mom had attended in her blue sequined dress soon after Dad had died.

"Stop. It was just a few times," Mom snapped. "And yes, but, he's not—"

"And you've been bringing this guy to our *house?*" Had Shaz seen him? I'd have to check in, make sure he was okay.

As Mom told me more about Joe, my desire to scream grew tenfold.

Mom had been seeing Joe for several months. He'd been in jail for years but had since become sober. He had a YouTube channel (which I later checked) where he went on rants about the government and also wellness, for some reason. He was not Muslim, but he'd "probably convert" for her. Also, he did not have a job.

Growing up, how many times had she yelled at me for even talking to a boy? All those lectures about how I had to marry the perfect Muslim guy or else she'd disown me? And now here she was, dating a guy named *Joe.*

"But he's seen the house, so he knows *you* have money," I said. "He's looking for an easy payday, and you're it."

"He's not like that! He's a good person, Farah. God, it's not healthy to be so suspicious of everyone. You can't *judge* people like that."

"Dad told me to look out for you, and this is exactly one of those times," I replied. "You cannot marry this guy. I can guarantee you, he wants your money. And even if on the off chance he doesn't, it's not healthy to jump into a whole new relationship with some guy you barely know so soon after your *husband died.*"

"Then what do you want from me, Farah?!" she yelled. "What the hell do you want from me?"

"I want you to act like a mom! To go to therapy and mourn in a healthy way! To, I don't know, give a shit about your kids!"

"That's not fair." Mom was crying. "That's cruel, even for you. You and your brother aren't children anymore. I am my own person, too. I *deserve* to have a life of my own!"

"Have you put any thought into how this would affect *us*?" I begged.

"I thought you would be happy for me!"

The profound, perhaps inevitable realization that your parents are just people—with flaws and imperfections—feels like mourning. The mom I'd hoped for—the mom I was so certain would appear if I was just a good enough daughter—was gone. That the same hands meant to raise me with love and care were also so easily capable of choking me the moment I didn't do as prescribed.

For so long it'd felt like the child in me had been screaming for her mother, only to be met with silence. For so long she'd made me feel like I didn't deserve her love.

But the reverse held true; if Mom was just a person, then maybe she didn't deserve my love, either.

Mom was a stranger.

"I'm *done*," I said, my voice grating through my throat, and hung up.

I called Shaz later that night. Shaz had, in fact, known that Joe visited the house, but he'd fled to the basement and locked himself down there to avoid meeting him. Later, in the same breath that she'd guilted Shaz for not being able to find a job, she'd told him she'd bought plane tickets for her and Joe to Quebec; she'd even paid for his hotel room since he couldn't afford it.

I'd never forgive her.

On the bright side, Mom had seemed to pick up on the fact that I never wanted to talk to her again and had thrown herself into the launch of her gym—which meant, for now, she was leaving me alone.

"Geez," I said, sighing. "How— God, how are you holding up?"

"I've sort of been more indifferent about her than usual," my brother answered, calm. "But I've been more responsible about my life now than I have been in the last few years. Eating healthy, and working out consistently. I'm staying in classes and doing well. I'm considering maybe becoming a therapist or something."

It was almost funny how the more our mom stopped acting like a mom, the more it forced us to grow up, to be more responsible and independent.

My eyes watered.

For the rest of our phone call, my brother and I talked about Kisa and Stella, about his friends on his Discord channel, about the new song he'd composed on the piano. "For some reason I've been listening to Carly Rae Jepsen's 'Boy Problems' on repeat," he'd told me, and I laughed at the randomness of it.

Even if our family was fractured now, we had each other. We had our own support systems.

And, by God, that was good enough for me.

My relationship with Stephen changed after we got married.

I began noticing little things about him I'd genuinely never noticed before: the way his tongue would flick his teeth whenever he was deep in thought, his smell that, for reasons I couldn't fathom, put me in an intoxicated stupor. His attentiveness, which I felt I didn't deserve.

Even our shoes, side by side at the doorway, made an unnamed warmth bloom in my chest.

Sometimes I'd catch Stephen humming the tune to the titular song in an old Bollywood film, *Kuch Kuch Hota Hai*. A story, funnily enough, about two best friends in college who, many years later, would find each other again and fall in love. I'd made him watch it in college. He'd never seen a Bollywood film before.

Eight years later, here he was: humming that song while standing over the kitchen stove. And I'd smile, watching him.

We'd known each other for so long.

Stephen was with me at all my doctors' appointments. Something in me would shudder when I'd hear him introduce himself: *Oh, I'm her husband.* He'd distract me as a nurse stuck a needle in my arm to draw blood. Helped answer any questions I had about my test results when my mind felt bursting at the seams.

My hair loss and muscle weakness, the doctors concluded, was, in fact, very likely because of trauma and stress.

"Trauma?" I asked my doctor, blankly.

"You'd be surprised," my doctor replied, "at what loss can do to a body. And you, clearly, have been through it." A pause. "Unfortunately, there's a chance your hair won't recover to the way it was."

Ah.

"Well, who needs hair, anyway?" I replied, trying not to cry.

"What do you need? What can I do?" Stephen would ask on those difficult nights, the ones when I mourned Dad, mourned my dismantled family. If I couldn't answer, he'd take the initiative and bring me food, rub my back. I was always holding back—my tears, my feelings, my anger with Mom and even God—and Stephen would remind me I didn't have to, not with him. My fury was eating me alive, a feeling so soul-shatteringly lonely, but Stephen provided an escape. He'd offer anything and everything if he thought it would make me feel better, and slowly, selfishly, I wanted to take it all. I couldn't recognize love, even if it was hiding in plain sight, and yet here he was, loving me when I was still struggling to love myself.

He'd become the throughline in the turbulence in my life. I didn't want to live without it.

It was all propinquity causing these new feelings, I told myself. Proximity and bonding through trauma. It would pass. One day, it would pass, and when everything settled, we'd have a peaceful divorce and move on with our lives. It wasn't exactly the life I'd imagined for myself growing up—getting married at twenty-five to the love of my life, a giant Pakistani wedding as our stage; being a high-powered wildlife attorney, a South Asian Erin Brockovich—but that ship had long sailed.

But still: What would loving him feel like? I wondered. What would it feel like, a love so soft and safe and warm in my palms, all earnest vulnerability? Like a baby bird cradled safely against my chest. A love you could release, knowing it would fly safely back to you in every scenario, in every universe.

Lately, I found myself wanting to try.

CHAPTER 28

The Day the Music Died

I got a text from my brother on a Thursday night; it was already nearly the end of September, and several months had passed since my legal marriage with Stephen. Since I'd cut Mom out of my life.

Shaz and I, though, continued to talk every other day; mostly to text each other memes and silly jokes, about upcoming video games we were excited about. Recently I'd surprised him by buying tickets to a *Kingdom Hearts*–themed orchestra performance in New York. I'd been a bawling mess beside him; *Kingdom Hearts* was the first game we'd ever played together.

I'd squeezed his hand when the song "Dearly Beloved" began to play, and he'd smiled.

Are you home? his text read.

Yeah, I'm at the apartment. Everything okay? I replied quickly.

Something felt wrong. I couldn't explain it, but my chest began to ache.

Hold on.

A minute later, he called.

"Hey!" I answered. I tried to sound as cheerful as I could. "What's up? You good?"

There was a sniffle on the other end.

My heart seized. "Shaz?"

"I'm really—" Another sniffle. "I'm not in a good place right now," said Shaz. He was crying. I'd *never* heard my brother cry, not like this.

"Oh. Oh, Shaz. What happened?"

Stephen, sensing something was off, sat beside me on the couch.

"Keith broke up with me."

I could feel the way his sobs racked his body. The anguish was like my own.

"Oh, sweetheart. I'm so sorry." I clutched my phone tight. My brother, in a sense, was the other man in the relationship, the interloper; Keith was already engaged.

But Keith had been stringing Shaz along, and Shaz had held on to false hope for years. He hadn't been prepared to be let go. To not be chosen.

"Hey, but you know what?" I asked. "I know it hurts right now. I know it sucks more than anything you've ever felt. But you are going to get through this. It's his loss, okay? You didn't do anything wrong." Hot tears flowed down my cheeks. "You did *nothing* wrong. And tomorrow you'll feel a little better. Every day, you're going to feel a little better, and this will just be some memory, a blip on the timeline of your life."

Shaz was quiet, but I could hear his breath, the wet inhales.

"We're going to get through this," I repeated, determined. "Tomorrow's Friday—you want to come here? We'll take you for a night on the town! Anything goes. Anything you fucking want, all weekend. Or I can come there and kidnap you. Okay?"

"I think . . . I think it'll be better if you came here," Shaz whispered.

"Sounds good." I pressed the phone harder against my cheek, willing him to feel it.

"I love you, little brother. I love you so much. And tomorrow's going to be amazing."

"I love you, too."

My heart hurt for him, but hearing him say *I love you* so earnestly—I found myself smiling through my tears.

We hung up, and Stephen handed me a tissue box.

"You want to go there now?" he asked.

"What? Really?" I looked at him, confused. "But you have work—"

"Yeah, but . . . I don't know. I'll take off. We should go to him. I'll drive." Stephen was already on his feet. "Go pack."

It was 10:00 p.m. I began to pack; twenty minutes later, we were ready to leave.

But then I got another text from Shaz.

I wasn't strong enough. I'm sorry, my dear sister.

The room spun. I nearly dropped my phone.

No. My panicked thoughts whorled in my brain. *No.* Don't you dare. Don't you dare leave me.

Shaz? I texted back, frantic.

Please call me.

Don't do anything, please.

Where are you?

A minute passed as Stephen and I stared at my phone screen. Still, Shaz didn't text back.

You are strong enough.

Shaz. Please. Pick up.

I chewed at my nails. Maybe nothing is wrong. But if Shaz was planning on doing what it sounded like he was doing—

"I'm calling the police," I told Stephen, already dialing 911.

I'd never called the police before. My heart was ramming in my chest, and I stumbled over my words—my throat felt so infuriatingly tight, dry—but I managed to explain what was happening to an operator, who then connected me with an officer in Shaz's area. He promised to put out an alert for his car; he'd begin looking for my brother right away.

I hung up. "I—I should text Mom."

Stephen nodded. "Call her."

I didn't want to hear her voice, but Stephen was right. Calling would be faster.

Mom picked up after three rings.

"I'm sorry, I—I don't know if I'm overreacting, but Shaz just sent me a cryptic text. Like he's"—I couldn't believe the words coming out of my mouth—"like he's going to kill himself."

Mom said nothing.

"I called the police already. Do you have any idea where he might be?"

"Well, I was in my room. I didn't know he'd left the house."

I bit back my irritation. Of course she didn't even know where he was.

"We need to find him," I said.

My mind could hardly keep up with all the possibilities of where Shaz could be—with questions all so bleak I could almost laugh.

If I wanted to narrow down his location, I had to think about how my brother might kill himself. It was a game, a riddle of the worst kind. It was the kind of bleak, fucked-up question you never wanted to consider: "If you had to kill yourself, how would you do it?"

Shaz wouldn't shoot himself. We didn't even have a gun.

It hit me then: cough syrup.

Like the fucking song. Hell, he'd practically told me.

"Check his debit card, then check with the local pharmacies," I told Mom. "Go to the CVS or something—he could be there. He might try to overdose on cough syrup or pills." Which meant if we found him in time—we could save him.

"I'll drive around," Mom said. "Maybe I can find his car."

I called the officer I'd spoken to earlier and gave him Mom's information; they'd talk to her as they investigated. The officer I'd reached had been helpful, like he actually cared. He'd sounded young, but he'd assured us he would do whatever he could.

"Pack for several nights, just in case," Stephen murmured at my side.

"Yeah," I said. I packed essentials: a toothbrush. Pj's. Underwear. Socks. Stella and Kisa's food. I was on autopilot. My brain had seemingly shut down.

Minutes later, Stephen and I, along with Stella and Kisa, were in our car and leaving New York City.

After a while, I found my voice again.

"I can't believe this is happening."

My body felt disconnected, like everything was a dream. Out of the corner of my eye, I could make out orange smears of highway lights rushing past us.

Stephen clamped my hand with his, a tether to something real.

⧉

Halfway through our drive, my phone began to vibrate.

"Mom?"

"They found him." Her voice on the other line was cold and metallic.

"And?"

"What do you think?" she spat.

My eyes filled. The world fell away. I tried to take deep breaths, but no air felt like enough.

"H-how?" I whimpered. *"Where?"*

"At a train station. Police found his car. You're coming here, right?"

A train station? "We should be there in an hour," I answered.

"I'll tell you everything when you get here." She hung up before I could ask anything else.

"He's gone," I told Stephen.

Stephen squeezed my hand, though I could barely feel it, and said nothing. Nothing he could say would help me.

Shuddering, I leaned back in the passenger seat.

This was real, I told myself. This was real.

My baby brother was gone, and now I was trapped in a world where he did not exist.

He was only twenty-two.

"I wanted him to stay," I sobbed, utterly breaking down, the kind of sobbing that rips you open from the inside and leaves scars on your bones. "He was supposed to *stay*."

CHAPTER 29

Dearly Beloved

They found his body—what remained of it—on the tracks at a nearby Amtrak station. Shaz had parked his car, walked to the train tracks, and lain down upon them.

The train, of course, didn't see him.

The police had footage. He'd already been at the train station when he'd called me. While I'd been frantically texting him, begging him to respond, he'd already been walking to the tracks.

That phone call, I realized later, wasn't a call for help. It had been my brother's goodbye.

In no world could I have imagined my brother capable of doing this to himself. In no world could I have imagined that his pain had been so immense that the idea of being run over by a fucking train—of the rattle of the tracks beneath him, of watching the train hurtling toward him—was less terrifying than the pain already inside him.

He'd chosen to end his life in a way that there would be zero chance of survival. He wanted to die, with 100 percent certainty. How could I ever be happy, knowing my brother had felt like that in his final moments?

Or maybe he *was* scared. Maybe in those final seconds, those final milliseconds, my baby brother was scared and alone and filled with regret.

I don't know which was worse.

It was late; by the time Stephen and I walked through the door of my family's house in Pennsylvania, it was nearly 1:00 a.m. Unlike the day Dad died, the house remained in a kind of stunned silence. Barely anyone spoke a word.

My mom's sister Amber arrived from Buffalo a few hours after we did. A scattering of my mom's friends came, sat with her on the couch in the living room.

Everything was a blur.

"Get some sleep," Mom commanded, while Stephen and I stood in the kitchen awkwardly. "There's nothing we can do now, anyway."

Stephen and I walked to my bedroom in a daze; he refused to leave my side. I curled up on my childhood bed, while Stephen grabbed a futon from a closet and slept on the floor.

Stephen left in the early afternoon to pick up my cousin Shaan, Amber's eldest son, from the airport. Shaan had been the one I'd lived with during my clerkship at the DOJ; he was my brother's age, and the two of them had been close. He hugged me firmly that day. The rest of Mom's family filed in one by one, and we spent the day talking about Shaz—favorite memories, favorite stories—and tried not to break from the reality of the situation.

Muslim burials happen fast, usually within three days; according to Islamic tradition, it was important to respect the body of the dead and allow it to be placed back into the earth as quickly as possible. There was talk of an autopsy. There was talk of how a proper autopsy would be impossible.

Silently, I was trying to make sense of my brother's death. When he'd told my mom his therapist wasn't helping, Mom had refused to find another, because this therapist was the only one who'd agreed to tell her the details of their sessions.

When I told her that was an extreme breach of confidentiality, Mom answered it was her right. She was his mom.

Shaz was bisexual in a community that found him, and the way he loved, taboo. It wasn't everyone, of course; there were those who, secretly, saw no harm or business in modulating who others like my brother loved, especially among the younger generation. But it was a support mostly unspoken. After all, even the topic was controversial enough to get people's hackles raised.

Sometimes I wondered if people used religion as an excuse to ignore the humanity of others, and instead reduce them to their sins.

The only meaningful support system my brother had gotten was on a Discord channel, filled with kids his age just as lost as he was.

Later that day I'd gotten panicked text messages from an unknown number. It was Keith; in the night, he'd gotten several messages from my brother but hadn't been able to contact him. He'd even attempted to call 911. Since then, their Discord channel had erupted into chaos.

I called him and told him what happened.

For a while Keith was silent.

"It feels like," he said slowly, "the curtains have just drawn on a play, and I'm waiting for the actors to come out, but—but the curtains aren't opening, and there's no applause, no actors." There was a sob. "God, this really is happening, isn't it?"

We talked for hours, only to realize that half of what Keith knew about my brother had been made up. Shaz told Keith he lived in Portland. He was part of a band, where he played piano. He had a college degree, a stable job. He had a dog named Stella. My brother had created a fictional double life, a persona, where he was and had everything he ever wanted. Everything he felt he should have been.

It shattered me.

"It always felt like he had one foot out the door," Keith choked through tears. "Now I know why."

✵

"We really need to stop meeting like this," said Maha gently as she walked into my bedroom.

I let out a wet laugh.

By the evening, the community had descended upon our house to give their condolences, food, and any support they could. It was crowded, with people huddled in corners, praying over Quran paras—smaller sections of the Quran.

Stephen and I remained holed up in my room. I couldn't bear to be around Mom, to hear her talking about how this was *a mother's worst nightmare*, how *the pain of losing a child was unbearable*. I couldn't help but think about how we hadn't been talking for the past few months. How that night she hadn't known Shaz had left the house.

The house quickly became, as Maha had put it, a "circus." Shameen aunty had returned, wailing even louder at the news of Shaz's death than she had at Dad's; we could all hear her through my bedroom door all over again. I was struck with a terrible sense of déjà vu.

"Oh, shit." I looked at Maha. "If Shameen aunty's here, you don't think Amina—"

But before I could finish, two girls—a pair of sisters named Eman and Zoya—burst into the room. I knew them from Sunday school; they'd been in Shaz's class and were several years younger than me. I liked them. Even Shaz had said they were kind. The last time I'd seen them, though, they'd been much tinier.

That was the strange magic about Sunday school, about the Muslim community. All the kids in the community, for better or worse, would grow up together and see each other every weekend for years. And collectively we'd experienced the feeling of being the children of immigrants, of the frustrations and traumas of straddling both a South Asian and American identity, of trying to find your own way to, or out of, one's faith. It was one big dysfunctional family.

Still, so many of us looked out for each other, even if we didn't truly know each other.

"Amina's here, and she's trying to see you," Eman, the elder sister, informed me. "She's already talking to your cousin—Shaan, I think?— to figure out where you are. He was trying not to laugh."

No one, I was learning, was a fan of Amina.

"This is a weird suggestion, but do you want to get out of the house?" Eman asked. "Get some food or something?"

"We're basically here to kidnap you," her sister Zoya added.

"Take her to the grocery store to get some snacks," suggested Maha. "I bet she hasn't eaten anything today."

The nearest grocery store was the one my brother and I would go to together. Going to the grocery store the day after he'd died felt absurd.

"Go," said Stephen next to me. "Get whatever you want. Hopefully by the time you get back, the chaos will have died down a little." He blinked. "Poor choice of words, but you get it."

Just then my bedroom door flung open, revealing Amina. Her eyes darted around the room, searching. Her gaze landed on me. Part of me wondered if she was about to tell me Shaz should have prayed his depression away.

Eman grabbed my arm and dragged me out, Zoya trailing behind us.

"We're going to the grocery store!" she announced as we passed a confused Amina and a very amused Maha.

❦

The janazah prayer and funeral were no better.

Kareem's parents had shown up, and Kareem's dad had been wearing designer sunglasses that he refused to take off even inside the mosque. At some point he'd approached Mom, demanding to know why she hadn't told him about Shaz's depression and all the hardships our family had been facing since Dad's death. He could have helped, he insisted—he was a respected physician, after all—and that by not reaching out, it was clear my mom didn't "value" his "voice."

Mom informed him that she didn't make it a point to call everyone in the community to tell them about Shaz's mental health. If anything, why didn't *he* reach out? Kareem's dad didn't like that; he stormed off to leave the funeral, but not before yelling that his red Maserati had been blocked by other people's cars (one of which was the hearse).

"Now I think we know why Kareem is the way he is," Maha had said.

It was an overture to the chaos to come. At the burial, when Shameen aunty began sobbing all over again and falling over my mom, it was Kareem's mom who, thankfully, picked her up off the floor and dragged her away.

Unlike Dad's body, which had been wrapped in white cloth, Shaz was kept in a biodegradable box the size of a small child; Stephen helped carry it to the grave.

It was so light, he whispered brokenly once he'd come back to my side. I held his hand, desperately trying, and failing, not to think about the implications of that tiny box.

After the imam finished the prayer and we made our duas for Shaz's soul, I approached his grave and grabbed a handful of dirt.

I'm burying my brother, I told myself. If I said it enough, maybe I could convince myself this was happening.

This is my brother's grave.

This is real.

This is real.

This is fucking real.

One of my favorite passages in the Quran comes from a surah—a chapter—called "Surah Ash-Sharh" (The Relief). It reads, *So surely with hardship comes ease. Verily, with hardship comes ease.*

Where, though, was my ease?

Something in me snapped. I bit back a laugh. This was absurd. Everything was absurd! We'd just buried my dad, and here we all were again, like no time had passed at all! This was so absurd, it was almost funny. Chopin, too—Shaz's favorite classical musician—had had a tragic end; he'd played piano to distract himself from the pain of illness, until he died at thirty-nine.

The tears wouldn't stop.

We watched in silence as the funeral home's little yellow excavator finished the job, barely covering the grave with scoops of wet earth. I wondered if it was the same one that had buried Dad.

I took a breath.

"You always did love pancakes, huh, Shaz?" I muttered softly, so only Stephen could hear.

Stephen stared at me in disbelief. But it was true: my brother had eaten pancakes for breakfast almost every day. And then for Shaz to have died by a train when he'd loved toy trains when he was little—it was another absurdity, a sick joke. I remembered when Dad had bought Shaz a model train set for his sixth birthday; we'd played with it for hours. And years later, while I was in law school, Shaz had even sent me a video of someone playing *Skyrim*, a popular fantasy video game, but they'd modded all the dragons to look like Thomas the Tank Engine. We'd cackled about it together.

"You really died the way you would've wanted to live," I went on, "getting pegged by a train."

This time Stephen snorted.

I was sobbing. I was laughing. Like my body couldn't decide on the appropriate reaction to seeing my baby brother buried, so instead it was firing on all cylinders, resulting in the most bizarre, indecent rites of death ever spoken.

"I know you wanted to lose weight, Shaz, but there are easier ways to do it," I concluded, my voice breaking.

"Jesus." Stephen nudged me with his shoulder, but he was covering his mouth with his hand.

An aunty I didn't recognize glanced back at us disapprovingly.

But I didn't care. She didn't know me, didn't know Shaz. I wasn't talking to her. This wasn't even directed at Stephen.

I looked up at the sky.

And I swear, for a moment, I could feel Shaz laughing, too.

❧

As people dispersed from the grave site, Mom stood by my side.

"You know people are saying we're cursed?" she said darkly.

Looking at the freshly churned earth before us—two mounds now—I found myself believing they were right.

❧

A few days later, Stephen and I went to the police station to pick up Shaz's car and phone.

My hand shook, and I plugged my brother's phone into his car radio, the way we'd done whenever we wanted to listen to his playlists. I increased the volume on the dial, opened his iTunes app.

Since news of his death, a single question had been haunting me: What was the last song he'd ever listened to? Now I'd finally know.

The song that played was a familiar one. It was called "Always in My Head."

A Coldplay song. The band that had inspired him to play piano. A band we'd both listened to on repeat when we were kids, sitting in the back seat of our parents' car.

The same band that had ushered him away from me.

CHAPTER 30

It Is What It Is

The week after the funeral, and with Mom's okay, I wrote a long Facebook post about my brother: about the importance of open discourse on Muslim queerness, on homophobia in the community, on the feeling of shame and stigma that people, like Shaz, carry through their lives. I even included a link to the Trevor Project for people to donate in his name. It wasn't meant as a big gesture of community callout, but an invitation for dialogue. If we didn't talk about the topics that made us uncomfortable, I wrote, then we'd continue to isolate those who needed someone to talk to.

The post wasn't much. It wasn't enough. But at least if it started a conversation—if it made people feel a little less alone—then it was something. And if not now, when? If not us, who?

Mom later received several angry phone calls, including from her two sisters and mother, my nani.

"They said you're dishonoring Shaz by telling everyone he was gay," Mom said, scrolling through her texts. "But they're also mad we didn't tell them he was gay? I don't know. Either way, they never want to talk to us again."

"So we're not supposed to talk about the stigma of being gay now that Shaz is dead," I replied slowly, "but we were supposed to out him while he was alive? To them? Am I understanding correctly?"

"Correct."

"Cool."

But the next day I was flooded with messages from distant relatives, from cousins I hadn't spoken to in years, from kids in the Muslim community. People who'd read the post and were offering support. Who'd confessed to knowing kids just like Shaz.

"I got a call from an aunty in the community saying she and her kids had a long talk about all this," said Mom, tired. "It's the only comfort I've got."

Shaz's death, it seemed, had created ripples.

But it also meant that other people I'd long avoided had also begun to reach out.

"Guess who I just got a text from?" Mom said, smirking like someone who'd sunk their teeth into a juicy bit of gossip.

My stomach clenched. "Who?"

"Kareem."

"Oh."

I stared down at my feet, at the patterns in the rug.

"Don't you want to know what he said?"

"Not particularly."

That night, apparently, they'd even talked on the phone; Kareem had heard about Shaz through his parents and wanted to give his condolences. He lived somewhere on the West Coast now and worked—I'd laughed at this—as a psychiatrist.

"He did say that the fact Shaz felt the need to invent a whole double life speaks volumes about the pain he felt. I thought that was pretty apt."

I said nothing. Stephen wasn't in the room with us; I wondered if that was why Mom had chosen the moment to discuss Kareem with me.

"He also says he just wants you to be happy. I think he wanted you to know."

I was caught in a torrent of emotions, suspended between the past and present. In some ways, life had molded me to be strong, but I still had an eggshell heart; Kareem's seemingly sincere well-wishes struck a tender chord in my childhood self. The tiniest part of me yearned to believe he really meant it. I couldn't forgive him for what he'd done, of course. I never would.

How like him it was to try to insert himself into my life now. But where old me would be bothered, I no longer cared. His well-wishes had come far too late, anyway.

"Kareem's grown up, it seems like," Mom said, heading to her bedroom. "You all have."

"Some of us more than others," I muttered.

※

When the dust had settled, about a month after Shaz's funeral, I moved to an apartment in Philadelphia. The apartment was on the top floor of a building in Old City, across from a church; the floors creaked beneath my feet, as if they hadn't been changed since the 1800s. They probably hadn't. The ceiling, though, was the best part. The people who'd renovated the building had left the enormous spoke and wheel of an 1850s grain elevator, which hung in the center of the living room area. You could even see where the floor had been changed and painted over just beneath it.

The rent was, thankfully, cheap.

I should be close to Mom, I reasoned once I'd made the decision. *Just in case.* I could hardly afford my share of the rent for the New York City apartment, anyway.

I was still angry at Mom about Shaz. About everything she'd done. I'd even gotten a phone call from Nyla, Mom's old friend, to commiserate about Mom's behavior. *It's why I pulled away,* she said. *I even told her—I told her she needed to be watching over Shaz. Make him food, spend time with him. But she just kept saying he wasn't a child anymore.* She sighed. *I don't know what else I should have done.*

But surely, I convinced myself, Shaz's death would change things. Now Mom and I could grieve and repair the damage and live our lives, slowly but surely. My therapist and I had spent hours talking about narcissistic parents: how they desire to be the center of attention, how they see their children as mere extensions of themselves. The gaslighting and blaming. The moment he'd described the traits of a narcissistic mother, it was like all the pieces, all the questions of my life, came together.

"In her mind, your mom could very well love you, in her own way," my therapist had said. "But many narcissists or those with narcissistic tendencies are often—not always, but often—unequipped with the language to show it in a healthy way. Love, or even healthy conflict, is a skill she hasn't quite learned."

I wondered if he was right. Sometimes I felt Mom wanted to love, and be loved. But she didn't know how. Instead of having the deep heart-to-heart conversations I craved, instead of taking my suggestion to commit to a therapist, Mom would dangle her affections in the form of money. *If you decide to move out of New York and live closer, I'll help you with your rent,* she offered out of the blue. *Then you can focus on writing, right?*

That's really nice of you, I replied—even if part of me wondered if her offer to pay rent was something she'd start telling other people over the phone like she always did, a public sign of how much she loved her daughter.

But there'd been this one magical moment we'd shared a few days after Shaz's funeral, where things between us had felt normal. Good, even. We'd been sitting in the kitchen together, talking about Shaz's piano, when a red-tailed hawk landed just outside the window only a few feet away from us. Mesmerized, we stared. The hawk, perched on the ledge of the deck, stared back at us, head tilted.

"Shaz . . . ?" my mom and I asked aloud at the same time.

We looked at each other, then burst out laughing. It felt like the first time I'd laughed in forever. Lately, if I found myself smiling, I'd hear a voice remind me that death was always lingering in the shadows, just waiting to pounce again. That it was just a matter of time. If I laughed about something, I'd think about my brother, who couldn't.

"So you thought it, too!" Mom choked through her laughter. "You know if Shaz were reborn, he'd come back as a bird. And I swear, it *looks* like him."

I wiped my eyes, wet with tears. "It really does!"

We watched the bird—its beautiful honey-gold gaze, the gorgeous, mottled pattern of its feathers—until it eventually flew off.

I wanted so badly to believe things could change for Mom and me. We shared memories. We shared loss.

Maybe now we could share more, the way a mother and daughter could.

❧

Stephen understood my decision to move. *Philadelphia's just a train ride away,* he'd assured me. He'd come visit often. And in the meantime—if I wanted, if I felt comfortable with it—he would search for jobs in Philadelphia.

I remembered the way he'd looked, hesitatingly hopeful, but not quite daring. He wasn't sure what I'd say, but here he was, being *vulnerable.*

"Of course I'd want you to," I replied. I'd lived with Stephen for the past two years. I didn't want to come home and not see his shoes in the doorway. I didn't want to go grocery shopping without him on weekends, or not bicker over the best way to pack the dishwasher.

And when he finally moved to Philadelphia, maybe—

Maybe it was time to talk about the future, to give a name to this strange dance we'd been doing for nearly nine years.

Until then I'd keep working on my book. The book-packaging company and my publisher had given me a month off from writing. I'd obviously need time to mourn, to be with family, the head of the packaging company told me over the phone.

But I was teetering on the edge of losing myself entirely. Writing was the only thing I felt I had to hold on to.

If I didn't have writing, I was afraid to imagine what else I could do.

⁂

"I'm signing up for a Reiki class," Mom informed me one weekend. A criminally *expensive* Reiki class that would require her to go on a retreat to Arizona, but a Reiki class, she said, that would be a *great* experience for her.

"Wow. First a skydiving class, and now this?"

Mom had come to stay with me for a day; we'd been sitting on the couch while I worked on my manuscript. Next to me, Mom looked through the gym financials on her laptop. I hadn't asked her how the gym was doing. In truth, I didn't want to know.

Mom shrugged, smiling. "Life is short. Oh, I forgot to tell you. Next week I'm going to a basketball game. We're seeing the 76ers. Not that I know anything about basketball."

"We?"

"Zaina and Usman. Their idea." She looked away. "And Joe."

"Joe? Joe? You're still seeing him?" I stared, dumbfounded. "What is this, a double *date*?"

"Oh, stop. It doesn't mean anything. We're all just friends."

"Weren't you telling me you were considering marrying this guy a few months ago?" I laughed darkly. "Come on, who are you fooling?"

Mom glared. "I should have known you'd act like this, so closed-minded. You still haven't even met him. You know he wanted to come to Shaz's funeral? But we knew you'd be like this. How can you—"

"He literally has a video on YouTube that sounds like a fucking manifesto!" I felt like I was yelling into the void. "You ever ask him why he has a shaved head? You ever ask him how he feels about Trump? And you wanted him to come to Shaz's funeral?!"

After my mom and I had fought about him, Stephen and I found Joe's channel on YouTube and watched one of his videos together in stunned silence. He'd made a rambling video about wanting to start a nonprofit for veterans—a video posted not long after he'd met my very charitable Mom, which I would bet was no coincidence.

This is the guy your mom wants to marry? Stephen had asked afterward. *Is he even a veteran?*

As far as we could tell, he was not.

"You're being unfair," Mom said. "You can't judge him based on one video!" my mom said.

"I'm *never* going to like him," I spat. "Okay? *Never.* I don't have to. I just—I don't understand how you can't see he's just using you. You paid for the Quebec trip, using *Dad's* money. Let me guess, you're paying for the basketball tickets, too? What else are you buying for him?"

It was as if she believed love was something that could be bought. Like the gym investment and the trip to Quebec—if she just kept throwing money at people, she could surround herself with those who would adore her the way she wanted.

"This is *my* life! You have no right to judge me!" Mom yelled, her face reddening. "I've done so much for you kids, and the *one time* I ask you to be happy for me—"

"YOUR SON JUST DIED," I screamed.

I couldn't believe it. Shaz's death hadn't slowed her down. If anything, it fueled her, made her believe that now, more than ever, she deserved to do whatever she pleased. Even if it meant hurting the only daughter she had left.

"I think it would be best for us both," I said, shaking, "if you left."

I'd never raised my voice like that at her. Never asked her to leave before, never set boundaries for myself.

But if I didn't do it, I knew I'd regret it for the rest of my life.

I put my laptop down on my coffee table and got to my feet.

"Just go. *Please.*"

Mom gave me a final disappointed look. Packed up her things.

And a few minutes later, she was gone.

CHAPTER 31

Creature of Doubt

I threw myself into writing.

It was the middle of the night when I finished the first draft of *I Hope You Get This Message*. It was late into the night when I typed THE END and lay down on the floor, feeling like I hadn't slept in years.

My first-ever book. I'd finally done it. I'd written an entire book.

But I didn't feel satisfied. Writing, I'd told Jeremy, was pain—it didn't come naturally to me, and sometimes every word felt like a tooth pulled. The satisfaction came when I'd reread what I wrote. Clumsy as my writing was, I loved seeing how the ideas that were once in my head had come alive on the page.

I'd never written a book before, but this—this felt wrong. The story wasn't coming together, and the characters I'd spent the past three hundred pages with were still total strangers.

I waited a week when Abby, the head of the book-packaging company and a well-known author in her own right, called me.

"So here's the thing," she said, sighing, "we've decided on a different direction for the book."

"What?"

"The draft itself is okay—your writing is good," she went on, "but plot wise, something's not clicking, and that's mostly on us. We're going to have to make some major changes."

"So what? What does that mean?" I asked.

"Bluntly? On our end, we're going to deconstruct the plot and make those fixes. We need to give the characters more concrete goals. We need to make sure the book ends on this big message of hope. But it means you'll have to rewrite the book, basically from scratch."

I swallowed. "Ah."

"This isn't a bad thing, though," Abby assured me. "It'll only make the book better. This is your debut novel—you want it to be good, and you want to feel good about it.

"And I can promise you, once we make the right changes, you *are* going to feel good about this book. The rewrite might even go by faster than the first time."

I took a deep breath, trying to stay calm.

I knew she was right. I'd hoped it was all in my head, but the more I wrote, the more I knew that something in the book was off. Still, though. The news of a rewrite had gouged out the remaining determination I had left.

We spent the rest of the phone call brainstorming fixes, which Abby wrote down to bring back to the rest of the team. One of the characters would now search across the country to find his lost sister before the world ended; another character would devise a scheme to steal money to save his house, but would find a love that would make him question his own morals. We made good progress. Good changes.

"Take a week off to clear your head," Abby instructed once we'd reached a good stopping point. "I'll reach out to you again once we have something, so all you have to do is hang tight."

"Okay," I replied, hollow.

We hung up, and I stared at my monitor.

It was going to be fine, I told myself. Lots of authors have to do rewrites. It wasn't the end.

You have to be strong now, okay? The words of my dad's cousin came to me then.

I was so tired of having to be. Dad was gone. Shaz was gone. For all intents, my own mother had abandoned me for people she thought were friends. And God—God was nowhere to be seen.

This book was all I had now, the only reason why I could wake up in the morning. But because of the rewrites, that same book would be delayed by almost two years. What if they decided it wasn't working and scrapped it altogether? What if it took me too long to rewrite, and my publisher didn't want it anymore? What if the book never saw the light of day?

It felt like my dream was dying. It felt like it'd already died. I wanted to write stories that would move people's hearts. But when it mattered more than anything else in the world, my words weren't enough.

So what was the point?

What was the point of anything?

Ah. This was more than ennui. This was what my brother was talking about. Maybe this was a taste of what my brother had felt.

Suddenly I became enveloped by a pain so great I could no longer feel my body, like every nerve had been set on fire. Since I'd gotten that text from Shaz, every day had felt like a long, silent scream, but now—

I suppose I should have felt lucky, honored to have called myself his sister, if even for a short while. But in those dark and lonely nights when I missed him more than I could bear, I found myself wishing Shaz had never existed, just so I wouldn't feel the pain of having lost him.

Yes, the decision came calmly, serenely, *I could end it all.* It was a simple matter of fact. I would end my life, and then the pain would finally be over, and then—I could see Shaz again.

Suicide is one of the biggest sins you can commit in Islam. But if I ended my life, at least Shaz and I would end up in the same place. Before we burned for all eternity, I could tell him I was sorry I couldn't save him. That I was his big sister, and I was supposed to protect him, even from himself, and I'd *failed.*

It was late, and my apartment was quiet. Peaceful. Kisa was sleeping on a chair somewhere, oblivious. Stella sat on a nearby couch, eyes half-shut. In the back of my head, I felt a brief flicker of guilt: Kisa and Stella would be alone with my body, but someone would find them. I filled their food bowls to spilling so they wouldn't go hungry.

As for Stephen—

The thought of Stephen made my head go blank, like it was trying to protect me from its emotional weight.

Slowly I walked to my coat closet, where I kept a toolbox, and pulled out a silver box cutter. I knelt on the rug in the center of my apartment, beneath the giant metal wheel embedded in the ceiling, and brought the blade to my wrist.

I'm so sorry. The apology came unbidden in my mind, though I'm not sure who it was directed at. Everyone, maybe. No one.

But as the blade began to sink into my skin, the sound of laughter woke me from the fugue state I was in.

Old City was a popular tourist destination, and on weekends, the streets were packed with families, with groups of friends, enjoying a night on the town. Though my apartment was on a tiny cobblestone alleyway off the main road, it seemed a group of young, drunken college boys had decided to use the alleyway as a shortcut.

Their laughter boomed, a loud, throaty *guffawing* that had completely ruined the dark intensity I was feeling.

My eyebrow twitched.

Excuse me, I'm trying to DIE over here! I thought indignantly. *Could you BE anymore disrespectful?!?!*

Furious, I got to my feet and stormed over to the window. The group of boys were loitering outside my apartment building, clad in white-and-green Eagles jerseys. Was some big football game happening? I swear I could smell the alcohol wafting off them all the way from there. One of the boys said something, and the group erupted in guffaws all over again.

Do I yell at them? I thought. *Tell them to keep it down so I can end my life in peace?* I *refused* to pass to the sound of a bunch of fucking frat boys having a good time!

Slowly, as if waking up from a bad dream, I felt my eyes flutter: the thought was so absurd, the laughter escaped my lips before I could even process what was happening.

I laughed, a stomach-clenching laugh that had me doubled over.

Stupid! How stupid! I was being dramatic and stupid. This whole thing was stupid! It was just a fucking *book*. Things sucked, but if I died now, there really would be no point to anything.

I needed to live. Deep down, I wanted to live. I wanted to live a life full of memories. I wanted more people to meet and befriend, more people to love, until my soul was filled to the brim with the love I kept for them. I wanted more books to read and escape into, more laughs to share, and more songs to hear—*someone* had to stay alive. So why not me?

And despite it all, I wanted to write. Write until I'd made sense of everything and found something in the world worth living for.

And one day, when I did die—I'd have a hundred stories to tell Shaz.

I threw the box cutter back in the toolbox. Gave Stella, who'd fallen asleep on the couch, a hug.

And sank into the chair in front of my computer.

꩜

A few days later, the Eagles won the Super Bowl, and the city blew up with life, with *euphoria*—like the world itself was telling me I'd made the right choice.

CHAPTER 32

The Thing with Feathers

It was the tail end of winter.

The months that followed my suicide attempt felt like driving in a beloved beat-up car, and you're soaring down the highway in June with the top down, and the wind is messing up your hair, but it's fine because you're on your way home to eat buttery-rich cake and watch silly movies with your friends and—

Right now you're singing with those same friends in the back seat to an old Tracy Chapman song on the radio, and even though you're usually shy about not knowing all the lyrics or being able to hit the right notes, your voices blend together just right, and it sounds so perfect, and it tastes like summer vacation on your tongue, and it's so damn good to be with them, in that moment.

With my mom out of my life, a great weight had finally been plucked off my chest, and I could move. So I did.

Kaya, my best friend from college, and I reconnected again; after years teaching in Japan, she was now living in New York City. She came over to my apartment in Old City, and we'd spent the evening playing video games like no time had passed. We settled, instantly, into a wonderfully comfortable, unfettered companionship where we could tell each other everything.

"My brother loved *Breath of the Wild*," I'd told her after an hour into the game. She gave me a sad look, but said nothing. Her eyes said everything. It was all I needed.

Stephen, too, was pleased Kaya had returned. They'd met several times in college, and seeing them getting along now made my heart soar, buoyed by the sheer glee of witnessing the comforting proximity between two people I loved so much.

At least once a week, we'd play co-op video games while on the phone. We'd talk, the three of us, for hours about the events of the week, our plans for the weekend. About nothing and everything, including my recent doctor's appointment for IBS symptoms, where I had to do a fecal test.

"I think the truest sign of friendship," I announced once, in the middle of a video game we'd been playing together, "is being able to openly discuss how many poops you've taken that day."

"That's disgusting," replied Kaya. "The answer is two."

"Three for me!"

"Literally no one asked you, *Stephen*."

"Wow, okay, *Kaya*."

And I'd wheeze with laughter, feeling happier than I'd ever felt in years.

❧

Maha came to visit once to tell me a piece of exciting news.

"We're trying for a baby," she said, smiling shyly. "Inshallah."

"Holy shit! Holy shit!" I sat in a daze. I had to remind myself that we weren't in college anymore: that we were both nearly twenty-eight years old, and Maha was well into a residency program. This was a perfectly normal age for people to start having babies. For as long as I'd known her, Maha had always said she wanted to have kids—a big, loving family, as she'd put it.

"Maha!" I hugged her close. "You're going to be such a great mom. Inshallah."

Inshallah: If Allah wills it. I wasn't sure what my relationship with God was, if I even had one anymore. But for Maha, I'd pray.

She smiled. "You know, if you had a baby, our kids could grow up together. Be friends."

I laughed softly.

"Yeah," I answered. "But I don't know. I'm not exactly in a great headspace to care for another person."

I did love kids. To help make ends meet, I'd even taken on a part-time job as a substitute teacher. Usually I'd get a phone call around six in the morning from a staffing company asking if I could fill in, and an hour later I'd be rushing out the door to a nearby Philadelphia public school. It was hell, but it gave me the chance to feel like a part of the community and help kids find new ways to learn.

But I was terrified about having picked up trauma from Mom, from internalizing an unhealthy way to care for my own child. I didn't want to perpetuate the cycle. The safest thing, I decided, was to not have kids at all.

"Plus, after everything that's happened, I kind of want to focus on me for a while. I've never even been on a vacation; the last I went on was in college, when Shaz and I went with Dad to Italy on his business trip, and all we really did was sit in the hotel."

"Okay, that's fair," said Maha, "that's *very* fair."

A comfortable silence settled between us.

"For what it's worth, though," Maha added, "I think you'd be a great mom."

I smirked. "I'll be the weird, quirky aunty you can drop your kids off with."

"Oh, God, no. They're never going to want to come home."

⁂

I started taking voice-over classes. I'd always been interested in acting—I'd gone to a summer acting camp in middle school and been in a couple of plays in high school—but Mom never let me do more for fear it would affect my grades.

Stephen had told me he liked my voice: *You know that time I called you for the class project to coordinate a meeting time? That phone call was what did me in. It was your voice.*

It was freeing, doing something unrelated to my writing. I loved being able to step in the shoes of another character, to experience a completely different physicality and emotion. If being me was too hard one day, for a short while, I could pretend to be someone else.

I'd also started rewriting my book, and this time, it felt easier—fueled, I think, by how voraciously I'd begun to read. I'd spent what money I could on new books across all genres, staying up late into the night reading. At Odyssey, we'd learned about the necessity of filling one's "creative well" from which to draw from, and that was exactly what I did. For inspiration, I even kept Rebecca's debut novel, *The Poppy War*, which had just been published, right by my computer.

If I wasn't reading for pleasure, I was researching satellite and radio communication. I was beyond giddy when the senior astronomer at the US-based organization searching for extraterrestrial intelligence graciously agreed to talk me through possible ways human–alien communication could work for my book.

"I'll have to read your book when it comes out," he said kindly. "Next year, you said?"

"Yep! Next year."

My smile was wide. It made me feel like a real author.

∽

What I didn't know was that Mom had begun having trouble walking. The change seemingly happened overnight; one day she'd been able to do push-ups and squats, and the next she couldn't balance on a single foot without toppling over.

It was like she had the legs of a fawn.

At first she thought her weakness was the result of overtraining; since befriending Malik and Anthony, she was at the gym six days a week, exercising for almost two hours. She took a week off, then another. Still, her legs were painfully tense.

We'd had nothing but radio silence between us for several weeks after our argument about Joe. She'd tried calling Stephen, tried to convince him to get me to talk to her again—to meet Joe. When Stephen offered to meet him first, Mom said *Never mind* and gave up trying.

But about a month after my twenty-eighth birthday, the texts about her health began coming in more frequently. Something was wrong, she said. Doctors suspected she might have multiple sclerosis; they'd already done blood work, even done an MRI that revealed a few brain lesions, but it didn't explain her sudden muscle weakness. When they did a spinal tap, they found nothing strange. Soon she'd see an endocrinologist.

It was just a matter of ruling things out.

We didn't discuss the fight. Instead, I began spending more time talking to Maha about possibilities, in a desperate rush to figure out what could be wrong. I began learning about all sorts of neurological diseases. Myasthenia gravis. Guillain-Barré syndrome. Alzheimer's.

None of it made sense. Why was this happening to Mom? Our theories became more and more ridiculous the fewer answers we got: Could Mom have contracted some weird virus? She'd apparently been traveling a lot, even swam in Puerto Rico. Was it the drugs she'd been dabbling in alongside Zaina and Usman? Was it all some wild side effect of unprocessed trauma?

Or were we really cursed?

I bought my mom a cane to use for walking. "It'll help put less stress on your muscles," I explained. Mom didn't want to use it, though. Using it felt too much like admitting defeat, she said. She didn't need a cane yet; her legs just needed time.

Except as time passed, it wasn't just her legs: soon, even her hand grip started failing her, and she had trouble opening bottles or jars. Her throat, too, always felt tight and dry; her voice had taken on a strange gravelly texture, like she had a bad cold.

Then one day, on June 28, I got a phone call from Malik. I picked up immediately, worried. Malik and I rarely spoke.

His voice shook as he explained he was with Mom at the Hospital of the University of Pennsylvania. The doctors had finally given her a diagnosis.

She had ALS.

CHAPTER 33

Murphy's Law and Other Truths

The next day Stephen and I had a long phone conversation with my mom to help plan her treatment.

Stephen, as usual, was incredibly helpful. He looked into dozens of ALS clinical trials, talked to several doctors and researchers who ran ALS clinics. She wouldn't have to lift a finger; Stephen would coordinate everything. It wasn't a cure, but some of the clinical trials seemed to slow the symptoms of ALS.

A week later, though, Mom wanted him to hold off. Several family members had told her that she should see a Lyme disease specialist instead; one of those family members had said just because Mom had gotten a negative result for Lyme disease didn't mean she was fully clear. And her symptoms were synonymous with Lyme disease, not just ALS.

Stephen was quiet when I told him. "It's not a bad idea, but . . ."

"You get the feeling that everyone's in denial and just grasping at straws?"

"Yeah."

But by the time Mom got back from the Lyme disease specialist, the denial had fully set in. She'd gotten another negative test result—and yet both the specialist and several of her relatives had still given her false hope that she wasn't dying. After all, it just made no sense—Dad and

Shaz had already passed. It was simply impossible. How could God give Mom a fatal disease after everything she'd already endured?

"I need to start living a more holistic lifestyle," she told us. "You know how many chemicals there are in the water we drink? The mercury, the arsenic? I could have lead poisoning."

"Have you talked with your doctors about this?" I asked. "Maybe you could get tested—"

"I can't trust doctors. They're all in bed with Big Pharma." Her lip quivered. "Those doctors don't care. They just look at me like I'm *dying*."

"Mom," I said gently, "the doctors aren't meant to give you the news you want. They're supposed to give you the news that's—that's *there*."

"You don't understand what it's like to be in my shoes right now. You don't understand what it's like to face death." Tears leaked down Mom's face. She was so scared. The fabric of reality had begun fraying at its edges, and Mom was powerless to stop it.

For so long I'd watched my mom treat her own life, for better or worse, as immortal. Impervious and infallible. Sometimes I had dreams where she died after trying something I'd told her not to do. In one dream she'd stolen my brother's bike and rode it down a hill; when I'd begged her to stop, she flew over the handlebars. In another dream she'd walked across the highway before I could pull her back.

And in my darkest, most horrible moments, secretly, I think I wished she'd disappear—if only to get a taste of the true consequences she was so certain would never touch her. But God, not like this. No one deserved this.

"It's *my* body, damn it," said Mom, her tone final, "so I get to decide the next course of action. You don't have to like it."

Mom had spent hundreds of dollars on vitamins and supplements, geared mostly for Lyme disease patients. She was already planning several other Reiki retreats—three, she'd said, all around the country. She'd also signed up with a personal naturopath who would work on "detoxifying her blood." Mom also found a doctor in Narberth who would inject her with stem cells; when Stephen looked him up, we learned that the doctor's license had been suspended.

Whenever I offered to accompany her on those appointments, she told me she had her "own people" to take her.

I told Stephen and Maha everything.

"But one of the clinical trials I'd sent her would have given her those injections for free! And they're actual ALS *specialists* at Harvard— with proper medical licenses!" Stephen said, frustrated.

"Do you want me to talk to her?" Maha offered. I'd been calling her every week, mostly to rant about all the strange treatments Mom was doing instead of seeing her medical team at Penn.

"God, no," I said, sighing. "It will only stress you out. Can you just come over instead? It'd be good to see you."

"Deal."

❧

Mom, meanwhile, had decided to finally sell the family house and move out. She'd already begun looking into new town houses, and had sold a majority of our furniture. Shaz's piano was, according to her, safely in storage somewhere.

Even Dad's garden, I'd noticed ruefully, had become overrun with weeds. I couldn't help thinking about how he'd walked me through the year before he'd died, telling me how he'd had plans to expand the garden, how he wanted to add trees to provide more shade. *I could read in the garden,* he'd said.

Now the house they were supposed to spend the rest of their lives in—the house I was supposed to be visiting every year for the holidays—would be occupied by some other family.

It was time to move on, whether I liked it or not.

But maybe, Mom suggested, once she'd sold the house, Stephen and I could live with her in her new place.

"First, you and Stephen should have a proper nikah."

"Where's this coming from?" I asked, thunderstruck. A nikah meant a real marriage ceremony, not just a legal one.

"Before I die, I need to make sure you guys are properly married in the eyes of Allah. Your dad would be upset otherwise. We can get the Sunday school to write up the nikah marriage certificate. Shaan can do the ceremony, since he knows Arabic and—"

"Hold on—"

"We can just do it at the house and save money. All you'd have to do is pick a date."

It was unfair for her to expect us to have a wedding just because she wanted it. Shaz had promised to play piano on my wedding day. The thought of being married without him there felt like fingernails on the walls of my stomach. And Dad wouldn't even be there to walk me down the aisle, to lead the dua that would bless our marriage. It didn't feel right without them.

I'd always wanted a small, intimate wedding, but a wedding now would feel like a horrible reminder of what we'd lost. Mom was too sick for the big, fancy wedding she'd used to want for me, anyway.

"I know she means well, but I don't really like that she's pressuring you," Stephen later told me. "Pretty sure, historically, being pressured into a marriage never ends well."

"Hard not to feel pressured when it's her dying wish," I muttered.

"True. But it's your life. You have to do what's best for you."

"Right. The thing is . . ."

I'd like to marry you, the thought came unbidden.

It'd always been Stephen, hadn't it?

We'd spent the past month job searching for him, and Stephen had been offered a job as a research coordinator at nearby Jefferson Hospital—the same hospital where my dad had been a pathology fellow, newly emigrated from Pakistan—just so I wouldn't be alone in dealing with Mom's diagnosis.

If it wasn't for Stephen, I'd have felt so alone through all of this.

One of my dad's sisters—Fouzia, the one who'd lived with Mom and Dad soon after they'd married—had recently called me to remind me to pray for Mom. My dad's side of the family had been coordinating reading sections of the Quran together to invoke blessings from God on Mom's behalf.

Sometimes I feel like I can't even call myself Muslim anymore, I'd confided in Stephen afterward, drowning in shame. *Sometimes I feel like I'm so angry at God, I can't even pray.*

There's a hadith, a saying, in Islam that "a time of patience will come to people in which adhering to one's religion is like grasping a hot coal." But those days, I felt that God had burned my hand, my arm, my whole heart, in a way I'd never recover.

Stephen ran his fingers through my hair. *It's understandable to feel that way,* he'd said. *Of course you'd feel that way after everything. But I think faith is never easy. That's why it's faith. You can always ease back into it when you're ready. For now, just focus on being a good person; the rest will follow.*

His words freed me.

Stephen, more than anyone, knew how much sadness I held behind my teeth. Anytime I put pressure on myself, anytime I told myself I wasn't good enough or couldn't do enough, there was Stephen, bringing me ease. Unlike Kareem or Yusuf, Stephen hadn't been looking for a woman to care for his needs first and foremost. For reasons beyond me, he'd only ever been looking and waiting for me. And those many kindnesses he had shown me throughout the years didn't come with the expectation I'd love him in return. His love would *never* be conditional. It never had been.

"Would you be against it?" I asked. "The nikah."

"You know I wouldn't. I *want* to marry you. I'll marry you a dozen times. But it's up to you, boss. It's always up to you."

I smiled and looked at the person in front of me with a clarity I hadn't felt for as long as I could remember.

I'd waited a lifetime for the feeling that filled me then: a wonderful, euphoric combination of gratitude and longing and nervousness and shameless want, want, *want*. I loved him. I so obviously did, even when I hadn't recognized it. Where there'd been uncertainty in my life, there'd been Stephen, dusting it all away. Where there'd been chaos, Stephen had been my rock. If strife came our way, we'd work through it together—he'd always proved as much.

It'd be dishonest to say our love was perfect (no love is, as bell hooks would say); we still argued over inconsequential things, like the occasional dishes lying around, laundry left in the dryer. But we'd always work it out with respect and kindness. We'd seen each other's flaws and put in the effort, had the difficult conversations to work through our own egos. Together we'd cry and forgive and be vulnerable. We'd grown, even if sometimes the growing pains hurt. But at the end of the day, we wanted the same thing: for each other to be happy. To make each other happy.

We were better together; it was as simple as that. If we got married properly this time—this time, I'd be in it. Fully and utterly and completely.

Verily, with hardship comes ease.

"Let's do it," I said. "I want to marry you, too."

❧

We held the nikah ceremony on September 1, 2018. We'd ended up telling only about twenty of our closest friends and family, including Amber, Mom's sister, and my cousins Shaan and Alina. Stephen's parents would be flying in from Florida, adorably thrilled that this wedding was finally happening.

Nani Jan didn't come. More to the point, I didn't want her to. Not only because she had so vehemently been against me talking publicly about Shaz's bisexuality, but because she—surprise, surprise—disapproved of Stephen. The reason? According to Mom, it was simple: he was Black.

"And his mom is South Indian, right? Uff," she'd complained in Urdu to Mom over the phone. "Their children are going to be so dark. What will people say?"

How very like her to have complaints despite having cut me off for the past year. Never mind that I didn't *want* children. Never mind the blatant, bigoted colorism of it all.

Mom had attempted to explain that yes, Stephen was a Muslim, and no one should question it—and that, maybe, could she not be racist about it? etc., etc., none of which pacified Nani's complaints, so Mom gave up trying to persuade her to see reason. Which, in my opinion, was a hopeless endeavor from the start.

"Damn. It's almost impressive that she can just say things like that with her full chest," said Stephen when I told him; I'd seen this coming, but still, he was far calmer about it than I.

"I'm sorry," I replied, sighing bitterly.

Her absence was a good thing, though. The nikah was lovely.

Maha was one of the first to arrive; she found me struggling to do my hair in the bathroom, and quickly smoothed it into something respectable. The long skirt I'd originally planned to wear fit too loosely—I'd lost weight from stress—so I settled for a cream-colored shalwar kameez that Nyla had gifted me a few years prior.

I half stumbled down the stairs, my new heels from DSW pinching my toes, and walked into the living room. My cousin Alina—Shaan's younger sister—had decorated the room with fairy lights and pink ribbon. A friend I'd grown up with at Sunday school, Madiha, gave Stephen and me traditional South Asian garlands made of roses and jasmine to wear around our necks.

The ceremony itself was short. Stephen and I sat at the front of the room by a beautiful display of flowers and lights made by Alina. Stella, our dog, sat in the middle. Shaan made a short speech about what marriage meant in Islam, how a small wedding surrounded by friends and family was Sunna.

There was beauty, he'd said, in simplicity. One only needed to look here, in this room, to see it firsthand.

Afterward, when everyone else had dispersed to grab food, I turned to Stephen.

"I'm going to slip into something more comfortable," I whispered conspiratorially. Five minutes later, after a bit of struggling to rip the shalwar kameez over my head, I was in pajamas. I loved having the excuse to wear such a lovely dress, of course—I couldn't remember the last time I'd dressed up—but I'd had my fill. I was exhausted. My feet hurt. As far as I was concerned, that was enough reason to be in my sleep clothes now.

When I'd come back down the stairs, I heard Maha laughing.

"There she is," said Stephen, wrapping his arms around me in a hug.

The doorbell rang just then, and I rushed to the door. It was Kaya; she'd donned a cute long skirt and held an intricately wrapped gift in her hands.

"Oh, shit," she said, looking me up and down. "Did I miss it?"

Behind me, Stephen and Maha were laughing all over again.

"Nah," I answered, smiling. "You're just in time."

Most of the wedding party piled ourselves in the basement, where we had one of the only pieces of furniture left—a giant L-shaped couch—and for the rest of the wedding, I played a video game while everyone watched. Unfortunately I'd never played the game before and had no idea it was an incredibly violent game. Nor did I know that it relied on speedy decision-making to avoid an untimely death. While I played, the rest of the wedding party would scream for me to choose something, anything. It was absurd. It was the strangest nikah I'd ever been to.

I was so glad we'd decided to hold it.

We were surrounded by people we loved—and not, this time, for a funeral. Mom looked more peaceful than she had in months. It reminded me of something I'd read in a book by bell hooks: "Rarely, if ever, are any of us healed in isolation. Healing is an act of communion." That was precisely what this wedding felt like: communion. Healing.

Wherever I'd go, I knew Stephen—and everyone else I loved— would make sure my house felt like a home. And despite everything, for the first time in so long, my family house felt like *home*.

Mom believed that love and happiness were a zero-sum game, that love was a finite resource to be earned from others. Others expect the best of love would swoop in and save them, like some big, dramatic storybook moment—like a knight in shining armor rescuing them in the nick of time. But even if Stephen's love had bolstered me in so many ways, so many times, I wasn't sure it was realistic to expect love to *save* you.

Love—maybe love simply sees you in a room when no one else does. Love was a pat on the head at the end of a hard day, a kind word of acknowledgment in a world so damn hard to live in.

Love was refuge. Love was comfort.

Love was *ease*.

And, sometimes, that was enough to hold on to.

CHAPTER 34

Solitary Places

Mom moved to an apartment closer to us in Philadelphia. I stayed with her most days; I'd bring my laptop and sit at her dining table to work on copyedits for *I Hope You Get This Message*. Thanks to Rebecca looking out for me and making the introductions, I spoke to a literary agent named Hannah, who agreed to represent me and help me get my writing career off the ground without a packager.

Focusing on my book, though, was another matter.

Mom needed help. A lot of help.

Everything she did took energy. Every task in her life became a series of equations. How much energy could she expel? What would be left? What could I add of my own energy to conserve hers?

Using the bathroom and washing up would drain her; even standing upright to wash her hands with soap took too much of her strength. She couldn't hold a toothbrush anymore. Wash her face. Her hair was full of tangles; brushing it was an impossible task. She struggled to make foods as simple as oatmeal or scrambled eggs because it required crossing the kitchen. What little strength and energy she had left, she had to use on breathing and leg exercises.

The independence she had finally gained and the vanity she had so coveted—even her *dignity*—had been stripped away.

The few bright spots we had to rely on were when she had visitors. Sometimes Nyla stopped by to drop off food she'd made herself, much of which she'd purée to ensure Mom could eat it. Sometimes she'd bring decorations—pretty jars or throw pillows—just to make Mom's apartment feel brighter, more welcoming.

I didn't like when Anthony and Malik stopped by, though. Several times when they'd come over, Mom would ask me to close her bedroom door, and I'd hear the three of them talking together in hushed tones.

Those days, Mom's unkindness would lash out.

Once, while Anthony and Mom were catching up, I'd excused myself to use the bathroom. By the time I'd returned, I found them laughing together.

"God, she pees so loud!" said Mom, covering her hand with her mouth.

"You pee like a fucking racehorse," added Anthony. "Just how bad did you have to go? Were you holding it in for days or something?"

This made Mom laugh harder.

I stood awkwardly, self-conscious. I didn't think I'd been peeing particularly *loud*, but I guess everything echoed in the apartment. What a strange thing, I'd thought, to pick on someone for.

It was moments like this that I realized no matter how much stronger I thought I'd become, how much better I'd become at standing up for myself, if I only spent enough time with Mom, I'd regress to my teenage self: passive and painfully unsure and desperate for a mother who'd accept me.

But when Anthony left, Mom went back to normal.

She'd tell me she was tired and her throat hurt, so we'd watch a movie, or old reruns of *Will & Grace* together. It reminded me of the times in high school when I'd come home and we'd watch TV together on the couch. Only now we'd watch in silence.

If I were lucky, and Mom had found another caretaker or nurse or friend she could pull, I was free to go home.

Eventually I'd collapse on the couch in the small row home Stephen and I now shared in Philadelphia, and scream into a pillow while Stephen—the ever-patient saint—waited for me to let it all out.

I wouldn't consider myself a particularly violent person—if pushed to anger, my go-to response was simply to cry, a lot—but lately Mom had been testing every ounce of patience I had.

"God, I swear—sometimes I want to punch her!" I'd say, squeezing my poor pillow-victim. "I know she's dying and she's my mom and she's the only family I have left, but GOD! Does that make me a bad person?"

"No," Stephen replied softly, running his fingers through my hair. "It just means you're a very, very tired person." He paused. "But if wanting to punch her becomes a recurring thing, then maybe it'd be a different story. Maybe."

❧

One of my mom's friends, Khulsoom—who was also very into Reiki—had helped Mom hire professional caretakers when she, Nyla, or I couldn't stay with her. The caretakers would keep her place tidy or make her breakfast. They'd clean her BiPAP machine, fluff her pillows, even wash her hair. Mom had begun having to stay in bed for so long that she was always at risk of bedsores; the caretakers, though, knew how to move her with ease to avoid them.

But Mom would dismiss them over the strangest things, then call me to care for her instead.

"This one lady who came, Shannon, was so nice, but I'm not. I can't fake it for more than half an hour," she said over the phone.

"You dismissed her because she was *nice*?"

"I don't know how to explain it. She was way too peppy, too chatty. *Like shut up,* you know what I mean?"

"Why don't you come stay with me for a few days?" I asked. "It'll give you a change of scenery."

"Maybe. I'd just need to figure out when; I have an appointment with a speech therapist later this week. For now, come over. I need help ordering groceries, anyway."

When I finally arrived, Mom also needed help with bathing.

She had a chair installed in her shower; she just needed someone to remove her clothes and help her get inside.

I nodded and helped her into her wheelchair, then guided her toward the bathroom. After I'd taken off her clothes—Mom only wore button-downs and oversize sweatpants those days—she let out a sad sigh.

Mom weighed little more than a hundred pounds; ALS had withered her once-strong body to bones, and there was no trace of the muscles that had once been the envy of the women in her life, the muscles she'd carved after hours every week at the gym. The ridges of her spine, a delicate, knife-sharp curve of thorns, jutted through her pale, blemish-free skin.

I tied her hair in a loose bun and turned on the water; when it was at a solid temperature, I carefully moved her to the chair. My hoodie grew damp; I should have removed it, I noted vaguely.

But I got to work. Using a washcloth, I lathered as much of her body as I felt comfortable with, in a clinical silence.

For a moment that could have been a tender, almost sacred memory for mother and daughter; the atmosphere was solemn.

Worse, I'd never felt more awkward in my life. This kind of intimate closeness between my mother and me had never existed before, and being thrust into this situation with her felt *incredibly* uncomfortable.

Mom seemed to feel the same.

"Your nickname used to be meow-billee, when you were a baby," she said. Her voice was half drowned out by the running water, and I had to strain to hear. "I just remembered. Your dad used to call you that."

"Oh yeah?" I didn't remember Mom ever calling me meow-billee. Since I'd been in middle school, she'd occasionally call me sweet pea, though—on good days when we didn't argue.

"You know what that means in Urdu? *Billee?*" she asked.

"Cat, right?"

Her head bobbed back a little. "I'm surprised you know."

Mom never taught me Urdu. She'd reasoned it was because I was born in America and I didn't need to know my mother tongue. But it felt like she'd done it purposefully to cut me off from Dad's family; most of them were far more fluent in Urdu than they were English. She'd denied me a connection to a part of our culture out of spite.

"You're still a meow-billee," she said, though I wasn't sure what she meant. "Just a silly little cat in a big, big world."

When I'd finished washing what I could, I grabbed some clean clothes for her, helped her get dry, and moved her back to her bed. I was grateful, then, that one of my coping methods for anxiety was exercise.

Mom was exhausted.

"You have to promise me not to let me turn into a vegetable, okay?" Mom begged me suddenly.

I knelt by her bed. Her bedside table, where one would expect a family photo or her wedding ring, had become a mess of pill bottles and tissue boxes; she couldn't control her mouth as well anymore, and sometimes she drooled. There was a tube of GenTeal Tears ointment for her eyes; lately she had trouble blinking or closing her eyes fully when she slept. There was Vaseline for her dry lips. An iPad so she could check her email, though lately, she'd been rarely using it. There was also the BiPAP machine, and a couple of bottles of distilled water.

I swallowed painfully. "Okay, Mom. I'll—I'll make sure."

"*Promise* me. I value my quality of life. You know I do. And I don't want to stay alive for the sake of staying alive."

She reached for my hand, though her fingers couldn't quite grip anymore.

"The moment I stop living, promise me, you'll make the decision that needs to be made."

My chest ached.

Mom wanted *me* to be the one to pull the plug. Another burden I was made to bear—the most excruciatingly heavy burden one could bear.

But I didn't want to make that decision. How could I make that decision? How was I, after everything, supposed to find the strength to honor her wishes?

And then to live the rest of my life with that guilt—

I couldn't believe we were even having this conversation.

Mom stared back at me, waiting.

Slowly, I nodded.

"I promise."

⁂

"I've made some changes to the will," Mom informed me one afternoon a few weeks later.

"All right," I replied, placid. I had never seen Dad's will, so I wasn't sure what to expect.

I'd been gearing up for a three-day trip to Utah, where I'd signed up for another writers' workshop. There I could finish the final edits for my book and begin brainstorming in earnest a new idea for my next novel, which I was stressed about. The book-packaging company I'd worked with had gotten in trouble when several of their employees came forward with allegations of gross mistreatment (a common occurrence in publishing, I was learning), among other things. Hannah, my agent, ended up renegotiating my book contract to finally make things more equitable, but it meant I was mostly on my own now.

On the bright side, the writers' workshop in Utah meant finally meeting my friends Marri and Kate, whom I'd found through Twitter when I'd first begun considering a future in writing during my 3L year. They'd encouraged me, in those early days, and I couldn't wait to see them face-to-face. And, selfishly, I also just wanted to get away from Mom, if even for a moment. I was with her nearly every day, prepping her meals, which had to be ground down to a paste, or helping her with her personal hygiene. I was at my breaking point.

But the timing of changing the will felt strange. Mom had told me months ago that her will was set. So what had brought this up? At this point Mom had finally accepted her ALS diagnosis; the Lyme disease treatment hadn't worked. In her own way, she was beginning to accept her impending death. Was that causing her to reevaluate the will?

Mom invited her lawyer to come to the apartment and talk me through the will, my future duties as executrix, and the breakdown of inheritance. In short, Mom would no longer pass everything to me. She wanted to donate most of her money to charity instead.

"That's fine," I'd said, "but do we know what charity? I just want to make sure it's legit."

"Your mom hasn't decided, but we'll be sure to fill that in once she makes her choice. Not everything in the will is set in stone just yet."

My eyebrows furrowed, but I said nothing. I'd learned it was better to stay quiet.

"Your mom will be giving you twenty thousand dollars."

I took a breath. It wasn't a wholly life-changing amount, but still: that was more than what I was getting under my current book contract with the book-packaging company. And if the rest was going to charity, I certainly couldn't complain.

"It'll be enough to take yourself on a very nice vacation," Mom chimed in. "Lord knows you're going to need a long vacation after all this. You and Stephen haven't even gone on a honeymoon."

She was right about that. I was twenty-eight and still hadn't taken myself on a single vacation. And with Mom's diagnosis, Stephen and I thought leaving for our honeymoon would just feel wrong.

"All right. Thanks."

"But Anthony and Malik are supposed to be paying me back a portion of the gym investment. Under our agreement, that money will go to you as a monthly stipend."

I glanced at Mom's lawyer, confused. "That's really nice, but the gym—it's not doing well. Right?"

The gym was complete and technically running, but Mom, Anthony, and Malik were struggling to find people to sign up for memberships. It didn't help that construction finished late; they'd aimed to open their doors in January, but it was already March, and most people had already signed up for yearly gym memberships. Anthony, according to Mom, was panicking. He'd heard rumors that a Planet Fitness was opening nearby. If they didn't draw in people soon, they'd be screwed.

Mom rolled her eyes. "Maybe the gym's not doing well *now*, but eventually! Businesses take time to grow. Give it at least five years."

"And all of this is written down in a contract somewhere?"

"It's not in a formal contract," Mom replied. "But you know them. They wouldn't lie."

Mom's lawyer's mouth clamped tight. Apparently she'd learned it was better to stay quiet, too.

CHAPTER 35

Take My Breath Away

The weeks that followed were a whirlwind of brief hospital visits. Mom had gotten a urinary catheter to help her use the bathroom; her bladder was failing. Though she was still alert and aware, she'd also completely lost her voice, and now relied on text messages and an app on her phone to communicate. Nor could she walk anymore, let alone stand. Her legs, her body, were slowly failing.

While I was in Utah—the day I'd arrived at the writing workshop— Mom began to experience a shortness of breath so debilitating, she couldn't eat or sleep. No matter how much breath she took, it never felt enough. Her nurse was certain it was because of her exhaustion and the stress on her body due to urinary retention. Or perhaps it was a panic attack; her body and entire way of life had so suddenly changed, it was sure to cause mental strain.

But as the day went on, it only got worse. She'd been with her nurse in her apartment when suddenly she'd begun seizing.

In the evening, when I'd sat down to work on my book edits, I got a phone call from Stephen.

"Your mom's in the ER. I'm here with her. I think—I think you have to fly back. I think this is it."

My throat went numb.

"What happened?"

"She had a seizure. She can't breathe on her own anymore, either. Doctors put her in an induced coma, and she's got an endotracheal tube to help with the breathing for now. They're going to need you when she wakes up."

I rushed back to my hotel room and explained the situation to Marri and Kate, who promised to let the workshop organizers know.

That night I took a red-eye flight back home.

By the time I'd reached the Penn Hospital ICU, Nani Jan had driven from Virginia and claimed the armchair in the corner of Mom's hospital room.

Stephen still had work, but he'd walked me through the labyrinth of patient rooms as soon as I'd arrived. He knew I didn't like hospitals. In the weeks before Dad's death, Shaz and I had spent hours during our visits sitting by Dad's side.

I hadn't seen Nani Jan since Shaz's funeral; the last Mom told me, Nani was still furious about the Facebook post I'd made.

"Asalamualaikum, Nani," I said. Dad had always instilled the importance of saying *salaam*, even to those you don't like.

"Walaikum asalaam," she replied stiffly, then left the room.

I looked at Stephen, who shrugged. "She's been pretty, uh, clammed up since she got here."

"Figures." I rubbed at my dry eyes. "Is anyone else here? I'm sure Mom would love to be with friends right now."

Nyla was at the hospital, but she was taking a phone call out in the hall. And Mom's sisters had arrived earlier that morning, but they were grabbing food in the hospital cafeteria.

We flagged the doctor, a younger, incredibly tall resident who explained the situation: Mom's breathing had gotten so bad they would have to keep the endotracheal tube in. Alternatively, they could install a tracheostomy tube, meaning they would make a hole in her throat and place the tube directly in her windpipe, which would be connected to a ventilator. It would be deeply uncomfortable, and recovery time would take at least a few weeks, but it could still be far better than the endotracheal tube—with the endotracheal tube, she couldn't even talk. With a trach, though, not only could she talk again, but she might—*might*—extend her life a little longer.

"How long do we have to decide? At least with the endotracheal tube, she still has a few more weeks, right?"

The doctor's face crumpled. "There's no way to tell. With ALS, it's—"

"Hard. Right."

Mom was no longer in a coma, but she was still dazed, half-asleep. Even if she were awake, knowing her, she wouldn't want to be. The endotracheal tube would make moving almost impossible.

She'd hate it.

"What about quality of life?" I asked. "Is there any guarantee her quality of life would be better with the trach?"

"Quality of life could be better, yes. But there's no guarantee that her body will be able to handle the procedure. Truthfully, I'm not certain her body could, and every day that passes . . ."

I bit my lip, hard.

Our options were to keep the endotracheal tube until she decided to go, but have a low quality of life, or get the trach that could eventually be more comfortable, but get a hole cut through her throat and risk a faster death.

Both options, I decided, sucked.

"When she's a little more awake, I'd suggest you all talk it out as a family. But if you can decide quickly, that would be preferable."

He looked at me and smiled sadly. "She's a very sweet lady, your mom."

Mom's hospital room quickly became a battle royal of opinions.

Nyla, Khulsoom, Zaina, and Usman were all Team No-Trach. The trach was too risky, and even if it extended her life by a few weeks, even a few months, having a hole in her throat could bring a dozen more possible complications to the fray, including potential infection; and with a trach, she'd also need a feeding tube. There were just too many uncertainties.

At one point even Maha stepped into the room to give her medical opinion, which matched the doctors': a trach, given Mom's current state, made no sense; it would put far too much stress on her already frail body. Even if it extended her life, Mom wouldn't have the autonomy she wanted.

So I agreed with Team No-Trach. It was perhaps the first time all of us had actually agreed on something. Mom had made me promise to put her quality of life above all else—to not keep her alive for the sake of staying alive—and now was that crucial moment.

We didn't say it, but we knew what it meant. It meant pulling out the endotracheal tube keeping her alive.

It meant letting her go.

Anthony and Malik had no opinion to share on the matter, but Anthony had done some research on his own, and he'd reported to us in the hospital room one afternoon that he'd found an ALS clinical trial called NurOwn that had shown promising results in slowing down neurodegeneration. To which Stephen had to inform him, through clenched teeth, that the NurOwn trial was the one he'd been trying to tell Mom to sign up for from the very beginning.

My aunt, Amber, was Team Whatever-Samia-Decided, which was both respectable and very on-brand for her. But my other aunt, mom's younger sister, and my nani had decided that a trach was the better option. Only a trach could prolong Mom's life now; to choose anything else, they'd claimed, was to *kill* her. We would be killing her! And this was a decision for *family* to make, anyway—even if, I thought quietly, it was my mom's friends who'd coordinated her care and been by her side the past few months.

Making matters worse, Mom was undecided on what she wanted to do, which meant that without her opinion, the opinions of others—close relatives, relatives I barely knew, community members—filled the tiny hospital room instead.

It'd been two days since I'd gotten back from Utah, and I still hadn't even had a chance to talk to her alone.

After a while of never-ending back-and-forth, Khulsoom and Nyla pulled me aside.

Khulsoom spoke first. "I hate to say this, but I don't think your aunts are thinking with straight heads. Amber means well, but your younger aunt—I don't know." She bit her lip in thought. "Okay, think of it this way. If your mom stays intubated for the next few days or weeks, it makes it far more difficult to take advantage of her, because she'll be stuck in the hospital, and you'll be with her. But if she survives the trach, she'll go home, and you won't always be around."

"What are you saying?"

"I'm saying I think there's a reason why some of your relatives want her to get the trach."

I looked away, unconvinced. This felt a little like conspiracy theory territory, but—could it be possible?

Maybe Khulsoom could tell I was doubtful, because she went on: "While you and your mom weren't speaking, she was staying in Virginia for a while with your younger aunt, right? Well, during that time, your aunt convinced your mom to give her thousands of dollars for a down payment for a new apartment in Virginia so she could live there close to them."

"What? Why?"

"You tell me. But after your mom put down the down payment, your younger aunt and her husband bought the apartment, and they were going to charge your mom *rent* to live there—knowing full well she wasn't healthy enough to live on her own. And, conveniently, when your mom came back to Philly, they never gave your mom that down payment money back."

My brain had gone blank, replaced instead by internal screaming.

Was it really true? This was absurd. Could my mom's own flesh and blood use her like that—and Mom didn't even tell me? It was *unbelievably* absurd, and yet . . .

"You can't trust anyone, jaani," Nyla added, "especially if money's involved. Not even us. And make sure you keep an eye on your mom's phone. She keeps blank checks in the back pocket, and you never know who might find them."

I needed to talk to Mom.

❧

Eventually—finally—everyone dispersed. I would stay another night at the hospital with Mom and sleep on the armchair in the corner of her room. Lack of sleep, though, was making everything look fuzzy, and sometimes I found my head rocking while I stood, like I was about to pass out.

And Mom—Mom was looking worse by the day. I hated seeing a giant tube in her mouth, hated how uncomfortable she looked. Only a year ago, she'd looked healthy and vibrant and strong. It wasn't right that things could change so drastically. It was terrifying.

The hospital was finally quiet. The silence was occasionally punctuated by the soft whispers of nurses outside the room, of beeping from Mom's heart monitor. A screen from a nearby computer illuminated the darkness. Mom liked the dark. It was easier on her eyes.

Because Mom was too weak to hold her phone to text, she relied on old-fashioned paper and pen to communicate. I used my phone to give her some light as she slowly wrote, her tiny hand trembling.

If I get extubated, what will you do?

"What do you mean?"

What are your plans?

My eyebrows furrowed. I honestly hadn't thought that far ahead. I hadn't thought about what life would look like after Mom died. Maybe part of me was still in denial, too.

"I don't know. Retire, maybe. Live in the woods."

Mom fluttered her eyes. She couldn't move her face the same way anymore, but she made subtle movements that told me how she felt. I knew she'd chuckle now, if she could.

I waited as she continued writing.

I want you to live in the forest. On a farm. With lots of animals.

And Stephen.

Her writing was so shaky, but I marveled at how she could still write, at the familiarity of her handwriting.

"Yeah?" I laughed softly. "I'll let him know."

Then I took a deep breath, readying myself. We needed to have the talk. This was our only chance; the longer I waited, the more tired she'd become.

But there was a knot in my chest, and the dull ache was suffocating. I should have been used to death by now, and yet I still couldn't shake off the fear of the unknown.

This was my mom. Regardless of everything—of how angry she made me, of how she'd hurt me over the years—she was the only family I had.

And yet the kindest thing I could do for her was tell her to leave me.

"So. The trach." I pulled a chair close to Mom's bed. "We need to talk about what you want to do."

Mom looked ahead, but I could see a muscle in her brow twitch. She knew this conversation was coming.

"You need to make a decision. I know it's hard. I can't even imagine—this is the biggest decision of your life. But if you don't make a choice, you might not have one. It's your life, right? What do you want to do?"

We talked for another half hour. We looked at videos of tracheostomies on YouTube. We read aloud an article from an ALS patient in hospice, and his experience with end-of-life care. We talked about her sisters and Nani Jan. We talked about Shaz, and how we missed him—how she might finally see him again.

"I know some doctors will let you listen to music while you—while you go," I said. "Is there any particular song you'd like to listen to tomorrow?"

Mom thought for a moment, then wrote down her answer.

Take My Breath Away by Berlin.

"Mom, I genuinely can't tell if you're joking."

Everyone would laugh though.

"I'm sure they would," I replied. "Damn, now I get where Shaz and I got our dark sense of humor from."

That night was the first time, I felt, that Mom had been fully honest with me about her life and the people in it. It was the first time we'd ever had a pleasant heart-to-heart conversation, and I wished—I'd wished this wasn't the last one. But at least she'd given me a good memory of her, one I could hold when she was gone: of Mom, acting like my mom, and not a fake version with the *Other* voice she used to keep up appearances.

The sun was peeking over the Philadelphia skyline when Mom told me her decision.

She didn't want the trach. She wanted the endotracheal tube removed, even if it meant she couldn't breathe. At least, she said, for a single, final minute, she'd be unassisted.

Mom wrote a list of whom she wanted to wash her body after she passed, per Islamic custom. Next, she wrote a list of whom she wanted to be at her bedside when she was extubated. I wrote out a text to everyone on her list, informing them that Mom had made her choice and to come back to the hospital whenever they could to say their goodbyes.

Mom chose to die on Monday, April 15, 2019.

Monday was not the worst day to die, I decided.

But it was still pretty fucking close.

❧

"Eat something, meri jaan," said Nyla, greeting me in the morning. "You've had a long night." She handed me a small package wrapped in aluminum foil: it was homemade banana bread.

My eyes watered. I couldn't eat—I couldn't stomach anything—but the gesture was so unexpectedly kind in such a chaotic maelstrom, I wanted to cry right then and there.

I told the doctors that Mom had decided to remove the tube, and a few hours later, when all her loved ones had arrived, we crowded around her bed.

"You won't be alone," said Khulsoom, kissing Mom's forehead.

As the doctor began preparing various medical equipment and checking Mom's vitals, Mom asked for some paper and a pen.

Wait, Mom wrote. *Where's Joe?*

Khulsoom looked at the paper, confused. "Joe wasn't on your list of people, honey. Remember?" She glanced over at me.

But I stared at the paper in disbelief.

Joe.

Joe?

Mom was about to get extubated. She was about to face the certain prospect of death and leave this world forever. She was about to leave me behind. And in her final moments—quite literally on her deathbed—instead of praying or asking for forgiveness or telling her loved ones just how much she loved them, she wanted to see *Joe*, of all people? The same guy she'd been too distracted by when her own son had left the house to kill himself?

Oh my God. Mom had been talking to him the whole time, even after Shaz died.

Mom wasn't abandoning me today. She'd abandoned her kids years ago. Maybe I'd always known.

The realization came like a kick to the gut.

Mom continued writing: *But Joe should be here. He texted earlier.*

"Why," I demanded, shaking, "the *hell* are you asking for Joe right now?"

Mom gave me a look. She was angry. She was hurt. More than anything, she looked at me like I was an inconvenience.

Stephen gently held my hand.

"What the hell is wrong with you?" I continued. "How could you even think having Joe here right now is remotely okay? Do you even stop to think how weird that would be?"

"Farah," interrupted Nyla, "I understand you're upset, but now is not the time, jaani."

I felt everyone's eyes on me.

"Come, hold your mom's hand. You need to let go. It's time."

Maybe Nyla was right. But I didn't want to hold her hand. It felt far too intimate, too *loving* a gesture, and in that moment I was more furious than I'd ever been with her, because the last thing we'd ever talk about was Joe.

I held Mom's wrist instead.

After a few minutes, the doctor removed her endotracheal tube.

It happened slowly, at first: Mom weakly cleared her throat of phlegm. Then she began to breathe, heavily. Then the gasps, the desperate gasps for life.

When people talk about pulling the plug, they imagine one's eyes closing, as if there was a peaceful falling asleep, until one's breath quietly fades.

Mom did not leave the world so gently.

She struggled. Struggled, as if against some unseen force.

As the seconds stretched, her doll eyes turned glassy, and her face began to turn a horrifying shade of blue. The light in her eyes faded. It was an image I knew would be forever burned in my memory, the kind that would reappear in my nightmares for years to come: Mom dying. Mom choking.

I couldn't watch anymore. I let go of her wrist. Looked away. Around me, Mom's sisters broke into sobs. Someone was whispering a prayer.

Eventually, finally, Mom was gone.

I took a deep breath.

CHAPTER 36

Music Sounds Better with You

After the funeral, I slept for fifteen hours. Stephen tried to wake me at some point for a bite to eat. But every piece of me was so exhausted, I couldn't even leave my bed, much less our home.

The strangest part about Mom being gone wasn't the lack of grief I felt—at most, I grieved for the loss of what could have been, the healthy relationship we could have had. It was the realization that I finally had the chance to build my own life. The possibilities were suddenly endless.

I felt relief.

The next day Maha and a few other girls I'd grown up with stopped by at our row home to bring food. One of my friends, Madiha, even cleaned our kitchen, which had grown messy the past few weeks; we'd barely been home to clean it. Later, we all watched *What We Do in the Shadows* together and laughed and reminisced. No one talked about the funeral. It was the best kind of reminder that I wasn't alone.

"You don't have to talk to anyone involved with your mom anymore, if you don't want to," Maha reminded me as I was bombarded with texts from Mom's friends and family. So often my mom had thrown out the phrase *blood is thicker than water* whenever my brother and I complained about having to visit her side of the family for holidays. I'd even asked her once why she was still in touch with Nani Jan, even though she told me time and time again how much she hated her, even though Nani Jan had begun complaining to everyone in the family that she thought she might have cancer because Mom was getting more attention since her ALS diagnosis.

Yes, but she's my mom, Mom would reply, as if it was the most obvious thing in the world. She probably didn't know the full quote was: *The blood of the covenant is thicker than the water of the womb.*

And my family, as far as I was concerned, was right here.

But once I was rested up, it was time to start my duties as executrix and sort through my mom's affairs, the thing I'd been dreading the most.

The first thing Stephen and I did was turn on her phone. I held it between us while we sat on the couch, waiting with bated breath as her texts and emails loaded.

Khulsoom, unfortunately, hadn't lied. With access to my mom's email, we could see that my aunt had indeed convinced my mom to put down money for a Virginia apartment that she'd never live in.

After the funeral, that aunt never reached out to me again.

We also learned that, over the past few days, Anthony and Malik had convinced my mom to change the will so they would get a large portion of the inheritance—one-fourth, to be exact. They'd just been waiting to find a time to bring a lawyer to the hospital. Khulsoom, though, had stalled Mom, saying it was better to hold off on making such big changes to the will so suddenly.

Mom had also invested far more into the gym business than she'd let on, using much of what had once been meant for Shaz's education.

Later, we also learned she'd been paying for Anthony's and Malik's dental care and rent, and had given Malik his own debit card, which, for reasons I could not fathom, she would fill every month with an allowance. Of course, Malik was helping Mom in return; when Mom's condition began to take a turn for the worse Malik had promised to help sell her G-Wagon. He'd use a trusted car salesman friend of his to get a fair price, he'd said. Mom would have one less thing to worry about.

The car, and the money it had been sold for, had disappeared since then.

With my blessing, Stephen did everything he could, pulling in lawyers and spending hours in communication with Mom's legal team to take back what had been stolen. When I was too tired to fight, Stephen took up the mantle.

Before she died, Mom had told me information about the storage unit holding Shaz's piano would be on her phone, but it wasn't there. Shaz's piano, where he'd poured so much of his soul, the piano that, in a way, knew my brother as well as I did, was lost forever.

But the worst piece of information we'd learned were the text messages Mom and Joe had been sending each other. Weeks before Shaz died, she'd demanded that my brother move out. What exactly she said to him, we had no idea; Mom, perplexingly, had deleted all the text messages from Shaz (she'd also deleted, I'd learn later, all her text messages with Kareem). But based on her texts with Joe, the plan was that after Shaz had moved out, Mom and Joe would be free to live in our family house together.

"Why didn't Shaz tell me what was going on?" I asked, gripping my mom's phone. All the wounds of Shaz's loss—the wounds I'd gotten so good at pretending weren't there—opened all over again.

In another life, in another world, Shaz and I were growing up together and would soon be celebrating his birthday. And maybe he'd learned to love himself, maybe as much as I loved him. But he hadn't and he wasn't, and our mom had done nothing to help.

"I don't know," answered Stephen wearily. "Maybe he didn't want you to worry."

The thought destroyed me.

What a curse it was to be trapped in a timeline where my brother no longer existed.

"We could have *saved* him," I said. "He could have lived with us."

Stephen wrapped his arms around me as I sobbed. For my brother. For my dad.

For the heart that, for years, had cried out for a mother who'd never respond.

❧

"Have you decided what you want to put on Samia's tombstone?"

I was on the phone with Elaine, the secretary at Wright Funeral Services. At this point we were practically friends.

"Yeah." I swallowed. "Just—just put *Samia Rishi. Wife. Mother.*"

"That sounds lovely," said Elaine.

❧

I got a huge box in the mail one day; the author copies of my debut novel had finally arrived, and soon the book would be on shelves. To celebrate the upcoming release and the end of the era Stephen and I had dubbed "The Rishi Family Curse," we took that long-awaited honeymoon. We went to Tokyo—as far away from home as we could go—and for almost two weeks spent a blissful vacation doing absolutely nothing. There was no itinerary, no scheduled plans or reservations. I wanted time to no longer matter. I wanted to live like my family hadn't died in some bizarre, seemingly never-ending series of unfortunate events, where the law of entropy need not apply.

A few weeks after we'd returned, unbeknownst to me, Stephen called every piano storage company in the Chester County area until, one day, he found Shaz's piano. Thankfully the storage company had still been charging Mom's credit card; otherwise they'd have sold the piano a long time ago. My mourning had been good for one thing: I'd still been behind on everything I needed to do in the aftermath of Mom's death, including canceling her card.

I cried the day Stephen told me, relieved. Music was the only trace I had of Shaz; even if, over the years, the memory of his face faded from the mind, at least I'd still have his piano.

Stephen's parents had moved to Pennsylvania a little after Mom's ALS diagnosis—to be closer to Stephen, to us—and they offered to keep the piano at their place. Their house was far bigger than our little row home, and I'd be able to see it whenever we visited them.

When I walked into their home and saw the piano again, Stephen wrapped an arm around me.

"It's not the same thing," he said gently, "but it almost feels like he's here."

I nodded. Nestled a little closer.

"Almost."

CHAPTER 37

Yes I Said Yes I Will Yes

Before I knew it, it was January, and my thirtieth birthday rolled in like a gloomy, uninvited guest.

The big 3-0. A momentous birthday, as far as birthdays go, and the first without any new messages in my family group chat. Stephen had asked if there'd been anything I'd wanted to do for my birthday, but I'd declined. I just wanted to chill at home, I'd said. I wanted to rest and relax in pajamas and not think about it. I sat on the couch, staring absentmindedly at the TV. I'd spent most of the day writing, like any other day, but now I was filled with an immense, agonizing loneliness that had lodged deep in my chest.

I hadn't even noticed Stephen approaching.

Quietly, he handed me a gift: a simple wooden mechanical pencil, wrapped in a silver bow.

The *pencil*. The goddamn pencil that he was supposed to give me on the day of our class project. For years I'd teased him about it, about how he'd chickened out. But here it was, finally: a pencil that, in some ways, represented the years we shared. And how fitting it was that Stephen would give me a pencil, the same tool that had also comforted me my entire life much in the same way Stephen had these past ten years.

"Oh my God," I said.

Stephen's gaze fell in embarrassment.

"Better late than never, right?"

It was silly, but this pencil felt like the most magical thing in the world. Soon a global pandemic would hit. The gym—Mom's gym—would burn down from an electrical fire in seemingly a divine act of providence. Slowly, I'd begin to pray again, rekindling my relationship with my faith; God and I had a *lot* to chat about, but faith is never easy. Stephen and I would visit Kaya in New York, and the three of us would reminisce and laugh until we'd snort. Maha's baby would be born; I'd be a proud aunty.

And I'd have miraculously written over four books, including one inspired by the time Stephen and I first met.

I remember how my dad once marveled at the mundane. This felt like one of those small marvels. Us, here, now. In the warmth of our little home, the world was quiet and kind and simple and *ours*.

But the pencil—it felt like the pencil had started it all. It felt like a culmination of everything. The past: us, in college, uncertain and scared to act on feelings we didn't understand. And the future: with Stephen, no longer bogged by a fear of rejection, replaced instead by a desperate willingness to build something, together. It was the offering of a tiny, modest pillar: a promise of the same support he'd always given, as I chased once-impossible dreams with a hundred possibilities.

The losses we endured changed the trajectory of my life in a way nothing else could have. I wouldn't say losing my parents and brother was a good thing; it was nothing short of a nightmare. But I found that losing them made me love harder. These small, brief moments of joy—I treasured them that much more.

I took the pencil—an OHTO Sharp Pencil, the label said in bold black letters—and kissed him, the way one did when they never wanted it to stop. Those days, we kissed often, as if to make up for lost time.

"Wanna marry me?" I asked. The words had fallen out of my mouth before I could think about it. But the feeling was true. I wanted to be with Stephen. I wanted to be his partner: not because of health insurance or because my mom wanted us to.

I simply wanted *this*.

But Stephen laughed, a warm, thawing sound that brought my veins aglow.

"Anytime," he said.

ACKNOWLEDGMENTS

My life is nothing without the people in it. And what a blessing it is to have so many people to thank, not just for bringing this memoir to life but for quite literally bringing my life to Life.

To the team at Amazon Publishing: my editor, Laura van der Veer, who believed in this story from day one; and Emma Reh, Deanna Ly, James G., Tashan Mehta, and all the others behind the scenes who worked so tirelessly to usher this book to publication—endlessly— thank you.

To Mindy Kaling, the legend herself: a huge thank-you to you and your team for choosing my book—what an incredible honor.

To Simone Noronha and Tree Abraham, for designing the cover of my dreams: I'm so blessed to have your art and design bless this story. Thank you.

To the team at Liza Dawson Associates, including Liza, Havis, Lauren, Lynn, and of course, Hannah Bowman, my agent and guide and champion, who heard my ridiculous pitch about writing this memoir even though I'm just a small writer with a small platform, and yet took me 100 percent seriously: thank you, thank you, thank you.

To my beautiful, ridiculously talented Odyssey family (because that is what you are to me—family): I miss you all every day.

To my parents: Thank you for making me stronger. I know you only wanted the best for your kids, and for that I'll always be grateful. Inna lillahi wa inna ilayhi raji'un.

To Seema and Nyla and Amber: I'm lucky to have so many strong women in my life.

To my cousins Shaan, Alina, and Nadia: I know I've said it before, and I'll say it again—you're the best cousins I could possibly wish for.

To Hiba and Farheen, my fierce, inspiring sisters: I'm always in awe of you both.

To Cara: one of my sincerest wishes is that we grow to be little old ladies together, forever sharing our awkward stories (and teasing Stephen).

To Shaz: Laughing doesn't feel the same without you. I'll always love you.

To you, the reader, for coming this far: How humbling it is to have someone read your words. Thank you so much for this gift.

And finally, to Stephen . . .

You know. You always know. And if somehow you still don't, well— now you have this book as a reminder.

ABOUT THE AUTHOR

Photo © 2023 Linette and Kyle Kielinski

Farah Naz Rishi (she/they) is the author of *I Hope You Get This Message* and *It All Comes Back to You*. A Pakistani American writer and voice actor, she received her BA in English from Bryn Mawr College, her JD from Lewis & Clark Law School, and her love of weaving stories from the Odyssey Writing Workshop. When Farah is not writing, she's probably hanging out with video game characters. For more information, visit www.farahnazrishi.com.